MASTERING

COMPUTER PR

MACMILLAN MASTER SERIES

Astronomy
Australian History
Background to Business
Banking
Basic English Law
Basic Management
Biology
British Politics
Business Communication
Business Law
Business Microcomputing
Catering Science
Catering Theory
Chemistry
COBOL Programming
Commerce
Computer Programming
Computers
Data Processing
Economic and Social History
Economics
Electrical Engineering
Electronics
English Grammar
English Language
English Literature
Financial Accounting
French
French 2
German

Hairdressing
Italian
Italian 2
Japanese
Keyboarding
Marketing
Mathematics
Modern British History
Modern European History
Modern World History
Nutrition
Office Practice
Pascal Programming
Physics
Practical Writing
Principles of Accounts
Restaurant Service
Social Welfare
Sociology
Spanish
Spanish 2
Spreadsheets
Statistics
Statistics with your Microcomputer
Study Skills
Typewriting Skills
Word Processing

MASTERING
COMPUTER PROGRAMMING

SECOND EDITION

P. E. GOSLING

MACMILLAN

First edition 1982
Reprinted 1982, 1983
Second edition 1984
Reprinted 1985, 1987, 1989

Published by
MACMILLAN EDUCATION LTD
Houndmills, Basingstoke, Hampshire RG21 2XS
and London
Companies and representatives
throughout the world

Printed in the People's Republic of China

British Library Cataloguing in Publication Data
Gosling, P. E.
Mastering computer programming. — (Macmillan
master series)
1. Basic (Computer program language)
I. Title
001.64'24   QA76.73.B3
ISBN 0–333–37196–8 (paper cover home edition)
ISBN 0–333–38777–5 (paper cover export edition)

CONTENTS

CONTENTS

PREFACE

This book is, I suppose, a guided tour of programming and what it involves. Its object is to introduce the techniques of writing computer programs, and all the mystique that this implies, to the many people who are now beginning to realise that the computer is here to stay. These people who are taking their first tentative steps into the new world of computing need (as a well-known general once said), to 'know the enemy'. Used properly and with understanding the computer ceases to be the enemy that the media sometimes make it out to be and becomes a powerful ally. Computers affect our daily lives more and more and hopefully can be used to improve the quality of our lives by releasing us from dull, repetitive tasks and allowing us to expand our minds.

In the preparation of this book I have had help from many people. Particularly I must thank Dave Pheasant of Alpha Micro, Roy Atherton, Eric Huggins, Keith Mackenzie-Ross, Barbara Robinson and Colin Martin. (I have to include the last-named because if I don't he won't write any more software for me!) My thanks also to Paul Hare of the Open University Student Computing Service for permission to use the ACE and MCSIM programs.

Producing a book of this type is very difficult because I find that the overriding problem is in deciding what to leave out rather than what to put in. Eventually I decided that it could never be an 'all you need to know about programming without actually doing it' type of book. Instead I have tried to produce, by means of as many examples as possible, a sort of 'Hitch-hiker's Guide to Programming' so that the reader will begin to get the flavour of the art, and I use the word advisedly, of computer programming. If I have encouraged readers to study other texts on programming in individual languages and actually to practise this art for themselves (with success I hope) then I shall consider that I have succeeded.

Peter Gosling

INTRODUCTION

The concept of programming has been with us for a long time without anybody really being aware of it. We simply used different words to express programming ideas. My father used to say 'Let's have a system, even if it's a rotten one!'. Whether we use the words 'system', 'method' or 'way of doing things' we are talking about the procedure to be adopted in order to solve some problem. Schoolchildren learning arithmetic by rote, in the 'bad old days', were an example of programming people to perform a simple repetitive task. These two examples, of course, date from before the computer age dawned, a time when the words 'system' and 'procedure' had rather different meanings from what they have in the context of computer programming. It might, perhaps, be noted in passing that the first 'computing' program was written in the nineteenth century by Ada, Countess Lovelace, the daughter of Lord Byron the poet. She wrote it for the mechanical *analytical engine* built by Charles Babbage.

So what is this programming business all about, if it has been with us for so long? First of all it has nothing to do with mathematics, in the conventional sense, as so many people tend to think. Being good at mathematics has practically nothing to do with computing. What programming does relate to is the use of one's native language, clearly and unambiguously, in order to put a set of instructions into execution in order to complete some task. Usually this not only involves the use of a series of positive statements about operations, which have to be performed, but also contains points where decisions have to be made and the steps which have to be taken resulting from these decisions. The questions that are asked must be clear and unambiguous and they must be phrased in such a way that whoever is carrying out the task is in no doubt what to do after each decision is reached.

A simple example of the concept of programming is in the instructions placed in a telephone call-box on how to make a call (see Fig. 1). This is fairly clear and to the point except that it does not tell the caller what to do if something goes wrong, nor does it tell the caller what to expect as

Fig 1

TO MAKE A CALL

Have money ready   5p **or 10p**

Lift receiver

Listen for continuous purring

Dial number or code and number

**When you hear rapid pips,
press in a coin**

**To continue a dialled call
put in more money during conversation or
when you hear rapid pips again**

a response from the telephone system. For example, the number you are ringing might be out of order or engaged and it would help if there were some directions regarding the procedure to be adopted in these situations. A properly written program of instructions should try and cover all possibilities. A different approach to the same problem is shown in Fig. 2, which is taken from a French telephone directory. Note that words have by and large been replaced by symbols which give the caller a better idea of how to proceed at each stage of the making of a call.

Fig. 3 is a Department of Health announcement regarding rent increases on property let to NHS staff. It was published in a newspaper as an example of 'officialese'. In fact, it is very clear and direct and far better than a paragraph of jargon. Fig. 3 does demonstrate that someone has, in fact, sat down and thought about the problem of communicating the method of calculating the new rents by breaking it down into a series of simple steps. This can be done by using a flowchart where the steps are indicated by a series of boxes joined by arrows. Each box contains an instruction or a question. If the box contains a question then it must be a question for which there can only be one of two answers, 'Yes' or 'No'. Not 'Yes', 'No' or 'Maybe'. By starting at the top of the chart the user can be guided to the correct rent, in this case, via the question boxes. Flowcharts play a very important part in the creation of a computer program and their use

Fig 2

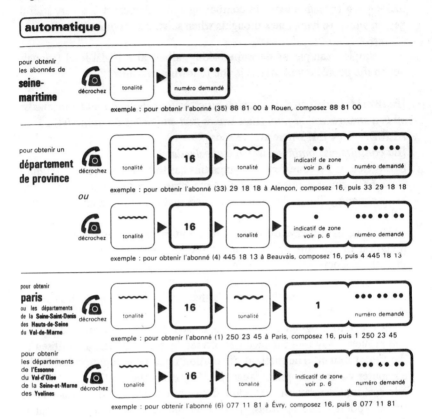

automatique

pour obtenir
les abonnés de
seine-maritime

décrochez — tonalité ▶ numéro demandé

exemple : pour obtenir l'abonné (35) 88 81 00 à Rouen, composez 88 81 00

pour obtenir un
département de province

décrochez — tonalité ▶ 16 ▶ tonalité ▶ indicatif de zone voir p. 6 — numéro demandé

exemple : pour obtenir l'abonné (33) 29 18 18 à Alençon, composez 16, puis 33 29 18 18

ou

décrochez — tonalité ▶ 16 ▶ tonalité ▶ indicatif de zone voir p. 6 — numéro demandé

exemple : pour obtenir l'abonné (4) 445 18 13 à Beauvais, composez 16, puis 4 445 18 13

pour obtenir
paris
ou les départements
de la Seine-Saint-Denis
des Hauts-de-Seine
du Val-de-Marne

décrochez — tonalité ▶ 16 ▶ tonalité ▶ 1 — numéro demandé

exemple : pour obtenir l'abonné (1) 250 23 45 à Paris, composez 16, puis 1 250 23 45

pour obtenir
les départements
de l'Essonne
du Val-d'Oise
de la Seine-et-Marne
des Yvelines

décrochez — tonalité ▶ 16 ▶ tonalité ▶ indicatif de zone voir p. 6 — numéro demandé

exemple : pour obtenir l'abonné (6) 077 11 81 à Évry, composez 16, puis 6 077 11 81

Fig. 3

1. Assess revised rent for each tenanted property.
2. Total revised rents under 1 to arrive at revised notional gross rent income.
3. Total existing rents to arrive at present gross income.
4. Deduct 3 from 2.
5. If 4 results in a negative sum, implement new assessed rents.
6. Otherwise, divide 4 by the total number of tenanted properties to arrive at average annual assessed increase for each property.
7. Divide 6 by 52 to arrive at average weekly assessed increase.
8. If 7 is £1.50 or less than £1.50 implement new assessed rents.
9. If 7 is more than £1.50 multiply change assessed for each rent under 1 by 1.50 over the amount calculated under 7 and implement the resultant scaled-down rents.

will be brought into a number of programs throughout this book. Decision-making is a crucial activity in computing and a flowchart is a very useful peg on which to hang one's thoughts when solving a problem.

A simple example of decision-making, albeit at a trivial level (though not to the people involved!), is in the following exchange.

[*PanWorld Tours offer five capital cities in four days. Ed and Alice wake up in a strange hotel room. Alice wakes first and prods Ed in the back.*]
ALICE: 'Hey Ed! Where are we today?'
[*Ed consults his combined watch and calendar.*]
ED: 'Gee, it's Wednesday, so I guess this has to be Paris, France.' [*Pulling back the curtains he points to the large steel tower dominating the skyline.*] 'What did I tell you? Guess that ain't the Statue of Liberty!'

Here we have a case of logical deduction made as a result of the inter-pretation of relevant information. If the information had been incorrect then the deduction could be in error. They could have been in Blackpool! It just goes to show the importance of presenting the correct information. A true saying in computing circles is that Garbage In equals Garbage Out (GIGO for short).

In order to program a computer one needs to be able to analyse a prob-lem in such a way that the facilities offered by the computer are utilised to the fullest extent. The method of solution must be communicated to the computer via an appropriate language. Very often the starting point will be a logical flow diagram of events and decisions (similar to Fig. 4 which takes up the point made previously). This technique is described in detail in Chapter 6 of G. G. L. Wright, *Mastering Computers*, a companion to this book. The flow diagram, as we shall see in later examples in this book, can then be converted into a computer language. There are a number of com-puter languages available as we shall also see later, but we shall be using the BASIC language to communicate many of the general programming tech-niques and ideas.

Many people feel that they would like to become programmers but have little concept of what the job really entails. The following is a transcript of a conversation the author had with Keith Mackenzie-Ross of Peterborough Data Processing Ltd.

P.G.: Keith, what qualities do you look for in a programmer?
K.M-R.: A logical mind. In fact, an aptitude for programming, which can be discovered from one of the standard aptitude tests, is better than paper qualifications in, say, mathematics.

Fig 4

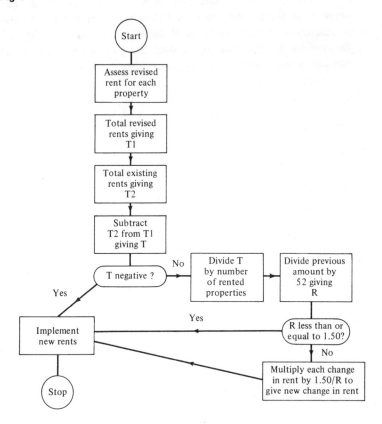

P.G.: Are programmers born, or made?

K.M -R.: Generally speaking they are made. Given that logical mind, and proper training, a person can become a programmer.

P.G.: In your opinion, is programming, as a skill, easy to learn?

K.M-R.: Yes. I do think, however, that people often have a mental block at first because they think the idea of programming a computer sounds complicated.

P.G.: Do you think that programming is merely just a skill?

K.M-R.: It is more than just a skill. Programmers tend to group them-selves into two types: programmers and coders. A programmer thinks about what he is doing in an effort to produce an efficient and elegant program. A coder on the other hand will merely do as he is told and will produce workable, but not very inspired programs.

P.G.: Finally, what do you think of the future of programming as a career?

K.M-R.: In the foreseeable future there is going to be a continuing high demand for skilled programmers. As the use of computers continues to rise there certainly looks as if there is going to be a very high demand for programmers to produce the software packages which commerce and industry are going to require.

CHAPTER 1

WHAT IS A COMPUTER PROGRAM?

1.1 INTRODUCTION

If one wanted to define what a computer is, then the following would probably fill the bill:

> a high-speed, automatic, electronic, digital, general purpose, stored program data processing machine.

It is not the purpose of this book to cover every aspect of this definition. In fact, the only part which really concerns us is the *stored program* concept. However, it is because a computer is electronic and high-speed that it is able to use a stored program in order to process data very quickly. In other words, there are pieces of electronic circuitry, which constitute the memory inside the computer, which are able to store a sequence of instructions, permanently if need be. These instructions can be brought into operation automatically in order to process the data which is presented to them. The concept of a computer being a device which produces the answers to a series of questions is very over-simplified and a rather romantic idea of what a computer really is, thanks to television and the popular press!

The concept of a computer program becomes easier to understand if we look on the computer as a kind of electronic filing cabinet. Let us take an example to illustrate the way in which data can be processed by such a machine. Consider a case where a computer is used to keep track of the amount of stock held in the stores of a factory. First of all we need a list of all the stock items held currently in the stores. This list will contain information, usually in part-number order, about the number of each item held in stock, its description, its cost, minimum reorder level and so on. All this information will be stored in the computer's memory on magnetic discs on what is generally called a *file*. If all the information about the movement of the stock, also in part-number order, is placed on another file on the disc then a program of instructions, stored in yet another part of the memory, is brought into action. This program will cause the information stored in the movements file to be merged with the current stock file so that a new, up-to-date, stock file is created. If all the data had been written down on pieces of paper then a clerk would have to made the amendments by hand in a ledger—which is another name for a file. This job is very boring, repetitive and error-prone. In fact it is exactly the kind of job computers are good at. Because computers never get bored and they are very unlikely—again despite what the media say—to make mistakes, they are ideally suited for taking over these boring repetitive tasks. People make mistakes; computers don't unless there is a malfunction in the electronics. TV and radio sets rarely go wrong so there is litte chance, given proper maintenance, that a computer should actually fail to work properly. After all, how many times do you tune a TV set to Channel 2 and get Channel 4? But that is the kind of 'mistake' a computer is supposed to make. If a computer program is used to perform routine tasks they will be performed as fast and as efficiently as the design of the computer *hardware* and the computer program, the *software*, will allow. If a further job has to be carried out on our stock file, such as scanning it to detect any stock levels below the reorder level and printing the necessary orders, another program needs to be called into action. One program is used for one job.

The whole attitude to programming can be summed up simply in the words of a student the author once taught. After about four weeks of a programming course the student suddenly said, 'I realise now that you need to know how to solve your problem before giving it to the computer!'

It is not difficult to see how raw data, which can only consist of numbers and/or names, can be stored. All that is needed is some code which enables alphabetic and numeric characters to be stored electronically (see P. E. Gosling and Q. L. M. Laarhoven, *Digital Codes for Computers and Microprocessors*, Macmillan, 1980). The storage of a sequence of instructions is also a matter of storing certain codes and we are going to start looking at programming from the bottom up, that is, from the point of view of the computer first of all. Then we will work up to the concept of programming which is orientated towards people rather than machines.

1.2 FIRST STEPS: A SIMPLE MACHINE CODE

In order to understand how a computer can carry out our instructions we will first of all look at the machine itself and for the present purpose we will examine a very simple machine and the codes we can use to make it perform as we want it. From our definition on p. 7 we have stated that our computer is *digital* by nature, that is, that it can only handle *numbers* of electrical pulses, and that it possesses some kind of *store*—memory in fact. The kind of numbers which can be retained in its store will be in the *binary* format, but for our purposes we will use numbers in the more familiar *decimal* notation and assume that the designer of the computer has arranged for the conversion between binary and decimal to be done for us. The processes which take place inside the computer consist of some arithmetic operations performed on a series of numbers which are placed into its memory from an input device according to a set of instructions which have previously been stored in the memory. The results of the calculations performed by the computer are then presented to the outside world on the output device. Note that the memory is used to retain two types of information, one is the numbers upon which it is working, called the *data*, and the other is the series of instructions which go to make up the stored *program*. The examples which follow will hopefully make this distinction clear. In the model computer which is used for the next examples we have a memory which is divided up into one thousand separate locations, or cells. These are numbered from 000 to 999 so that every one of these memory locations can be indentified by a three-digit decimal number. Each one of these locations can only store one number and one number only. That number may be, however, the numerical representation of an instruction or a piece of numerical data.

The operations our computer can perform, there are only 10, are denoted by the code numbers

$$00, 10, 20, 30, 40, 50, 60, 70, 80, 90$$

and the instructions which make up the program are stored in a sequence of locations and are executed one at a time. This is done by copying an instruction from memory into a special part of the central processing unit where it is decoded and then the decoded instruction is executed. Then the next instruction is called in to be decoded and executed, and then the next, and so on. The central processing unit contains a series of special small memory units called *registers*. For our example we only need to be aware of two of these; one is called the accumulator and the other is called the *sequence control register*. The accumulator is the register where the results of all arithmetic operations are placed—the arithmetic having been performed in a special part of the central processor called the *arithmetic unit*. The sequence control register is the register which holds the address where the next instruction to be carried out is to be found. Once the address of the first instruction in the program has been placed in that register, the central processor knows where to start looking for instructions. Once the instruction has been loaded into the part of the central processor which decodes it, the sequence control register is incremented by 1. Now it may be that the instruction which is decoded is one which causes a jump from one part of the program to another, and in order to do this it will change the address held in the sequence control register. Examples of this will be shown later.

The code 00 is to be used by our computer to signal an instruction which will cause a number to be transferred from an input device (a piece of equipment which will allow the outside world to communicate with the computer—the keyboard of a terminal for instance). The instruction

00297

will mean

Open a channel from the input device to location number 297 and then transfer the number given to that device into location 297.

Code 10 signals an instruction which will cause the contents of a location in memory to be transferred to an output device—the screen of a VDU for instance. By this means the computer can communicate with the outside world. So that

10356

will mean

Open a channel from location number 356 to the output device and send a copy of the contents of that location to the output device.

Typical input devices, such as a card reader and a paper tape reader, are shown in Fig. 1.1. A line printer and a paper tape punch, typical output devices, are shown in Fig. 1.2. Fig. 1.3 shows a teleprinter and a VDU, both examples of *terminals*, which act both as input and output devices.

In order to enable our computer to perform arithmetic we have to use a special register called an *accumulator*. All numbers have to be loaded into this register before any arithmetic can be carried out. For example

40321

means

Add the contents of location 321 to the contents of the accumulator.

50163

means

Subtract the contents of location number 163 from the contents of the accumulator.

Fig 1.1 *paper tape reader and card reader*

Two instructions are needed to move numbers into and out of the accumulator. 20 is the code for loading the accumulator so that

20436

means

Fig 1.2 *paper tape punch and line printer*

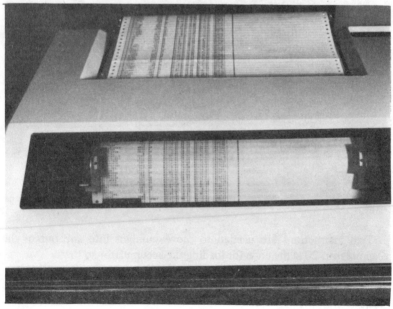

Fig 1.3 *teleprinter and VDU terminal*

Place a copy of the contents of location 436 into the accumulator.

The above instruction will always destroy what was already in the accumulator by replacing it with the new number.

The instruction

30199

means

> copy the contents of the accumulator into location 199.

Again this will overwrite whatever was previously in location 199.

All the foregoing means that a typical sequence of events would be
(1) Place a number into a specified memory location.
(2) Copy the number into the accumulator.
(3) Perform some arithmetic on the contents of the accumulator.
(4) Place the contents of the accumulator in a specified memory location.
(5) Output the contents of the location specified in step 4.
(6) Stop.
The code for stop is 90000.

A simple program to read in two numbers, compute their sum and then print the answer might look like this.

Location	Contents	
150	00100	Input a number to location 100
151	00101	Input a number to location 101
152	20100	Load accumulator with contents of 100
153	40101	Add contents of location 101 to accumulator
154	30102	Store contents of accumulator in 102
155	10102	Output contents of 102
156	90000	Stop

Note that the instructions themselves are stored in locations 150 to 156. After all, the instructions have to be stored somewhere. This also goes to show that the memory of a computer must store both data and instructions and they should be kept well apart. This is because they are both stored in the same form, namely a numeric code, and if the worst happened the computer has no way of knowing the difference between data and instructions—it's all numbers to the computer.

In a sense a computer program is rather like a treasure hunt in which we have the sequence control register to tell us where the next clue is to be found. For a simple calculation-type program such as this one, the use of this register is simply to hand us over from one memory location to the one following it in sequence. In the next few pages we shall see how certain instructions can make our program jump out of sequence.

Fig. 1.4 shows our first program in action. Notice that the first thing we have to do is to load in our instructions, in their numeric form, one at a time starting at a specific location. When this phase has been completed we have a series of instructions stored as numbers sequentially in a known series of memory locations. In order to run the program we have to tell the computer where to find its first instruction, in location 150, and then

Fig 1.4

```
    RUN

    TRACE,START,RESTART,FINISH,LOAD,DUMP OR EXECUTE ? LOAD

    FIRST STORE ADDRESS
     ? 150
    NUMBER OF LOCATIONS TO BE FILLED ? 7
    ENTER MACHINE CODE INSTRUCTIONS OR DATA
     ? 00100
     ? 00101
     ? 20100
     ? 40101
     ? 30102
     ? 10102
     ? 90000

    TRACE,START,RESTART,FINISH,LOAD,DUMP OR EXECUTE ? DUMP
    SEQUENCE CONTROL REGISTER = 000
    OPERAND = 000    OPERATOR CODE = 000
    INDEX REGISTER =  0000000 ACCUMULATOR = 0000000
    FIRST STORE ADDRESS
     ? 100
    NUMBER OF LOCATIONS TO BE OUTPUT ? 3
       ADDRESS        CONTENTS
         100          0990000
         101          0990000
         102          0990000
    END OF DUMP

    TRACE,START,RESTART,FINISH,LOAD,DUMP OR EXECUTE ? EXECUTE
    ADDRESS OF FIRST INSTRUCTION TO BE EXECUTED ? 150
    INPUT ? 6
    INPUT ? 8
    OUTPUT:  0000014

    TRACE,START,RESTART,FINISH,LOAD,DUMP OR EXECUTE ? DUMP
    SEQUENCE CONTROL REGISTER = 000
    OPERAND = 000    OPERATOR CODE = 009
    INDEX REGISTER =  0000000 ACCUMULATOR = 0000014
    FIRST STORE ADDRESS
     ? 100
    NUMBER OF LOCATIONS TO BE OUTPUT ? 3
       ADDRESS        CONTENTS
         100          0000006
         101          0000008
         102          0000014
    END OF DUMP

    TRACE,START,RESTART,FINISH,LOAD,DUMP OR EXECUTE ? FINISH
```

leave it to the sequence control register to step through the memory from location 150 to location 151, location 152, and so on. After the instruction has been decoded and executed the next instruction is decoded and executed until the STOP Instruction is reached. Note that we can look inside the memory to see exactly what is stored in any location by using the command DUMP. In our example we have used this to find out what is in locations 100, 101 and 102 and we see that just as we had hoped there are the numbers we had input in the first two of these and the result of their addition in location 102.

If we wished to amend out program we could change the contents of location 153 so that it contained the code 50101—we could do this by instructing the computer to LOAD the number 50101 into location 153—and then on the command EXECUTE the program would ask for the address of the first instruction to be executed, 150 again, and ask for a number to be placed in location 100. Then it would execute the instruction in location 151, which requires a number to be placed in location 101. Then comes the instruction stored in 152 which copies the number stored in 100 into the accumulator. Now the instruction in location 153 is executed and the contents of 101 are subtracted from whatever is now in the accumulator. The instruction in location 154 places the contents of the accumulator into location 102 and the instruction in 155 prints the contents of 102. The instruction in 156 says STOP.

There are three more codes left. These are 60, 70 and 80 and are used to cause the execution of the program to jump out of sequence. In other words they alter the contents of that very important register, the sequence control register. For example, the code

> 60429

means

> Place the number 429 in the sequence control register.

The result is that whatever the instruction following that one in the next location in memory it will be ignored and the instruction stored in location 429 will be the next to be executed.

If the coded instruction

> 70277

is executed it is instructing the computer to examine the number currently in the accumulator. If this number is zero then the contents of the sequence control register must be changed to 277. If the accumulator has anything but zero in it then the sequence control register is left alone. This is an example of a *conditional* jump instruction.

In the same way the code

> 80611

will be interpreted as

> If the accumulator contains a number which is less than zero then execute the instruction found in location number 611.

If the contents of the accumulator are anything but a negative number then the instruction immediately following is executed.

As an example of the use of the *jump* instructions the following program accepts a pair of numbers as input. If the two numbers are not equal they are printed and the program stops. However, if they are equal then a jump is made back to the start of the program and a further pair of numbers are input and the test for equality is made again. This cycle is repeated until a pair of numbers which are not equal are input; only then will the program stop. Fig. 1.5 shows the program and a *flowchart* (of which more later). The flowchart is merely a pictorial representation of the sequence of events. A run of the program using our machine simulator is shown in Fig. 1.6.

Fig 1.5

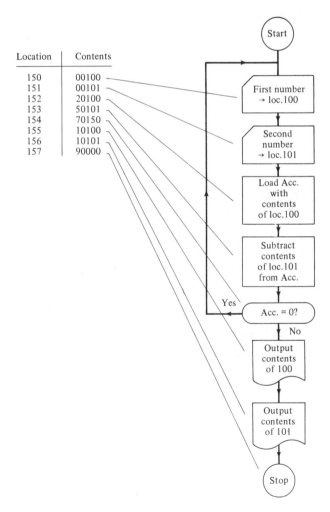

Fig 1.6

```
TRACE,START,RESTART,FINISH,LOAD,DUMP OR EXECUTE ? LOAD

FIRST STORE ADDRESS
 ? 150
NUMBER OF LOCATIONS TO BE FILLED ? 8
ENTER MACHINE CODE INSTRUCTIONS OR DATA
 ? 00100
 ? 00101
 ? 20100
 ? 50101
 ? 70150
 ? 10100
 ? 10101
 ? 90000

TRACE,START,RESTART,FINISH,LOAD,DUMP OR EXECUTE ? EXECUTE
ADDRESS OF FIRST INSTRUCTION TO BE EXECUTED ? 150
INPUT ? 4
INPUT ? 6
OUTPUT:  0000004
OUTPUT:  0000006

TRACE,START,RESTART,FINISH,LOAD,DUMP OR EXECUTE ? EXECUTE
ADDRESS OF FIRST INSTRUCTION TO BE EXECUTED ? 150
INPUT ? 6
INPUT ? 6
INPUT ? 5
INPUT ? 7
OUTPUT:  0000005
OUTPUT:  0000007

TRACE,START,RESTART,FINISH,LOAD,DUMP OR EXECUTE ? DUMP
SEQUENCE CONTROL REGISTER = 000
OPERAND = 000   OPERATOR CODE = 009
INDEX REGISTER =  0000000 ACCUMULATOR =-0000002
FIRST STORE ADDRESS
 ? 100
NUMBER OF LOCATIONS TO BE OUTPUT ? 2
  ADDRESS        CONTENTS
    100          0000005
    101          0000007
END OF DUMP


TRACE,START,RESTART,FINISH,LOAD,DUMP OR EXECUTE ? DUMP
SEQUENCE CONTROL REGISTER = 000
OPERAND = 000   OPERATOR CODE = 009
INDEX REGISTER =  0000000 ACCUMULATOR =-0000002
FIRST STORE ADDRESS
 ? 150
NUMBER OF LOCATIONS TO BE OUTPUT ? 8
  ADDRESS        CONTENTS
    150          0000100
    151          0000101
    152          0020100
    153          0050101
    154          0070150
    155          0010100
    156          0010101
    157          0090000
END OF DUMP
```

Notice again that in both of the previous examples the instructions and the data on which they operate are stored in different parts of the memory. Remember that a computer has no way of telling that a particular set of digits in its memory is an instruction, or a piece of data. Despite popular belief, computers cannot perform magic!

A final example of a program written in our simple machine code is the one shown in Fig. 1.7. In this case the program asks for two numbers to be input and then proceeds to calculate their highest common factor. Again it illustrates the repetitive nature of many computer programs where a *loop* of instructions is executed time and time again until a particular condition is satisfied. A run of the program is shown in Fig. 1.8.

If one writes programs using this type of code then it becomes very easy to see just how a computer interprets its instructions and carries them out. In addition, the programmer can make very efficient use of the memory because he can specify exactly where every variable is to be stored. However, such a programming method is both time-consuming and prone to error. At one time it was the only way a computer program could be written. Luckily a method of programming eventually became available which made it unnecessary to use numerical codes and the actual addresses in memory where the various parts of the program, and the data associated with it, were to be stored.

1.3 ASSEMBLER CODE PROGRAMS

An assembler code takes the burden of deciding where every piece of data and instruction has to be located away from the programmer and shifts it to the computer. This allows the programmer to concentrate more on the logic of the program and less on the machine. In order to achieve this the programmer is allowed to use single words instead of numeric codes for the instructions. Letters of the alphabet are used as *symbolic addresses* instead of the actual memory locations used. Our simple program to input a pair of numbers, add them together and print their sum, as on p. 14, is written as

INPUT A	Input a number to location A
INPUT B	Input a number to location B
LOAD A	Copy the number in A into the accumulator
ADD B	Add the contents of B to the accumulator
STORE C	Store the contents of the accumulator in C
PRINT C	Copy the contents of C to the output device
STOP	Stop

Fig 1.7

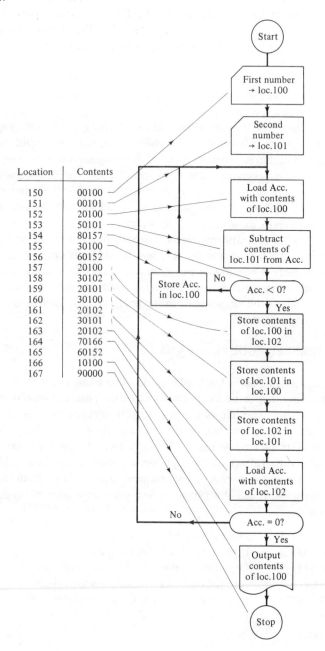

Location	Contents
150	00100
151	00101
152	20100
153	50101
154	80157
155	30100
156	60152
157	20100
158	30102
159	20101
160	30100
161	20102
162	30101
163	20102
164	70166
165	60152
166	10100
167	90000

Fig 1.8

```
TRACE,START,RESTART,FINISH,LOAD,DUMP OR EXECUTE ? LOAD

FIRST STORE ADDRESS
 ? 150
NUMBER OF LOCATIONS TO BE FILLED ? 18
ENTER MACHINE CODE INSTRUCTIONS OR DATA
 ? 00100
 ? 00101
 ? 20100
 ? 50101
 ? 80157
 ? 30100
 ? 60152
 ? 20100
 ? 30102
 ? 20101
 ? 30100
 ? 20102
 ? 30101
 ? 20102
 ? 70166
 ? 60152
 ? 10100
 ? 90000

TRACE,START,RESTART,FINISH,LOAD,DUMP OR EXECUTE ? EXECUTE
ADDRESS OF FIRST INSTRUCTION TO BE EXECUTED ? 150
INPUT ? 12
INPUT ? 4
OUTPUT:  0000004

TRACE,START,RESTART,FINISH,LOAD,DUMP OR EXECUTE ? DUMP
SEQUENCE CONTROL REGISTER = 000
OPERAND = 000    OPERATOR CODE = 009
INDEX REGISTER =  0000000 ACCUMULATOR = 0000000
FIRST STORE ADDRESS
 ? 100
NUMBER OF LOCATIONS TO BE OUTPUT ? 2
   ADDRESS      CONTENTS
    100         0000004
    101         0000000
END OF DUMP


TRACE,START,RESTART,FINISH,LOAD,DUMP OR EXECUTE ? DUMP
SEQUENCE CONTROL REGISTER = 000
OPERAND = 000    OPERATOR CODE = 009
INDEX REGISTER =  0000000 ACCUMULATOR = 0000000
FIRST STORE ADDRESS
 ? 150
NUMBER OF LOCATIONS TO BE OUTPUT ? 18
   ADDRESS      CONTENTS
    150         0000100
    151         0000101
    152         0020100
    153         0050101
    154         0080157
    155         0030100
    156         0060152
    157         0020100
    158         0030102
    159         0020101
    160         0030100
    161         0020102
    162         0030101
    163         0020102
    164         0070166
    165         0060152
    166         0010100
    167         0090000
END OF DUMP
```

The program instructions, in machine code form of course, are placed in a sequence of locations by a program which already resides in the computer's memory and is supplied by the manufacturer. This program is part of the *software* supplied by the computer manufacturer and installed when the machine is delivered. The software converts the instructions from the words supplied by the programmer into the numeric equivalent and then allocates a memory location for each instruction and for each symbolic address. Eventually the program, which the programmer has written in this very simple form of English instructions, is converted into the only thing the computer ultimately recognises—a numeric code. For the mathematically minded reader, there is a one-to-one correspondence between the instruction in this *assembler code*

INPUT A

and the ultimate numeric code

00100

In the third machine code example, on p. 20, there is a point in the program where a decision has to be made. The test instruction is stored in location 154 and says

If the contents of the accumulator are less than zero then the next instruction to be carried out is found in location 157.

Similarly, the instruction stored in location 156 says

The next instruction to be carried out is to be found in location 152.

The programmer who writes a program in an assembler code need know nothing about where his instructions are to be stored, these being supplied by the computer software, so there has to be a way of attaching *labels* to particular instructions. This program can then be written in assembler code and is

```
P) INPUT A
   INPUT B
   LOAD A
   SUB B
   BZ P
   OUTPUT A
   OUTPUT B
   STOP
```

The first instruction in the program has the label P attached to it. Labels can be alphabetic or numeric characters, so the instruction BZ will know where to send the program should the test prove to be true. In other words **BZ P** means

> If the contents of the accumulator are zero then the next instruction to be carried out has the label P attached to it. Otherwise carry on in sequence.

If the test fails and the accumulator contains anything but zero then the last three instructions, to output the contents of locations A and B followed by STOP, will be carried out. If a program contains the instruction

GOTO T

then it means that the next instruction is that which has the label T attached to it and the program must carry on in sequence from that point until told otherwise.

There are a number of implications in the use of an assembler code. One of these has already been mentioned and this is that the computer software handles the translation of the mnemonic instructions of the code into machine language. The other is rather more subtle in that it must be realised that the computer has to keep track of the symbolic addresses and the labels hung on to certain instructions. This is done by using what is called a *symbol table* where the relationship between symbols and actual locations is noted. The action of the software associated with a assembler code will be made apparent in the next section which deals with a very simple *high-level language*. Machine codes and assembler codes are known as *low-level languages*. The rest of this book is devoted to programming in various high-level languages, which are easy for us to understand as programmers. They have to be translated into low-level machine code which is ultimately the only language the computer can understand.

1.4 ACE: A HIGH-LEVEL LANGUAGE

Although assembler codes are easier to use than machine codes, they still require the programmer to write a lot of repetitive code. A high-level language enables a considerable compression to be made in the code written by a programmer thus allowing even more thought to go into the logic of the program and even less to go into the internal organisation of the computer which executes the program. In other words, more work is given to the computer software, which is all the time becoming more and more sophisticated. Thus the computer is given tasks to do which it is good at, namely the high-speed execution of repetitive but essentially very simple tasks. A high-level language takes a lot of drudgery out of the job of a programmer and releases him more for the task which he is best suited to do—creative thought.

The program written in machine code on p. 14 (see Fig. 1.9) and then in assembler code on p. 9 can be written in a high-level language called ACE as follows

```
INPUT A, B
LET C = A + B
PRINT C
END
```

thus producing a program which is short, to the point and fairly easy to understand.

What ACE does is to take each line of program as it is typed in and allocate memory space to both the instruction and the constants and variables in that instruction. In the first example the first program line contains the word INPUT followed by the names of two variables A and B. They are called 'variables' because their values are not known at the time the program was written and so memory space has to be reserved for them. ACE allocates memory locations for program instructions starting at location 150, for variables and constants starting at location 50. This means that every time the variable named A is referred to in the program the location numbered 50 is meant. Similarly whenever B is referred to location 51 is the one used.

When the next line of the ACE program is input we have

```
LET C = A + B
```

to be interpreted. ACE knows where the variables A and B are stored in memory and it now encounters a new variable called C. This is allocated to memory location 52, which is the next free one. The complete translation of the ACE instruction will result in the construction of a set of machine instructions to load the contents of location 50 into the accumulator, add the contents of location 51 and finally store the results in location 52.

The next line of the program

```
PRINT C
```

will be interpreted as an instruction to output the contents of location 52, since by this time ACE knows where C is located.

```
END
```

is interpreted as STOP and the end of the program is denoted by a star.

At this point ACE prints what is called a *symbol table* which is its list of each variable and constant, when there are any, and its precise location in memory. We shall deal with the use of labels a little later.

Fig 1.9

```
? INPUT A,B

C-STRING
  150              INPUT           50
  151              INPUT           51

  ? LET C=A+B

C-STRING
  152              LOAD            50
  153              ADD             51
  154              STORE           899
  155              LOAD            899
  156              STORE           52

  ? PRINT C

C-STRING
  157              OUTPUT          52

  ? END

C-STRING
  158              STOP

  ? *

END OF COMPILATION

SYMBOL TABLE:-
***********

CONSTANT SECTION
-------------------


VARIABLE SECTION
-------------------

  50               A               50
  51               B               51
  52               C               52

LABEL SECTION
--------------


YOU WILL NOW GET THE NECESSARY INPUT TO THE "MCSIM" PROGRAM

LOAD
  150
  9
 0000050
 0000051
 0020050
 0040051
 0030899
 0020899
 0030052
 0010052
 0090000
EXECUTE
  150
```

Program outline: The first line of the program, which accepts the values of two variables A and B, is converted into a pair of statements in assembler code allocating the first variable to location 50 and the second to location

51. The next line is converted into five separate assembler instructions and at first sight two of these might appear redundant. The first two instructions load the contents of location 50, A, and add to this number, which is now in the accumulator, the contents of location 51, B. We would expect that it would be sufficient to then move the contents of the accumulator to the location reserved for C, namely 52, and that would be an end to it. However, we have to allow for more complex arithmetic operations than the simple addition of two numbers so the contents of the accumulator are stored temporarily in location 899 in case there was another piece of arithmetic to do on that line. An example of this is shown in Fig. 1.12 where one calculation to be carried out is

LET C = E * 5 + 1050

A more extreme case might be if we had to divide the sum of two numbers by the difference between them. Here we would have to arrange for the temporary storage of the sum, the temporary storage of the difference and then the division of one of these answers by the other. Having placed the result of the addition in location 52 the next instruction is to output the contents of that location. The signal that the end of the program is reached is the * and then ACE produces the symbol table which consists, in this case, of the locations of the three variables mentioned in the program, namely A in location 50, B in location 51 and C in location 52. There are no constants or labels used in the program, but examples of these are shown later. Finally a list of the machine code instructions is printed out. Each of the assembler instructions generates one machine code instruction.

ACE, of course, is a teaching language invented by the Open University which enables us to examine step by step the transformation from the original *source* program written in a high-level language into the final executable *object* program in the low-level language. This low-level machine code can be directly converted into the electronic instructions which cause the data stored in memory to be processed according to the programmer's requirements. What is happening is that we present each line of our program to ACE, then, provided the rules of the language (called its *syntax*) are obeyed, that line is converted into assembler code first of all and then into the final machine code. The machine code can then, as we shall see, be presented to our machine simulator program and run.

The program shown on pp. 17 and 22 can be written in ACE as

```
10  INPUT A
    INPUT B
```

```
IF A = B THEN 10
PRINT A
PRINT B
END
```

Note that we use numeric labels in ACE to define particular instructions. This means that the line INPUT A has the label 10 attached to it. The third line of the program allows us to make direct comparisons between the contents of the memory location holding the variable called A and the one holding the variable called B. ACE takes care of what goes on in the accumulator. Fig. 1.10 shows this program processed by ACE and producing the final machine code program.

This example shows the use of labels and after the symbol table, which shows again that the variables A and B are to be stored in locations 50 and 51, comes the information that the label 10 is attached to the instruction in location 150. As can be seen, the result of presenting the first instruction, with label 10, to ACE is that it is placed in location 150. Hence the program has been converted from a high-level language into a machine code via an assembler code.

Finally a program which actually does something useful. The program shown in Fig. 1.11 is written in ACE and is used to calculate the amount of an electricity bill. For the purpose of this example we shall assume that there is a standing charge of £3.25 on all bills and that there is a minimum charge of £3.64 for electricity consumed in addition to the standing charge. The first 150 units used are charged at 7p per unit and all units above 150 are charged at the reduced rate of 5p per unit. There is a VAT rate of 15 per cent charged on all bills. The program is designed to accept as input a number representing the number of units used and will output the amount to be charged by the electricity company.

Now here is a more complicated program which contains constants, variables and several labels. ACE is given more work to do than in the previous program because the jumps in the program tend to be forwards rather than backwards. A backward jump is easy for ACE to deal with since when the labelled statement is entered, ACE is put on the alert ready to receive an instruction to jump to that label. If a forward jump is to be made then use has to be made of a very clever feature of low-level languages. This feature is called *indirect addressing* and uses mnemonics such as

IGOTO, IBN, IBZ

in the assembler code. What these are saying is that a jump is to be made to a particular location in memory and in that location is found the address of the actual location where the next instruction is to be found. An instruction such as

Fig 1.10

```
    ? 10 INPUT A

C-STRING
 150            INPUT          50

    ? INPUT B

C-STRING
 151            INPUT          51

    ? IF A=B THEN 10

C-STRING
 152            LOAD           50
 153            SUB            51
 154            BZ             150

    ? PRINT A

C-STRING
 155            OUTPUT         50

    ? PRINT B

C-STRING
 156            OUTPUT         51

    ? END

C-STRING
 157            STOP

    ? *

END OF COMPILATION

SYMBOL TABLE:-
***********

CONSTANT SECTION
-------------------

VARIABLE SECTION
-------------------

 50             A              50
 51             B              51

LABEL SECTION
-------------------
 100            10             150            0


YOU WILL NOW GET THE NECESSARY INPUT TO THE "MCSIM" PROGRAM

LOAD
 150
 8
0000050
0000051
0020050
0050051
0070150
0010050
0010051
0090000
EXECUTE
 150
```

Program outline: This program starts with an instruction which is labelled with label 10 in this case and ACE will keep a note of this fact so that it knows that the instruction in location 150, the first instruction produced by ACE always goes into location 150, is the one bearing the label 10. The next line of program generates a single input instruction and then follows a test to see if the variables called A and B contain numbers which are equal or not. This line of program will cause the number stored in location 50, the variable A, to be loaded into the accumulator and the number stored in location 51, B, subtracted from it. If the contents of the accumulator are zero then the program will jump to the instruction labelled 10–BZ 150 which means 'if the contents of the accumulator are zero jump to location 150'. If the test fails then the next instruction, to print the contents of location 50, is carried out. The next program line generates another output statement and the program stops. Again the * is used to tell the computer that program input has ceased. Then the symbol table is printed out. There are no constants in this program, the two variables are present and the single label, label 10, is attached to location 150. The zero at the end of the label section entry for label 10 tells us that a jump backwards has been made—forward jumps are dealt with in the next example. Finally the machine code instructions, one again for each of the assembler instructions, is printed out. You may notice that the machine instructions are of exactly the same form as those used in the program shown in Fig. 1.6 except that in that case the variables were stored in locations 100 and 101 instead of 50 and 51.

      IGOTO 166

will mean

> Find out what number is stored in location 166 and then execute the instruction which is stored in the location in memory with that address.

If location 166 held the number 231 then the instruction stored in location number 231 would be the next one to be executed.

What ACE does is to leave a space after an indirect jump instruction so that this empty memory location will be filled with an address as soon as a suitably labelled instruction is typed in. The label section of the symbol table gives the label, the address of the instruction bearing that label and the address of the location containing the address of the labelled instruction. This all sounds a bit tortuous, but a certain amount of detective work at this point will be well rewarded. Let us just examine one of the labels in the symbol table. Immediately following label 30 are the numbers 161

Fig 1.11

```
      INPUT E
      IF E<150 THEN 30
      IF E=150 THEN 30
      GOTO 90
 30   LET C=E*7
      IF C<364 THEN 50
      GOTO 60
 50   LET C=364
 60   LET C=C+325
      LET C=115*C
      LET D=C/10000
      LET C1=(C-D*10000)/100
      PRINT D,C1
      END
 90   LET E=E-150
      LET C=E*5+1050
      GOTO 60
      END
```

*Program outline: The first line of the program requests a value for E, the
number of units used. Then the value of E is tested to see whether it is
equal to or less than 150. A jump is made to the instruction labelled 30 if
either of these conditions are met, otherwise a jump is made to label 90.
All the calculations are performed in pence so that at label 30 the number
of units used is multiplied by 7 and that value assigned to the variable
called C, for Cost. If C is less than 364 a jump is made to the instruction
labelled 50 where C is given the value of 364, the minimum charge for
electricity. The sequence of instructions which starts at label 60 will
increase the value of C by 325, the standing charge, then multiply by 115
for the cost plus VAT. Notice that a statement such as LET C = C + 325
means that whatever the value of C was it must be increased by 325. The
last two lines before the printing of the cost takes place are to extract
the pounds and the pence from the total cost in pence; remember that
ACE only works in whole numbers so that the result of dividing 567 by
100 will be 5 since the decimal part will be lost. Finally at label 90 the
cost of units which exceed 150 in number is calculated. The 1050 comes
from the fact that the first 150 units will cost 1050p at 7p per unit.*

and 155. The first of these is the address of the instruction which bears the
label, the second of these numbers is the address of the location, which
holds the address of the labelled instruction and is the object of the indirect
jump instruction.

The processing of the program by ACE is shown in Fig. 1.12 and Fig.
1.13 shows the output from ACE being run by our machine simulator.

Fig 1.12

```
? INPUT E

C-STRING
150            INPUT          50

? IF E<150 THEN 30

C-STRING
151            LOAD           50
152            SUB            51
153            IBN            155
154            GOTO           156

? IF E=150 THEN 30

C-STRING
156            LOAD           50
157            SUB            51
158            IBZ            155

? GOTO 90

C-STRING
159            IGOTO          160

? 30 LET C=E*7

C-STRING
161            LOAD           50
162            MUL            53
163            STORE          898
164            LOAD           898
165            STORE          52

? IF C<364 THEN 50

C-STRING
166            LOAD           52
167            SUB            54
168            IBN            170
169            GOTO           171

? GOTO 60

C-STRING
171            IGOTO          172

? 50 LET C=364

C-STRING
173            LOAD           54
174            STORE          52

? 60 LET C=C+325

C-STRING
175            LOAD           52
176            ADD            55
177            STORE          898
178            LOAD           898
179            STORE          52

? LET C=115*C

C-STRING
180            LOAD           56
181            MUL            52
182            STORE          899
183            LOAD           899
184            STORE          52
```

```
? LET D=C/10000

C-STRING
185          LOAD          52
186          DIV           58
187          STORE         899
188          LOAD          899
189          STORE         57

? LET C1=(C-D*10000)/100

C-STRING
190          LOAD          57
191          MUL           58
192          STORE         899
193          LOAD          52
194          SUB           899
195          STORE         898
196          LOAD          898
197          DIV           60
198          STORE         897
199          LOAD          897
200          STORE         59

? PRINT D,C1

C-STRING
201          OUTPUT        57
202          OUTPUT        59

? END

C-STRING
203          STOP

? 90 LET E=E-150

C-STRING
204          LOAD          50
205          SUB           51
206          STORE         898
207          LOAD          898
208          STORE         50

? LET C=E*5+1050

C-STRING
209          LOAD          50
210          MUL           61
211          STORE         899
212          LOAD          899
213          ADD           62
214          STORE         898
215          LOAD          898
216          STORE         52

? GOTO 60

C-STRING
217          GOTO          175

? END

C-STRING
218          STOP

? *

END OF COMPILATION
```

SYMBOL TABLE:-
****

CONSTANT SECTION

10	150	51
11	7	53
12	364	54
13	325	55
14	115	56
15	10000	58
16	100	60
17	5	61
18	1050	62

VARIABLE SECTION

50	E	50
51	C	52
52	D	57
53	C1	59

LABEL SECTION

100	30	161	155
101	90	204	160
102	50	173	170
103	60	175	172

YOU WILL NOW GET THE NECESSARY INPUT TO THE "MCSIM" PROGRAM

```
LOAD
 51
 1
0000150
LOAD
 53
 1
0000007
LOAD
 54
 1
0000364
LOAD
 55
 1
0000325
LOAD
 56
 1
0000115
LOAD
 58
 1
0010000
LOAD
 60
 1
0000100
LOAD
 61
 1
0000005
LOAD
 62
 1
0001050
LOAD
 150
```

```
0000050
0020050
0050051
1080155
0060156
0000161
0020050
0050051
1070155
1060160
0000204
0020050
0200053
0030898
0020898
0030052
0020052
0050054
1080170
0060171
0000173
1060172
0000175
0020054
0030052
0020052
0040055
0030898
0020898
0030052
0020056
0200052
0030899
0020899
0030052
0020052
0210058
0030899
0020899
0030057
0020057
0200058
0030899
0020052
0050899
0030898
0020898
0210060
0030897
0020897
0030059
0010057
0010059
0090000
0020050
0050051
0030898
0020898
0030050
0020050
0200061
0030899
0020899
0040062
0030898
0020898
0030052
0060175
0090000
EXECUTE
150
```

Program outline: In this example the program listed in Fig. 1.11 is presented line by line to ACE which translates it first into the assembler code equivalent together with the location of each variable and constant, thus the variable E has been allocated the address 50 in memory. The second line of the ACE program contains a reference to an instruction labelled 30 which has not yet been typed in. Thus a direct jump to the location in memory where that instruction is held cannot be made. The instruction stored in location 153 therefore has to be of the indirect variety followed by a jump to the next instruction to be executed which will be in location 156. 155 is reserved for the address of the instruction labelled 30 when eventually it is typed in. Notice that a similar instruction is placed in location 158 since the label 30 is referred to again in the third line of the program. The fourth line of the program, GOTO 90, again refers to a jump to a label which does not yet exist. Hence the IGOTO 160 instruction and the fact that the next instruction to be set up is in location 161 leaving 160 to be filled when the labelled instruction finally appears. Eventually the rest of the program is input and the symbol table showing where the constants are to be stored is first printed. This shows, for instance, that the number 150 is stored in location 51, the number 7 is in location 53, and so on. Then the variables are listed together with their storage locations: the variable E is in location 50, C in location 52, and so on. Finally the symbol table lists all the labels showing, for example, that the instruction labelled 90 resides in location 204 and that location 160 contains that address. The space was left for it to be filled as soon as the labelled instruction was input. Similarly the other labels refer to the locations where the labelled instructions are stored and the addresses which hold the key to these labels.

After the symbol table comes the machine code version of the program which is derived exactly from the assembler code on a one-to-one basis. The program in this form is input to the machine code simulator program and run in Fig. 1.13.

Fig 1.13

```
TRACE,START,RESTART,FINISH,LOAD,DUMP OR EXECUTE ? EXECUTE
ADDRESS OF FIRST INSTRUCTION TO BE EXECUTED ? 150
INPUT ? 0
OUTPUT:   0000007
OUTPUT:   0000092

TRACE,START,RESTART,FINISH,LOAD,DUMP OR EXECUTE ? EXECUTE
ADDRESS OF FIRST INSTRUCTION TO BE EXECUTED ? 150
INPUT ? 150
OUTPUT:   0000015
OUTPUT:   0000081
```

```
TRACE,START,RESTART,FINISH,LOAD,DUMP OR EXECUTE ? EXECUTE
ADDRESS OF FIRST INSTRUCTION TO BE EXECUTED ? 150
INPUT ? 300
OUTPUT:   0000024
OUTPUT:   0000043

TRACE,START,RESTART,FINISH,LOAD,DUMP OR EXECUTE ? EXECUTE
ADDRESS OF FIRST INSTRUCTION TO BE EXECUTED ? 150
INPUT ? 261
OUTPUT:   0000022
OUTPUT:   0000019

TRACE,START,RESTART,FINISH,LOAD,DUMP OR EXECUTE ? DUMP
SEQUENCE CONTROL REGISTER = 000
OPERAND = 000    OPERATOR CODE = 009
INDEX REGISTER =  0000000 ACCUMULATOR = 0000019
FIRST STORE ADDRESS
 ? 50
NUMBER OF LOCATIONS TO BE OUTPUT ? 12
     ADDRESS        CONTENTS
       050          0000111
       051          0000150
       052          0221950
       053          0000007
       054          0000364
       055          0000325
       056          0000115
       057          0000022
       058          0010000
       059          0000019
       060          0000100
       061          0000005
END OF DUMP


TRACE,START,RESTART,FINISH,LOAD,DUMP OR EXECUTE ? DUMP
SEQUENCE CONTROL REGISTER = 000
OPERAND = 000    OPERATOR CODE = 009
INDEX REGISTER =  0000000 ACCUMULATOR = 0000019
FIRST STORE ADDRESS
 ? 150
NUMBER OF LOCATIONS TO BE OUTPUT ? 69
     ADDRESS        CONTENTS
       150          0000050
       151          0020050
       152          0050051
       153          1080155
       154          0060156
       155          0000161
       156          0020050
       157          0050051
       158          1070155
       159          1060160
       160          0000204
       161          0020050
       162          0200053
       163          0030898
       164          0020898
       165          0030052
       166          0020052
       167          0050054
       168          1080170
       169          0060171
       170          0000173
       171          1060172
       172          0000175
       173          0020054
       174          0030052
       175          0020052
       176          0040055
```

```
177        0030898
178        0020898
179        0030052
180        0020056
181        0200052
182        0030899
183        0020899
184        0030052
185        0020052
186        0210058
187        0030899
188        0020899
189        0030057
190        0020057
191        0200058
192        0030899
193        0020052
194        0050899
195        0030898
196        0020898
197        0210060
198        0030897
199        0020897
200        0030059
201        0010057
202        0010059
203        0090000
204        0020050
205        0050051
206        0030898
207        0020898
208        0030050
209        0020050
210        0200061
211        0030899
212        0020899
213        0040062
214        0030898
215        0020898
216        0030052
217        0060175
218        0090000
END OF DUMP
```

CHAPTER 2

BASIC:

A HIGH-LEVEL LANGUAGE

2.1 Introduction

The languages described in Chapter 1 are 'invented' languages in the sense that they are used to introduce the newcomer to programming to the general concepts of the subject. The languages are not used for serious programming although each computer, whether it be a small micro or a large mainframe will have its own machine code and assembler language. However, they will be rather more complicated than the introductory examples, which are actually 'simulators' of the real thing and are used purely for teaching purposes. There are a very large number of high-level computer languages of which the 'main line' families of languages are BASIC, COBOL, PL/1, FORTRAN, ALGOL and Pascal, to name the most common. The use of the word *families* in connection with languages is deliberate since each of them exists in a number of dialects, just like any other language.

For most of this book the language called BASIC (Beginner's Allpurpose Symbolic Instruction Code) is going to be used to introduce the most important aspects of programming. This is not a book about programming in BASIC, but it is a book about programming and some of the techniques required to write good computer programs. To find out the details of writing programs in BASIC, or any other of the languages available, the reader should consult either programming manuals issued by the computer companies or books devoted to the specific language which is chosen to be studied in depth. Each computer will have its own special variation of each language and even though the differences between dialects of the language may be slight they can often cause endless trouble if they are not fully understood.

All computer languages need instructions which will cause a specific set of computer operations to take place. With high-level languages one statement can generate a large number of machine instructions, as we saw with the use of the ACE language in the last chapter. High-level languages need to be able to generate instructions which will

(1) Control the input of data to, and the output of data from the computer's memory. These are usually called input/output (I/O) instructions.

(2) Cause the computer to perform arithmetic operations. These are usually called *assignment* instructions since they cause arithmetic to take place and assign the results to particular locations in memory.

(3) Tell the computer how the data it is processing should be stored. (This may not make a lot of sense at the moment but soon you will see that it is important that data is stored in different forms.)

(4) Allow logical decisions to be made; these are called *conditional jump* instructions.

(5) Control the order in which the set of instructions which make up the program are executed.

A computer program has to start somewhere, usually as a problem to be solved, and the first step in writing a program is to decide, in outline at least, how the problem is to be tackled. This is dealt with in more detail in Chapter 8 but at this stage let us take the example of totalling up a shopping list. The data which is needed occurs in the form of pairs of numbers. These numbers represent how many of each item is bought and the amount paid for each of them. The output from the program would be the total cost of the goods bought. In other words the computer is not really interested in the fact that three tins of baked beans were bought at 24p each, only that there were three items at 24p. In fact only the numbers 3 and 24 are relevant to the program. Only the programmer knows, or cares, that they represent numbers of tins and amounts of money. So far, so good. The solution to the problem falls into several phases. The first of these is the phase in which the computer is supplied with a set of pairs of numbers representing, in order, the cost in pounds and the number purchased of each of these. The pairs of numbers input would be, say

1.41, 1, 0.66, 2, 1.78, 1, 0.24, 3, . . .

meaning that there was one item bought at £1.41, two at 66p, one at £1.78, three at 24p and so on. To total the bill we need to multiply the pair of numbers together and add the answer into the running total for the bill until we reach the end of the list of goods purchased. This all implies that the data, which is the set of pairs of numbers, has to be placed in the computer's memory, and a multiplication sum performed on each pair of numbers; the answer is then added into a running total, which is also held in the computer's memory. When the input of data comes to an end another part of the program has to be executed so that the final total is printed out. Then the program will stop. This means that the computer must have some way of knowing that the input list has come to an end so that the repeated operation of multiplication and addition into the total ceases and that loop is broken out of before the final total is printed. Therefore there must be some mechanism which is constantly asking, 'Have we reached the end of the list?' If the answer is 'Yes' then the final stages of the program are executed. If the answer is 'No' then the loop in which two numbers are input, their product calculated and the answer added into the total is carried out yet again. Luckily computers never get tired of asking the same question and then carrying out the same old boring calculation if the answer to that question tells them that the calculation must be carried out again, even if it is for the millionth time. This is of course, in direct contrast to the parent who, 100 yards from home on a car journey, is asked by a child, 'Are we there yet?'

The BASIC instructions which allow the various types of operation to be signalled to the computer are dealt with in this and the next five chapters. How other languages handle them is dealt with in Chapter 10.

2.2 BASIC

You may have noticed that computers operate on both *variables*, whose values are not known at the time when the program was written, and *constants* which are numbers supplied by the program itself. A good example of this is the electricity bill program where the number of units is input by the person running the program. The number of units will be a variable, as indeed will be the cost which is calculated according to the number of units. The constants are the numbers which represent the cost per unit, standing charges, VAT rate and so on.

In most versions of BASIC the variables are referred to by letters of the alphabet, or a letter followed by a single digit, for example, A, K, X1, H7, and so on. They are, in fact, *symbolic addresses* as referred to in the previous chapter.

BASIC is very similar to the ACE language mentioned in Chapter 1 in that it uses *assignment* statements of the form

$$LET\ P = Q + R - 4$$

which means that the variable Q contains a number which must be added to the value of the variable stored in R and the constant 4 must be subtracted from that sum and the answer assigned to variable P. This implies that there are four memory locations involved in this operation, three are reserved for the variables P, Q and R and one for the constant 4. The word LET is optional in most versions of BASIC but it is very useful for the novice to use it since the equals sign in an assignment statement is not used in the conventional mathematical way. In BASIC the equals sign is used to stand for 'takes the value of'. There can only be one variable name on the left-hand side of the assignment statement so that the assignment operation consists of performing the arithmetic on the variables and constants on the right-hand side and the result of that calculation assigned to the variable name on the left-hand side.

Constants in BASIC can be positive or negative decimal numbers with or without a sign preceding them. The absence of a sign implies that the number is positive. Very large or very small numbers can be written in a very special standard form which is of the following structure

dEe

where d is a decimal number and e is a power of 10 so that

3497.973

can be written as

3.497973E3

which stands for

3.497973×10^3

The letter E stands for 'times 10 to the power of'. Similarly the number

0.000005697

can be written as

5.679E−6

standing for

5.679×10^{-6}

In addition, the number

−0.0010203

is written as

−1.0203E−3

Arithmetic operations in BASIC are indicated by the following symbols

+	add
−	subtract
*	multiply
/	divide
↑	exponentiate (raise to the power of)

Brackets are used to group operations together and reduce ambiguity. There is a hierarchy of arithmetic operations which bears a distinct relationship to the old-fashioned BODMAS (Brackets, Of, Division, Multiplication, Addition, Subtraction) rule of arithmetic. The rule in BASIC is

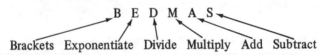

Brackets Exponentiate Divide Multiply Add Subtract

Any arithmetic expression in BASIC is always evaluated according to this rule for example

$$(4 + 6) \uparrow 2 + 3 * 4$$
$$\Rightarrow \quad 10 \uparrow 2 + 3 * 4$$
$$\Rightarrow \quad 100 + 3 * 4$$
$$\Rightarrow \quad 100 + 12$$
$$\Rightarrow \quad 112$$

     INPUT

means

connect the input device to memory and load whatever is typed into memory.

     PRINT

means

Copy the contents of a specific memory location on to the output device.

     STOP

means stop.

     END

is usually optional and acts in a very similar manner to STOP. Refer to the computer manufacturer's manual to find if it is essential. Sometimes it must be the very last statement in a program.

Every BASIC instruction is prefixed by a line number and the program is always executed in line number order beginning at the lowest numbered line. A simple BASIC program which illustrates these points is shown in Fig. 2.1. It accepts two numbers from the input device, which will usually be a teletype or a VDU, calculates their sum and prints it. The command RUN causes the program to start execution from the lowest numbered line.

We now know sufficient BASIC to use the language to perform simple arithmetic calculations for use and some examples of these are shown in

Fig 2.1

```
10 INPUT A,B
20 C=A+B
30 PRINT C
40 STOP
RUN
? 3,4
7

STOP AT 40
RUN
? -3,4
1

STOP AT 40
RUN
? 1.08E+4,-3.07E+6
-3059200

STOP AT 40
RUN
? -9.786E-7,-5.6754E-8
-1.035354E-06

STOP AT 40
```

Program outline: The first part of this illustration shows the program instructions which are retained in memory as they are typed in. The programmer then types RUN and the program starts execution at the first line, line number 10. Because it has the instruction INPUT to execute the computer will print a ? prompt and will expect two numbers, since there are two variable names after the word INPUT. In the first instance the value 3 will be assigned to the variable A and 4 to the variable B. The program will then continue to its next line where the value of the variables A and B are added together to give a value to the variable C. Finally the value of the variable C is to be printed and the program will stop. Notice that the answer, 7 in this case, is printed followed by a statement, STOP AT 40, which tells us that it has reached the STOP instruction at line 40. The program can now be run again for different pairs of numbers input. Each time the RUN command is given the program will start executing at the statement with the lowest line number. Luckily BASIC keeps a note of the starting address of the program, unlike the machine code programs we have seen earlier where we have to tell the computer where to look for its first instruction.

Fig. 2.2. What we are doing is using the computer to evaluate formulae for us. The FORTRAN language was developed specifically for this purpose—hence its name, FORmula TRANslator.

As well as allowing us to evaluate simple formulae, BASIC allows us to call for such operations which would usually send us hunting in sets of

Fig 2.2

```
10 INPUT A,B,C
20 D=B↑2 - 4*A*C
30 PRINT D
40 STOP


10 INPUT U,F,T
20 S=U*T + 0.5*F*T*T
30 PRINT S
40 STOP


10 INPUT P,T,R
20 I=P*T*R/100
30 PRINT I
40 STOP


10 INPUT A,B
20 X=(A+B)/(A-B)
30 PRINT X
40 STOP
```

Program outline: In each of the programs in this figure the first line will request numbers to be input and the ? prompt will be printed. Once the appropriate number of items have been typed in, three in the first three programs and two for the last one, line 20 will cause the evaluation of some formula, specified according to the rules of BASIC, and then the value of the variable which has been specified on the left-hand side of the expression in line 20 is printed out when line 30 is reached. Then the program stops.

tables. Such things as square roots, sines, cosines, and so on, are easily available to the BASIC programmer. All that is needed is the code SQR for a square root to be evaluated, like this

$$A = SQR(X)$$

where A is the square root of the number stored under the name of X. The square root is evaluated, in much the same way that the square root key on a pocket calculator sets a set of calculations in train, by the code SQR, and the result of the calculation is assigned to the variable called A. Computers don't need to store sets of tables because all the functions, and more, shown in Table 2.1, are calculated as and when required.

Fig. 2.3 shows a slection of programs which use the SQR function.

The next example, Fig. 2.4, is a BASIC program which will solve a simple quadratic equation. Notice how brackets are used liberally and that the SQR function is used. The two roots are calculated separately since

Table 2.1

Code	Meaning
SQR	Square root
SIN	Sine (of angle in radians)
COS	Cosine (of angle in radians)
TAN	Tangent (of angle in radians)
EXP	Raise e to the power
LOG	Logarithm to the base e
INT	Largest number less than or equal to the expression
ATN	Arctangent

Fig 2.3

```
10 INPUT A,B,C
20 D=SQR(B↑2-4*A*C)/(2*A)
30 PRINT D
40 STOP


10 INPUT L,G
20 P=3.14159
30 T=2*P*SQR(L/G)
40 PRINT T
50 STOP


10 INPUT L,C
20 P=3.14159
30 F=1/(2*P*SQR(L*C))
40 PRINT F
50 STOP


10 INPUT X,Y
20 Z=SQR(X↑2+Y↑2)
30 PRINT Z
40 STOP
```

Program outline: These four programs follow the same pattern as those in Fig. 2.2 except that the expression to be evaluated contains the SQR instruction which tells the computer that the square root of whatever follows is to be calculated.

there is no way of indicating the 'plus or minus' part of the quadratic equation formula.

BASIC works in an *interactive* manner and this means that a programmer sitting at a terminal can control the development, testing and running of a program almost instantaneously. BASIC allows the programmer to modify and edit the program he is writing quickly and easily. It is a language which offers a quick reaction to errors and says why it fails to understand what has been presented to it. This is particularly useful if

Fig 2.4

```
10 INPUT A,B,C
20 LET R1=(-B+SQR(B†2-4*A*C))/(2*A)
30 LET R2=(-B-SQR(B†2-4*A*C))/(2*A)
40 PRINT R1
50 PRINT R2
60 END
RUN
? 1,4,1
-.26794919
-3.7320508

STOP AT 60
RUN
? 1,10,0
0
-10

STOP AT 60
```

Program outline: Don't be put off this one just because you may not be very good at mathematics. All that is happening is that we are telling the computer to evaluate the formula

$$x = \frac{-B \pm \sqrt{(B^2 - 4AC)}}{2A}$$

where ± means 'plus or minus'. This means that we have to instruct the program to calculate two numbers, one using the + sign and one using the − sign. Hence the two lines, 20 and 30.

certain things written in a program might just set a computer on to a disaster course, such as setting up an endless loop. For example, if the program in Fig. 2.4 were given a set of numbers such that the program is asked to find the square root of a negative number, then this can be detected and a message sent to the programmer as the program reaches the point where the error occurs. At this point the program would stop and output an error message. Fig. 2.5 shows this happening. We would get a similar result if a calculation involving a division by zero were encountered. As division is performed by a series of repeated subtractions this is a situation we can do well without.

Fig 2.5

```
RUN
? 1,0,1
ERROR - FUNCTION ARGUMENT IN 20
```

In order to help the programmer, BASIC allows lines to be altered or deleted very easily. A single line number typed in will cause the deletion of the line with that number. The replacement of one line of instructions by another is simply done by typing in the new line with the same line number as that to be replaced. Some versions of BASIC additionally offer an *editor* which enables one or more characters in a line of BASIC program to be changed: a + sign to a − sign for example. An example of these amendments to a program is shown in Fig. 2.6.

Fig 2.6

```
10 INPUT X,Y
20 Z=X*Y
30 PRINT Z
40 STOP

RUN
? 3,4
12

STOP AT 40

20 Z=X/Y

LIST

10 INPUT X,Y
20 Z=X/Y
30 PRINT Z
40 STOP

RUN
? 3,4
.75

STOP AT 40
```

Program outline: Here we have a program which accepts two numbers, called X and Y, multiplies them together and prints this product, called Z. However, after the program has been run once, the programmer wants to amend the program so that the operation of multiplication is changed to that of division. So he types in a fresh line 20, LIST confirms that the new line has replaced the previous line and runs the program again.

Apart from program instructions BASIC allows us to issue *commands*. These are distinguished from program instructions by their lack of line numbers. We have already come across the RUN command in Fig. 2.4. There is another command which is of great use to a programmer when he wishes to see the current state of his program after, for example, some changes have been made to it. The command LIST will cause all the program instructions to be listed out at the terminal in the order of their line numbers. A program can have its instructions entered in any order, last line first should you wish, but the program will always be listed and run in line number order.

2.3 EXAMPLES

Finally here are some examples of simple BASIC programs, together with the results after they have been run. Fig. 2.7 shows a program which calculates the simple interest on the sum of money over a period of time at a particular rate of interest. Notice how we have made the program more 'user friendly' by using PRINT followed by a series of characters placed inside quotation marks. BASIC causes these lines of program to be printed

Fig 2.7

```
10 INPUT "RATE PERCENT ? ";R
20 INPUT "TIME IN YEARS ? ";T
30 INPUT "NUMBER OF POUNDS INVESTED ? ";P
40 LET I=P*T*R/100
50 PRINT P;"POUNDS INVESTED FOR";T;"YEARS AT ";R;"PERCENT PER ANNUM INTE
REST"
60 PRINT"WILL GIVE YOU ";I;"POUNDS IN SIMPLE INTEREST"
70 END

RUN
RATE PERCENT ? 4.5
TIME IN YEARS ? 2
NUMBER OF POUNDS INVESTED ? 100
100 POUNDS INVESTED FOR 2 YEARS AT 4.5 PERCENT PER ANNUM INTEREST
WILL GIVE YOU 9 POUNDS IN SIMPLE INTEREST

END AT 70
```

exactly as they appear inside the quotes, thus giving the impression that the computer is 'talking' to us. The characters within the quotes are called *literals* and can be any of the printing characters on a keyboard. Note also that the programs include REM statements—REMarks which are intended to help the programmer rather than the user, who will never see them unless he obtains a copy of the program instructions. REM statements are included to help anyone who wishes to know exactly how the program works. In these examples the REM statements give little more than a program title and a very brief description. In later programs we shall see how these statements can be included in order to give 'signposts' which describe what the program is doing at that particular point. REM statements form a useful part of the program *documentation* (of which much more later) in that if a program is to be modified by someone who was not its original author then it helps the understanding of what the author was doing at specific places in the program.

Perhaps an apology might be in order at this point since some of the following programs are slightly mathematical. If the sight of the words 'sine', 'degrees' and 'radians' fill you with dread, don't worry, the next page is not essential except as an indication that a computer program written in BASIC does save us a lot of time by performing calculations which would otherwise have us rushing for books of tables or slide rules.

The program shown in Fig. 2.8 calculates and prints the sine of an angle. Now, the SIN function requires that the angle is supplied in radians and not in degrees. This means that there must be a preliminary piece of arithmetic carried out to convert degrees to radians. This takes place in line 30 where the number of degrees is multiplied by $(\pi/180)$ and thus converted into radians. The resulting number of radians is then fed to the SIN function for the final calculation.

Fig 2.8

```
5 REM***PROGRAM TO CALCULATE SINE OF AN ANGLE GIVEN ITS SIZE IN DEGREES*
**
10 PRINT"ENTER NUMBER OF DEGREES"
20 INPUT D
25 REM***CONVERSION OF DEGREES TO RADIANS***
30 R=D*3.14159/180
40 S=SIN(R)
50 PRINT "SINE OF";D;"DEGREES IS";S
60 END


RUN
ENTER NUMBER OF DEGREES
? 45
SINE OF 45 DEGREES IS  70710631


END AT 60
```

Program outline: Note that the line numbered 30 is used to convert from the number of degrees, held in the variable D, into a number of radians, held in the variable R, by multiplying the value of D by 3.14159 (π) and then dividing it by 180. Then the value of SIN (R) is calculated and assigned to the variable S which is then printed out together with the text which surrounds it.

Fig. 2.9 is a program which calculates the area and circumference of a circle given its radius. Note that this program has its printing controlled by semicolons (;) but in Fig. 2.10 these have been replaced by commas (,) in lines 50 and 60. Note also that on line 10 a semicolon has been added on to the end of the line with the result that the input request, which is always a question mark (?) in BASIC, is printed on the same line as the contents of line 10. This is a very common practice in order to make a program look more conversational. Another way of doing this is to use the single line

Fig 2.9

```
5 REM***PROGRAM TO CALCULATE AREA AND CIRCUMFERENCE OF CIRCLES***
10 PRINT"TYPE IN RADIUS IN MM"
20 INPUT R
25 REM***CALCULATION OF AREA***
30 A=3.14159*R↑2
35 REM***CALCULATION OF CIRCUMFERENCE***
40 C=2*3.14159*R
50 PRINT "AREA =";A;"SQUARE MM."
60 PRINT"CIRCUMFERENCE =";C;"MM"
70 END


RUN
TYPE IN RADIUS IN MM
? 300
AREA = 282743.1 SQUARE MM.
CIRCUMFERENCE = 188954 MM

END AT 70
```

Program outline: All this program is doing is to use the formulae

$$A = \pi R^2$$

for the area of a circle and

$$C = 2\pi R$$

for its circumference in lines 30 and 40. These values, assigned to A and C respectively are printed out with the relevant text in lines 50 and 60.

10 INPUT "TYPE IN THE RADIUS IN MM.", R

instead of the two lines 10 and 20. This technique is used in a number of examples in later chapters.

Fig 2.10

```
10 PRINT"TYPE IN RADIUS IN MM";
20 INPUT R
30 A=3.14159*R↑2
40 C=2*3.14159*R
50 PRINT "AREA =",A,"SQUARE MM."
60 PRINT"CIRCUMFERENCE =",C,"MM"
70 END


RUN
TYPE IN RADIUS IN MM ? 300
AREA =          282743.1       SQUARE MM.
CIRCUMFERENCE =                1884.954    MM

END AT 70
```

Lastly, with Fig. 2.11 we have a program which illustrates one way in which the output from a program can be placed exactly where it is wanted on a page by using the TAB instruction. This is particularly useful if the printing is to be done on pre-printed stationery. TAB indicates exactly at

Fig 2.11

```
10 PRINT TAB(10);"HEADING"
20 PRINT TAB(8);"_____"
30 PRINT
40 PRINT TAB(10);"JOHN";TAB(20);"JANE";TAB(30);"JIM"
50 PRINT TAB(8);"JOANNA";TAB(21);"AMY";TAB(27);"ARTHUR"
60 PRINTTAB(11);"BOB";TAB(17);"ANTHONY";TAB(25);"RODERICK"
70 END


RUN
      HEADING
      _____

      JOHN      JANE      JIM
    JOANNA       AMY    ARTHUR
       BOB   ANTHONY  RODERICK

END AT 70
```

what position across the page the next character in the output is to be printed: TAB(15) at the fifteenth position, TAB(55) at the fifty-fifth position, and so on. It is very similar to the tabbing arrangements on a normal typewriter. The use of TAB will be used in a number of the programs illustrated in subsequent chapters.

CHAPTER 3

DECISIONS, DECISIONS

3.1 CONDITIONAL AND UNCONDITIONAL JUMPS

In both the previous chapters it has been said that a program will proceed to execute in the order of its instructions once it has been given the RUN command. In BASIC programs the order of execution is determined by the line numbers allocated to each line of the program. The order in which the program instructions are executed can be changed by two types of instruction. One of these is the *unconditional* jump which simply says

GOTO 400

so that the next line of program to be executed is that bearing the line number 400 irrespective of where in the program the directive is placed ('Go to gaol; go directly to gaol, do not pass Go, do not collect £200').

On the other hand the computer can be made to take logical decisions and select one of two alternatives and this gives it a power quite beyond that of a simple calculating machine. In the first chapter we saw instructions of this type where a branch was made after the contents of the accumulator had been examined.

BASIC allows the programmer to write a far more meaningful test than just examining the accumulator. This register is never mentioned or even recognised as existing. It is the variables within the program which concern the programmer and so the software which backs up BASIC is left to worry about accumulators and the like. All the programmer has to write is a test such as

100 IF X > Y THEN GOTO 200

which will cause the execution of the instruction on line 200 if the value of the variable held in X is greater than the value of the variable held in Y. If the test fails, that is, if the value of the variable in X is less than or equal to the variable held in Y, then the instruction immediately following the test is executed. This is a *conditional* jump. BASIC looks after the loading and testing of the contents of the accumulator and leaves us to concentrate on the more important problems of program logic.

The tests which can be made part of a conditional jump instruction can come from six possible types. These are

Greater than	>
Less than	<
Equal to	=
Not equal to	<> or #
Greater than or equal to	> =
Less than or equal to	< =

and so we can write tests of the form

100 IF X > Y THEN GOTO 200

or

100 IF X < Y THEN GOTO 200

or

100 IF X = Y THEN GOTO 200

or

100 IF X <> Y THEN GOTO 200

or

100 IF X > = Y THEN GOTO 200

or

100 IF X < = Y THEN GOTO 200

All six of the above tests are based on the truth, or otherwise, of the assertion which follows the keyword IF. The first of the six examples could be written in a form closer to English as

IF (the assertion that the value of X is greater than the value of Y is true) THEN the next instruction is to be found on line 200.

In general, we can write any testable assertion in the brackets; for example we can write a test which determines whether or not B^2 is greater than 4 AC or that K = 0 or any relationship between variables and constants that can have either a true or a false value. (This is another example of the binary nature of the workings of a computer.)

So far we have seen that if the assertion is true then a jump is made to a particular line of program. This, however, may not always be the case since many forms of BASIC allow the IF test to be followed by any executable BASIC statement such as PRINT, STOP or LET as well as GOTO. For example we could write

        10 IF X = Y THEN PRINT "EQUAL"

or

        10 IF X <> THEN LET X = Y

3.2 PUTTING DECISIONS TO USE

Now let us see some programs written in BASIC which illustrate the use of decisions to cause the repetition of parts of the program in order to, as in the first three examples, accumulate a total. Fig. 3.1 is a program which inputs 10 numbers, adds them up and prints their total and their average. Notice that this is done in a loop where the number of numbers input is kept track of by a variable called C. The running total of the numbers is held in a variable called T. It is very tempting to write a program which looks like this

        10 INPUT A, B, C, D, E, F, G, H, I, J
        20 T = A + B + C + D + E + F + G + H + I + J
        30 PRINT "TOTAL IS"; T
        40 PRINT "AVERAGE IS"; T/10

but a moment's thought will show that this is not a very useful program since it could not be expanded—as the program in Fig. 3.1 can—to accept, total and calculate the average of, say, 100 numbers. We would soon have a very unwieldy program and find that we had run out of letters of the alphabet!

Fig. 3.2 shows the program adapted to do the same as in the previous figure except that at line 25 the program is told how many numbers to expect and hence the number of times the loop has to be executed.

Fig 3.1

```
 5 REM***PROGRAM TO AVERAGE A SET OF 10 NUMBERS***
10 C=0
20 T=0
30 INPUT X
40 T=T+X
50 C=C+1
60 IF C=10 THEN 80
70 GOTO 30
80 PRINT "TOTAL IS";T
90 PRINT "THE AVERAGE IS";T/10
100 STOP
```

Program outline: In this program the variables C and T are used to hold a count of how many numbers have been input to the program and their total respectively. Lines 10 and 20 set these variables to be zero, since at that point we have had no numbers input and their total so far is therefore zero. The numbers are input one at a time whenever line 30 is reached and at line 40 the value of T is increased by the number input at line 30. Line 50 sees C increased by one as each number is processed. Then line 60 tests the value of C to see if it has reached 10. If it has then the total and the average are printed and the program stops at line 100. If less than ten numbers have been input then line 30 is executed again to input another number. Notice that only the current value of X is retained, and as soon as line 30 is executed again a new value overwrites the previous value so that we could get the following sequence. Initially, C = 0 and T = 0. At line 30 X becomes, say, 21. Then T becomes 21 and C becomes 1. The test at line 60 fails and so we go back to line 30 where X may be assigned the new value of 15. T then becomes 36 and C will increase to 2. At this point the program has retained to running total of 36, the number of items input, 2 and the last value of X which was 15. The 21 has been lost for ever having been replaced by the 15. And so the program continues.

Fig 3.2

```
5 REM***BETTER VERSION OF AVERAGE PROGRAM***
10 C=0
20 T=0
25 INPUT"HOW MANY NUMBERS ?";N
27 REM***N CONTROLS THE NUMBER OF ITEMS INPUT***
30 INPUT X
40 T=T+X
50 C=C+1
60 IF C=N THEN 80
70 GOTO 30
80 PRINT "TOTAL IS";T
90 PRINT "THE AVERAGE IS";T/N
100 STOP
```

Program outline: This is basically the same as Fig. 3.1 except that a request is made for a number to be input at line 25 which will tell the program how many numbers it will have to total. This number will be held in the variable N instead of always being 10 as in the previous program. This means that line 60 tests C against the value of N, which could be 5 or 79 or 100 or whatever, instead of 10 and that line 90 computes the average by dividing the total by this of N.

The program in Fig. 3.3 is an even more refined version in that the person who uses the program need have no idea of how many numbers are to be input before the program is run. To use the program in Fig. 3.2 properly the user would have to count the number of items to be processed before the program is run. Computer people are notoriously bad at arithmetic! Fig. 3.3 uses a 'trigger', in this case a rogue value of X which is −1. The value −1 has no special significance, any number which does not exist

in the rest of the list will do. Other common numbers used as triggers are
0, 999, 99 and so on.

In Fig. 3.4 decisions are put to use in a program which is used to convert currencies at the current rate of exchange.

Fig 3.3

```
5 REM***AVERAGE PROGRAM USING -1 AS A TRIGGER TO STOP INPUT***
10 C=0
20 T=0
30 INPUT X
40 IF X=-1 THEN 80
50 T=T+X
60 C=C+1
70 GOTO 30
80 PRINT "THE TOTAL OF";C;"NUMBERS IS";T
90 PRINT "THE AVERAGE IS";T/C
100 STOP
```

Program outline: This is an even better version of the averaging program since it does not require the programmer to know in advance how many numbers are to be added up. All that is necessary is to terminate our list by the number −1 which acts as a rogue value or a 'flag' to say to the program 'You've had all the numbers now. Compute the average please'. This it does by dividing the total, T, by the value of C which has kept track of the number of items processed.

Fig 3.4

```
5 REM***CONVERSION PROGRAM - POUNDS TO DOLLARS OR VICE VERSA***
10 PRINT "THIS PROGRAM WILL ALLOW YOU TO CONVERT POUNDS STERLING"
20 PRINT "TO AMERICAN DOLLARS OR VICE VERSA"
30 INPUT "WHAT IS THE CURRENT RATE OF DOLLARS TO THE POUND ?";R
40 PRINT "TYPE 1 FOR CONVERSION FROM POUNDS TO DOLLARS"
50 INPUT "TYPE 2 FOR CONVERSION FROM DOLLARS TO POUNDS: ";N
60 IF N=1 THEN 100
70 IF N=2 THEN 140
80 PRINT "ONLY 1 OR 2 TO BE TYPED IN"
90 GOTO 40
95 REM***CONVERSION £ TO $***
100 INPUT "HOW MANY POUNDS ?";P
110 D=R*P
120 PRINT P;"POUNDS STERLING =";D;"AMERICAN DOLLARS"
130 STOP
135 REM***CONVERSION $ TO £***
140 INPUT "HOW MANY DOLLARS ?";D
150 P=D/R
160 PRINT D;"AMERICAN DOLLARS =";P;"POUNDS STERLING"
170 STOP
```

Program outline: This program uses the concept of a using a variable as a 'switch'. If N is assigned the value 1 then the section of program from lines 100 to 130 is executed. If N is given the value 2 then the section from lines 140 to 170 is executed. Any other value which might by accident be given to N is trapped out in line 80 since both tests will fail because N will neither be 1 nor 2 and the program returns to line 40 for the user to have another try.

An example of a computer program which is non-computational is shown in Fig. 3.5 where the program sorts three numbers into ascending order of size. It is non-computational in that the program consists of nothing but a series of tests and interchanges as a result of those tests. This is a good example of the fact that not all programs are mathematical.

Fig 3.5

```
5  REM***SORTING THREE NUMBERS INTO ORDER***
10 INPUT A,B,C
20 IF A>B THEN 200
30 IF B>C THEN 300
40 IF A>B THEN 400
50 PRINT A,B,C
60 STOP
190 REM***SWAP OF A AND B***
200 T=A
210 A=B
220 B=T
230 GOTO 30
290 REM***SWAP OF B AND C***
300 T=B
310 B=C
320 C=T
330 GOTO 40
390 SWAP OF A AND B***
400 T=A
410 A=B
420 B=T
430 GOTO 50
440 END
```

Program outline: This program does no calculations but makes a number of decisions. Three numbers are input and adjacent pairs are compared in size. Should the first be larger than the second their positions are reversed. The sequence is

(1) Compare first pair—swap if necessary.

(2) Compare second pair—swap if necessary.

(3) Compare first pair again—swap if necessary.

(4) Print all three numbers.

The swapping procedure requires a little examination. At first sight it might be thought that to interchange the values of the numbers held in A and B all we need do is write A = B and B = A. If you think about it for a little and remember that we are exchanging the contents of a pair of storage locations in memory then we have to be rather more subtle. Imagine you have two glasses, one full of beer and the other full of water. If we want to put the water in the beer glass and the beer in the water glass, what do we need? That's right, another glass!

Another example of a test being made and the outcome of the test determining which part of the program is executed after the test is in the mathematical routine which is used by all computers to calculate square roots (see Fig. 3.6). This is an example of what is called an *iterative* process where a better and better approximation to the answer is obtained every time the loop of calculations is traversed. What is happening is that every square root starts with an approximation, which is 1. Then the number to be rooted is divided by this approximation and the answer is added to the approximation. The next move is to divide the sum of these two numbers by 2 and this provides a new, and better, approximation. Then the calculation is performed using the new approximation. This produces a better approximation still until finally the number fed into the approximation part of the loop is the same as the number which emerges from it. For example, if we wish to calculate the square root of 3, we must start with a first approximation of 1

$$\frac{1}{2}\left(1 + \frac{3}{1}\right) = 2$$

The second approximation is 2, then

$$\frac{1}{2}\left(2 + \frac{3}{2}\right) = 1.75$$

The third approximation is 1.75, then

$$\frac{1}{2}\left(1.75 + \frac{3}{1.75}\right) = 1.732 \quad \text{(to 3 places of decimals)}$$

The fourth approximation is 1.732, then

$$\frac{1}{2}\left(1.732 + \frac{3}{1.732}\right) = 1.732 \quad \text{(to 3 places of decimals)}$$

so that now we have the number put into the calculation producing an identical number from the calculation and if we are working to three decimal places only we can say that the square root of 3 is 1.732. So who needs tables to calculate square roots?

The program written in machine code in Fig. 1.7 is now written in BASIC in Fig. 3.7. Notice how much easier it is to follow when written in a language that is closer to the programmer's own tongue.

Some versions of BASIC allow us to go even further with decisions by allowing the use of the word ELSE, so that we can write

IF X > Y THEN PRINT X ELSE PRINT Y

Fig 3.6

```
5  REM***SQUARE ROOT CALCULATION USING ITERATION***
10 INPUT A
15 REM***SETS FIRST ATTEMPT AT ROOT TO BE 1***
20 X=1
25 REM***CALCULATES A BETTER APPROX. OF ROOT***
30 X1=(X+A/X)/2
40 IF X=X1 THEN 70
45 REM***REPLACES PREVIOUS APPROX. WITH BETTER ONE***
50 X=X1
60 GOTO 30
65 REM***PRINTS ROOT***
70 PRINT X
80 END
```

Program outline: The theory behind this program is as in the main text, but just notice that the number whose square root is required is input at line 10 and assigned to the variable called A. Then in line 20 the first approximation for the square root is given to the variable X in line 20 so that the first approximation to the square root always starts at 1. A better approximation is calculated on line 30 and the answer is assigned to the variable called X1. The value of X1 is obtained by calculating the average of X and A divided by X. Line 40 tests to see if the values of X and X1 are the same. If they are, then we have reached the required answer, namely the square root of the number called A. If X and X1 differ in size then, even if that difference is small, X is assigned the value of X1 and the calculation on line 30 is performed again. This process of 'iteration' proceeds until the test on line 40 is satisfied, at which point the program terminates. This iteration procedure is a very useful tool by which an original, not very good, guess at the answer to a problem is fed into a calculation and is 'refined' to produce a better approximation to the true answer. As an example of this program in action the following table shows the values of the variables as the program proceeds. The object is to calculate the square root of the number 100, which will be assigned to the variable A, X is initially set to be 1 by the program and then the values of X and X1 change until the text of X becoming the same size as X1 is successf'

X	X1
1	50.5
50.5	26.2401
26.2401	15.0255
15.0255	10.8404
10.8404	10.0326
10.0326	10.0001
10.0001	10
10	10

Notice how the initially widely differing values of X and X1 rapidly con-
verge to a value quite close to the final answer. Then the value of X
slowly 'homes in' on the final answer which is, of course, 10 (10 × 10 =
100), so we can easily see that our answer is correct.

Fig 3.7

```
5 REM***HIGHEST COMMON FACTOR PROGRAM***
10 INPUT A,B
20 IF A-B<0 THEN 50
30 A=A-B
40 GOTO 20
50 C=A
60 A=B
70 B=C
80 IF C=0 THEN PRINT A
90 IF C=0 THEN STOP
100 GOTO 30
110 END
```

*Program outline: The program first of all establishes which is the larger of
the two numbers input in line 10 and assigns the value of the larger to A
by interchanging A and B if required by lines 50 to 70. B is then repeatedly
subtracted from A until the result is negative. If by this time A has reached
zero then the value of B is printed and the program stops. (I know that line
80 says that if C = 0 then A is to be printed, but look at the lines it executes
just before it reaches line 80.)*

meaning that if the value of X exceeds the value of Y then the value of
X is printed, otherwise the value of Y is printed. This is a particularly useful feature since it cuts down the number of GOTO instructions in a program and thus reduces the 'spaghetti' look of some BASIC programs. This
feature is found in a number of other programming languages.

3.3 LOOPS

In some of the preceding examples a loop of instructions has been traversed
by setting up a starting value of a counting variable, going through the
loop, incrementing the variable and then testing to see how many times
the loop has been traversed. Fig. 3.2 was a good example of this. All high-
level languages allow us to define loops by means of special instructions
thus reducing the amount of code the programmer has to write. In BASIC
this is done by means of a FOR ... NEXT ... loop. At the start of the
loop we could, for example, write

FOR I = 1 TO 10 STEP 1

and at the end of the loop write

> NEXT I

The first of this pair of lines states that the counting variable is to be called I and it is to be set intially at 1. I is to be increased in steps of 1 until it has reached 10. When I has reached the value of 10 the loop is no longer executed and the instruction immediately following the NEXT I line is to be executed. The loop of instructions is therefore bracketed by the FOR . . . and the NEXT . . . so that

> 10 FOR I = 1 TO 10 STEP 1
> 20 PRINT I
> 30 NEXT I

will cause the numbers 1 to 10 to be printed. In the same way

> 10 FOR I = 10 TO 1 STEP –1
> 20 PRINT I
> 30 NEXT I

will cause the numbers 10 down to 1 to be printed.

If the step size is 1 then it can usually be omitted so that

> FOR I = 1 TO 10

implies a step size of 1.

Fig 3.8

```
1 REM***ANOTHER AVERAGING PROGRAM USING 'FOR - NEXT' LOOP FOR INPUT***
5 T=0
10 FOR I=1 TO 10 STEP 1
20 INPUT X
30 T=T+X
40 NEXT I
50 A=T/10
60 PRINT T,A
70 END
```

Program outline: Here is yet another version of the program which averages a set of numbers. It uses the BASIC facility of defining a loop of instructions which are bracketed by the statements on lines 10 and 40. Line 10 says that the value of a variable called I must go from 1 to 10 in steps of 1 and line 40 states that it is at the point in the program that the value of I is to be incremented. This means that every instruction contained within lines 20 and 30 will be repeated ten times. After the loop has been executed ten times line 50 will be executed followed by the rest of the program.

The foregoing may be trivial examples, but look at Fig. 3.8 where 10 numbers are read in and summed prior to their total and average being printed. Fig. 3.9 shows the same process taking place but for a number of inputs governed by the number allocated to N in line 10. Both these programs are similar to those in Figs 3.1 and 3.2.

Fig 3.9

```
1 REM***THE VALUE OF N CONTROLS THE NUMBER OF TIMES THE LOOP IS EXECUTED
***
5 T=0
10 INPUT N
20 FOR I=1 TO N STEP 1
30 INPUT X
35 T=T+X
40 NEXT I
50 A=T/N
60 PRINT T,A
70 END
```

Program outline: This is basically the same as the previous program except that the number of times the loop is to be traversed is held in the number N which is input at line 10.

The program shown in Fig. 3.10 shows an example of a FOR . . . NEXT . . . loop used to control the printing of the values of the expression

$$4x^2 + 3x - 2$$

over a range of values of x.

Fig 3.10

```
5 REM***EXAMPLE OF A LOOP WITH START, FINISH AND INCREMENT DETERMINED AT
  RUN TIME***
10 INPUT F,L,S
20 FOR X=F TO L STEP S
30 Y=4*X↑2+3*X-2
40 PRINT Y
50 NEXT X
60 END
```

Program outline: This program would be very useful if a table of values of a certain expression were required. At line 10 three numbers are input which will define the starting value, F, of the variable called X, the largest value, L, for X and the size of step, S, by which F is to be incremented from F to L. In other words, if F was made 1, L was made 6 and S was made 0.5 then the values of Y would be calculated for values of X which would be in turn

1, 1.5, 2, 2.5, 3, 3.5 . . . . 5, 5.5, 6

Once X has reached 6 the last calculation and print are made and the program stops.

Loops do not have to be traversed a predetermined number of times, as in the previous examples. The program in Fig. 3.6 could be written as in Fig. 3.11. Here, once the assertion is found to be true, the program breaks out of a loop and finishes. If the loop goes its full course then the best approximation of the root is calculated and printed. This prevents the possibility which exists in the previous version of the program that it might go into an infinite loop if the test in line 40 fails each time round—it could happen!

Fig 3.11

```
5 REM***SQUARE ROOT CALCULATION - EXAMPLE OF AN ITERATION***
10 INPUT A
20 X=1
25 REM***CALCULATION ISONLY ALLOWED TO CONTINUE A MAXIMUM OF 100 TIMES**
*
30 FOR I=1 TO 100 STEP 1
40 X1=(X+A/X)/2
50 IF X=X1 THEN 90
60 X=X1
70 NEXT I
75 REM***JUST IN CASE AN EXACT MATCH IS NOT FOUND IN LINE 50***
80 X=(X+X1)/2
90 PRINT "THE SQUARE ROOT OF";A;"IS";X
100 STOP
```

Program outline: This is basically the square root program again but with the addition that the repeated calculation can only be made 100 times at most. This is because there is always the possibility that at line 50 the values of X and X1 may not be exactly equal and so the program is saved from going into an endless loop by saying, 'If you cannot get an exact answer after 100 tries then take the average of the values of X and X1 and use that as the answer'.

Finally, Fig. 3.12 is the electricity bill problem, written in ACE in Fig. 1.11, but now written in BASIC. It will appear again in some of the other languages later on in this book.

Fig 3.12

```
 5 REM***ELECTRICITY BILL PROGRAM***
10 INPUT E
15 REM***TESTS FOR NUMBER OF UNITS ABOVE 150***
20 IF E<=150 THEN 30
25 GOTO 90
27 REM***CALCULATES COST AT 7P PER UNIT***
30 C=E*0.07
35 REM***TESTS IF LESS THAN £3.64 WORTH OF UNITS USED***
40 IF C<3.64 THEN 50
45 GOTO 60
47 REM***SETS C TO MINIMUM CHARGE***
50 C=3.64
55 REM***ADDS ON STANDING CHARGE***
60 C=C+3.25
65 REM***ADDS ON V.A.T. CHARGE @ 15%***
70 C=C*1.15
75 REM***PRINTS TOTAL CHARGE***
80 PRINT "£";C
85 STOP
87 REM***CALCULATES NUMBER OF UNITS OVER 150***
90 E=E-150
95 REM***CALCULATES COST OF UNITS AT 5P PLUS COST OF FIRST 150 UNITS ***
100 C=E*0.05+10.5
110 GOTO 60
```

Program outline: This program follows exactly the same form as the one described in Fig. 1.11. The only difference is that it uses the better facilities offered by BASIC over ACE by being able to work in decimals instead of whole numbers only.

CHAPTER 4

STORING DATA IN MEMORY

4.1 BITS, BYTES AND WORDS

Once one understands the basic workings of a computer then the concept of the storage of data is quite simple to follow. The majority of computers, whether mainframe, mini or micro, are designed around the concept of the computer *word*. A word is the basic unit of information used by a computer and is a collection of *bits* (*bi*nary dig*its*) and contains 8, 16 or 32 bits as a rule. Eight bits are collectively known as one *byte* and if we stick to the byte concept we shall be able to follow the descriptions of data storage used in this and subsequent chapters. Basically a computer can store three types of data: *integer* numbers, *floating point* numbers and *characters*. An integer, a whole number, can be either positive or negative and needs 2 bytes of storage, that is, one word of a minicomputer's memory. A floating point number, one which contains a decimal part as well as an integer part, needs 4 bytes of storage, that is if it is to contain a maximum of 6 significant digits. If more storage is allowed for a floating point number then its number of significant digits is increased. If 6 significant digits are stored then the number is said to be stored with *single precision*. A character, which can be any letter of the alphabet, the digits 0 through 9 and special characters such as @, %, +, =, &, etc., need 1 byte of storage and so one 16 bit word of a minicomputer's memory can store two characters (see P. E. Gosling and Q. L. M. Laarhoven, *Digital Codes for Computers and Microprocessors*, Macmillan, 1980).

The version of BASIC available on most minicomputers does not distinguish between integers and floating point numbers and stores everything in floating point. This can lead to some peculiar *rounding* and *truncation* errors. Many of the microBASICs now available do allow a distinction to be made between integers, single and double precision floating point numbers, with a consequent increase in the accuracy of the arithmetic operations. The distinction between the use of integers and floating point numbers may not be easy to grasp initially but suffice it to say that we should always do our counting, as in many FOR . . . NEXT . . . loops, using integers and our arithmetic using floating point numbers. If counting is done using floating point numbers then some very odd results can be seen—see Chapter 9.

4.2 STORING LISTS

However, now we must get down to business. We have already seen that variable names in BASIC act as 'symbolic addresses' for the storage location where the number associated with that variable is stored. The symbol table keeps track of just where each variable is stored in memory. In addition to this it is also possible to store lists of numbers in memory by using the concept of the *base* address for a list. To do this we use a DIMension statement in BASIC and this reserves space for a set of variables which all bear a common family name. For example

10 DIM K(100)

will cause a set of locations in memory to be set aside for a list whose members will be known as K(1), K(2), K(3), etc., up to K(100). The first address reserved for this list is known as the base address of the list. The address of any element of the list can easily be computed by offsetting the number of the item in the list from this base address. In other words the address of K(12) will be 12 steps up from the base address. As programmers we do not have to worry about this calculation—it's just another job performed for us by the computer software.

Fig. 4.1 shows a simple program in BASIC to read a set of numbers into a list and then print them out. The object of the program is to place a series of numbers into a series of related memory addresses ready for immediate access while the program is running. But beware, if another program is then entered and run then the set of numbers previously put into the list cannot be retrieved. Any subsequent program cannot access variables stored in memory by a previous program. The only way this can be done is to store the data away on a disc or tape file, not in main memory. The technique used for this method of storage will be dealt with in the next chapter.

Another example of the simple use to which the storage of data in a list is put is in the program featured in Fig. 4.2. In this a randomly organised set of numbers are read into a list and then the list is scanned in order to find the smallest number in the list. (Note that the method used for triggering off the end of the input list is also used in the program shown in Fig. 3.3.) The program scans through the list from the start comparing each number with the smallest number found so far as it goes. This routine has to be started off and this is achieved by first of all allocating the very

Fig 4.1

```
5  REM***USING A LIST OF NUMBERS STORED IN MEMORY***
10 DIM L(50)
20 INPUT N
30 FOR I=1 TO N STEP 1
35 REM***ALLOCATES INPUT NUMBERS TO THE LIST - ONE AT A TIME***
40 INPUT L(I)
50 NEXT I
60 FOR I=1 TO N STEP 1
65 REM***PRINTS LIST L STORED IN MEMORY ONE AT A TIME***
70 PRINT L(I)
80 NEXT I
90 END
```

Program outline. This program serves no really useful purpose except to show how we can set up lists of numbers in memory. What we can do with these lists is a matter for explanation in other programs which will follow later. A list of numbers is stored in memory for rapid immediate access hence the name sometimes given to what we often now call RAM (Random Access Memory) and what we used to call core memory; that is, 'Immediate Access Store' (IAS). Any data stored in this type of memory can be read from far faster than if it were stored on a backing store consisting of discs or tape. Immediate access store has no moving parts and is all-electronic whereas backing store will always, until new technology provides something faster, contain much slower mechanical devices. However, there is a disadvantage to storing data in an IAS in that it has to share the memory with the program which is used to manipulate that data and as soon as another program is loaded into memory or the computer is switched off, everything in that memory is lost.

The first line of the program prepares the ground for a list called L which is to have up to 50 numbers stored in it. They will be known as L(1), L(2), L(3),..., L(50). At line 20 the variable N is given a value which determines just how much of the list we actually wish to use. N can take any value so long as it does not exceed 50—see below for the effect of N exceeding 50. Once N has been given a value then the number of times the first of the two loops is to be executed is established. By this the required number of items are placed in the list. If N is 20 then only 20 items are placed in the list, for example. The first number input will be assigned the name of L(1), the second L(2), and so on, so that the Nth number is placed in L(N). By this time the numbers in the list have been placed in memory and can then be accessed for whatever processing the program requires. In our preliminary example all we are going to do is simply copy the list from memory on to whatever output device (video screen or printer) our computer happens to use. The second loop starts off a counter, called I, back to 1 and then proceeds to copy the list, starting at L(1) and finishing at L(N) on to the output device.

If, in line 20, N had been given a value of, say, 55 then the program would have gone well and accepted the first 50 numbers input putting them into the list L. However, when I reached the value of 51, which is one more than the DIMensioning statement on the first line of the program has allowed for, an error message would be printed out saying

SUBSCRIPT ERROR IN LINE 30

which tells you that we are trying to use an item in a list with a subscript (the number in brackets) which has not been allowed for, in this case the 51st. Only by reDIMensioning the list with a larger number, by writing, say, DIM L (55) and starting again from the beginning will the problem go away.

first number in the list to be the smallest number, which it is at that point. Then the second number is compared with the smallest and if it is smaller then this number takes over the role as the current smallest. Then the third number in the list is compared with the current smallest and so on until the end of the list is reached. At that point the smallest number is printed out. The repetition of the operation 'test—replace the smallest so far by the number it is tested against if this is now smaller—go on to the next number in the list' is just the kind of repetitive operation which a computer can do, never get tired of and perform faster than we can.

4.3 SORTING LISTS INTO ORDER

The example in Fig. 4.2 may appear at first sight to be trivial but in fact it forms the basis of a very useful program which is used to sort numbers into ascending order, another time-consuming and boring task when done by hand. The technique is to scan the unsorted list to find the smallest number. This number is placed at the head of a new list and the original

Fig 4.2

```
5   REM***PROGRAM TO LOCATE THE SMALLEST NUMBER IN A LIST***
10  DIM L(50)
15  I=1
20  INPUT L(I)
30  IF L(I)=-1 THEN 100
40  I=I+1
50  GOTO 20
100 N=I-1
101 I=1
105 S=L(I)
110 I=I+1
120 IF I>N THEN 200
125 REM***CURRENT SMALLEST FOUND AND ASSIGNED TO S***
130 IF S>L(I) THEN S=L(I)
140 GOTO 110
200 PRINT S
210 END
```

Program outline: The maximum size of the list L is DIMensioned in line 10 and then a number of numbers are read into that list, counted in by the variable I. The list is terminated by a −1 trigger. Since the last item in the list is to be ignored because it is −1 the actual length of the list is called N which is equal to I − 1, line 100. The list is now scanned from the first, where I = 1, to the last, when I = N, to establish which is the smallest number in the list, S. In line 130 the current smallest, S, is tested against each element of the list in turn, L (I), and if S exceeds L (I) then S assumes that value. That all sounds fine but remember that S has to have some initial value and that is why we have line 105 which sets the first value of S to be the value of L (1). After all, if we are looking at the members of the list one at a time in order then while we are looking at the first in the list that is the smallest so far. Notice that the loop never takes the program back to line 105 again; the loop takes us from line 140 to line 110 and we only drop out of the loop by succeeding in the test on line 120 when we have reached the end of the list and print S. Then the program stops.

list scanned again to find the next smallest number. This is then placed in the second position in the new list and the next smallest is found, placed in the new list and so on. The problem that immediately arises is that once the smallest number in a list has been found, how do we find the next smallest? This is easily solved if, once the smallest number in a list has been found and copied into the new list, its place in the old list is taken by a large number, say 99999 as in our example. The routine for finding the smallest in the list can then be used again. Once the next smallest has been found it too can be replaced by 99999 and the routine continues until such time as the original list contains nothing by 99999s. At that point the new list must contain all the numbers in ascending order. The program is shown in Fig. 4.3.

If the program in Fig. 4.3 is used to sort very long lists of numbers it soon becomes very inefficient. This is because the whole list is continually scanned from end to end each time and there will be more and more unnecessary tests. The version of the program shown in Fig. 4.4 is a more elegant approach to the problem. In this case the list becomes shorter and shorter as the smallest number is pulled out of the list. Once the position of the smallest number in the list has been established, all those members of the list which follow it are squeezed up one place. The sorting process then becomes faster and faster as the list becomes shorter and shorter. When the list contains only one number the sorting process is complete.

Figure 4.5 shows another program for sorting numbers, but this time the list is scanned from start to finish and pairs of numbers which are such that the first is greater than the second are switched round. This method is

Fig 4.3

```
5 REM***SORTING BY SELECTION OF THE CURRENT SMALLEST IN A LIST***
10 DIM A(100),B(100)
15 REM***INPUT PHASE***
20 I=1
30 INPUT A(I)
40 IF A(I)=-1 THEN  70
50 I=I+1
60 GOTO 30
70 N=I-1
74 REM***END OF INPUT PHASE***
75 L=1
80 S=A(1)
81 J=1
85 K=0
90 FOR I=1 TO N
100 IF S>A(I) THEN  200
110 IF A(I)=9999 THEN K=K+1
120 NEXT I
140 GOTO 250
200 S=A(I)
210 J=I
220 GOTO 120
250 B(L)=S
255 L=L+1
256 REM***REPLACEMENT OF CURRENT SMALLEST BY 9999***
260 A(J)=9999
265 IF K=N-1 THEN  300
270 GOTO 80
300 B(L)=S
304 REM***PRINTING OF SORTED LIST***
305 FOR I=1 TO N
310 PRINT B(I);
320 NEXT I
325 END
```

Program outline: This program uses two lists A and B which can contain up to 100 items each. First of all the unsorted list is read into list A, lines 20 to 70 using the −1 trigger again to indicate the end of the list. The variable L set to 1 in line 75 keeps track of how many of the numbers have been placed in to list B. Line 80 sets the first value of S, the smallest number, to be the first number in list A. The variable J, initially at 1, tells us which number in list A contains the current smallest. This is because when we have been right through list A and found the smallest number it contains, we need to know where it is so that we can replace it with 9999 in list A. The variable K keeps count of the number of 9999s which have been placed in list A. Once list A has been scanned and the current smallest has been found it is placed in the next available place in list B, its place in list A is filled by 9999 and the list is scanned again for the next smallest. When there is only one number in the list A which is not 9999, tested in line 265, then that number is placed into list B and list B is printed out, lines 305 to 320. Then the program stops.

Fig 4.4

```
5 REM***FASTER VERSION OF SELECTION SORT***
10 DIM A(100),B(100)
20 I=1
30 INPUT A(I)
40 IF A(I)=-1 THEN  70
50 I=I+1
60 GOTO 30
70 N=I-1
75 L=1
80 S=A(1)
85 J=1
90 FOR I=1 TO N
100 IF S>A(I) THEN  200
110 NEXT I
120 N=N-1
130 IF N=0 THEN  400
140 GOTO 300
200 S=A(I)
210 J=I
220 GOTO 110
300 B(L)=A(J)
310 L=L+1
315 REM***THIS SECTION MOVES REST OF LIST UP ONE PLACE***
320 FOR K=J TO N
330 A(K)=A(K+1)
340 NEXT K
350 GOTO 80
395 REM***PRINTING OF SORTED LIST***
400 B(L)=A(1)
401 FOR J=1 TO L
410 PRINT B(J);
420 NEXT J
430 STOP
```

Program outline: This is very similar to the previous program except
that instead of replacing the elements of list A by a rogue value of 9999
as the current smallest is discovered the list is made to shrink so that if
at any point, say, the fifth element of the list is found to be the smallest
then after it has been copied into the sorted list, list B, all the rest of the
list from A (6) to the end is shifted up one place. This is done in lines
320 to 340. The effect of this is to shorten the list by one item each time
it is scanned, thus making the scanning faster and faster as there are less
and less elements to scan. Notice that the value of N is reduced by one in
line 120 each time the list is scanned until N becomes zero in line 130. At
this point the program is directed to line 400 when the last remaining number in list A is placed at the end of list B which is then printed out. Then
the program ends.

Fig 4.5

```
5 REM***SORTING USING THE 'BUBBLE' SORT TECHNIQUE***
10 DIM L(100)
20 I=1
30 INPUT L(I)
40 IF L(I)=-1 THEN 70
50 I=I+1
60 GOTO 30
70 N=I-1
80 F=0
85 REM***START SCANNING THE LIST***
90 FOR I= 1 TO N-1
95 REM***COMPARE ADJACENT ITEMS IN LIST***
100 IF L(I)>L(I+1) THEN 200
110 NEXT I
115 REM***TEST TO SEE IF ANY EXCHANGES HAVE BEEN MADE***
120 IF F=0 THEN 150
130 GOTO 80
140 REM***PRINT SORTED LIST***
150 FOR I=1 TO N
160 PRINT L(I);
170 NEXT I
180 STOP
190 REM***EXCHANGE ROUTINE***
200 T=L(I)
210 L(I)=L(I+1)
220 L(I+1)=T
230 F=1
240 GOTO 110
250 END
```

Program outline: The method of placing the unsorted numbers into the list L is the same as in the previous programs. However, once the list has been established we set a flag called F to zero. Then the list is scanned from start to finish testing pairs of adjacent numbers. Should the first be greater than the second they are swapped over and the flag F is set to 1. After the whole list has been scanned the state of the flag is tested, line 120. Should this be zero then the whole list has been scanned without any exchanges having been made and so the list has been sorted and it is printed in order—lines 150 to 170.

known as a *bubble* sort since the numbers are constantly moving along the list and the larger numbers rise towards the top of the list, like the bubbles in a fizzy drink. When the list has been scanned without any interchange of adjacent numbers taking place the list is sorted and the program stops. The program can sense that no interchange has been made by the use of a variable called a *flag* which is set to 1 whenever an interchange routine has been performed. At the start of the scan the value of the flag is set to zero and at the end of the scan the flag is tested to see if it has changed in value. If it has not then no changes have been made to the list and hence this implies that the sorting process is now complete. Again, this method is not very efficient if very long lists of numbers are to be sorted.

Fig. 4.6 shows a more efficient method called a *shell* sort. It is a version

Fig 4.6

```
5 REM***SORTING USING THE 'SHELL SORT' TECHNIQUE***
10 DIM A(100)
20 I=1
30 INPUT A(I)
40 IF A(I)=-1 THEN 70
50 I=I+1
60 GOTO 30
70 N=I-1
120 M=N
140 M=INT(M/2)
160 IF M<=0 THEN 440
180 K=N-M
200 J=1
220 I=J
240 R=I+M
260 IF A(I)<=A(R) THEN 380
280 T=A(R)
300 A(R)=A(I)
320 A(I)=T
340 I=I-M
360 IF I>0 THEN 240
380 J=J+1
400 IF J<=K THEN 220
420 GOTO 140
440 PRINT"SORTED LIST"
460 FOR I=1 TO N
480 PRINT A(I);
500 NEXT I
520 END
```

Program outline: This shell sort program starts off by reading in the list of unsorted numbers into list A. then a scanning takes place, but only of corresponding elements in two halves of the list. Should the order of size of the numbers compared be such that the first exceeds the second they are exchanged, lines 260 to 320. Then the list is subdivided into four parts and comparable elements from the four parts are tested. This testing, moving and subdivision continues until the number of subdivisions of the list is equal to the number of elements in the list. At this point the list is sorted and can be printed out, lines 440 to 520. This method of sorting is at least three times faster than the bubble sort shown in Fig 4.5, but the principle is complex and its details rather beyond the scope of this book.

of the bubble sort. It is always a good idea to test out a program such as this with dummy data and trace its progress through the program with pencil and paper. This is often called a *dry run* and can be very revealing.

4.4 TABLES

An extension of the concept of a list can be made by adding a second dimension so that the contents of a *table* can be stored in the computer's memory. A table, or *array*, of numbers, say with three rows and four columns is stored row by row from the base address of the table. A list called A with 50 elements could be stored from a base address of, say, 200 in the manner shown in Table 4.1.

Table 4.1

Address	Contents
200	A(1)
201	A(2)
202	A(3)
248	A(49)
249	A(50)

An array called P with three rows and four columns would represent the table

P(1, 1)	P(1, 2)	P(1, 3)	P(1, 4)
P(2, 1)	P(2, 2)	P(2, 3)	P(2, 4)
P(3, 1)	P(3, 2)	P(3, 3)	P(3, 4)

where the order of the number in brackets refers to the *R*ow followed by the *C*olumn number—P(R, C). The array would be stored in memory from a base address of, say, 600 in the manner shown in Table 4.2.

Table 4.2

Address	Contents
600	P(1, 1)
601	P(1, 2)
602	P(1, 3)
603	P(1, 4)
604	P(2, 1)
605	P(2, 2)
606	P(2, 3)
607	P(2, 4)
608	P(3, 1)
609	P(3, 2)
610	P(3, 3)
611	P(3, 4)

It is part of the computer's software to convert a statement such as

10 DIM A(50)

or

20 DIM P(3, 4)

into a series of related addresses in memory and to generate the necessary instructions to point to address 609 when, for example, the array element P(3, 2) is referred to in a program.

A good example of the use of an array is in a program which creates a league table for, say, a series of football teams. The program in Fig. 4.7 demonstrates this. Note that all that is required is a set of four numbers in order: these represent the home team number, the away team number and the goals scored by each. For example, if team number 4 was at home to team number 2 and the scores were 3 for the home team and 1 for the away team then the four numbers 4, 2, 3, 1 would be input to the program. This gives sufficient information to the program for the appropriate rows and columns of the league table to be amended. The contents of the first column gives the number of matches played by each team, so that the element 3, 1 will contain the number of games played by team number 3. The fifth column contains the number of goals scored by the teams, so that element 6, 5 contains the number of goals scored by team number 6.

Fig 4.7

```
10 DIM R(10,7)
20 INPUT T1,T2,G1,G2
30 IF T1=-1 THEN 290
40 R(T1,1)=R(T1,1)+1
50 R(T2,1)=R(T2,1)+1
60 IF G1=G2 THEN 150
70 IF G1>G2 THEN 220
80 R(T1,3)=R(T1,3)+1
90 R(T1,5)=R(T1,5)+G1
100 R(T1,6)=R(T1,6)+G2
110 R(T2,2)=R(T2,2)+1
120 R(T2,6)=R(T2,6)+G1
130 R(T2,5)=R(T2,5)+G2
140 GOTO 20
150 R(T1,4)=R(T1,4)+1
160 R(T2,4)=R(T2,4)+1
170 R(T2,5)=R(T2,5)+G2
180 R(T2,6)=R(T2,6)+G1
190 R(T1,5)=R(T1,5)+G1
200 R(T1,6)=R(T1,6)+G2
210 GOTO 20
220 R(T1,2)=R(T1,2)+1
230 R(T2,6)=R(T2,6)+G1
240 R(T2,5)=R(T2,5)+G2
250 R(T2,3)=R(T2,3)+1
260 R(T1,5)=R(T1,5)+G1
270 R(T1,6)=R(T1,6)+G2
280 GOTO 20
290 PRINT"TEAM  P    W    L    D   FOR AGT PTS"
300 PRINT"================================================"
310 FOR I = 1 TO 10
320 PRINT I;
330 PRINT SPC(2);R(I,1);SPC(2);R(I,2);
340 PRINT SPC(2);R(I,3);SPC(2);R(I,4);
350 PRINT SPC(2);R(I,5);SPC(2);R(I,6);
360 PRINT SPC(2);R(I,7)
370 NEXT I
```

4.5 MATRICES

For the mathematically minded programmer an array can be used for holding the elements of a matrix. A program which multiplies one matrix by another, by multiplying the appropriate elements of the arrays, is shown in Fig. 4.8. Some versions of BASIC actually provide matrix functions as part of the software so that by writing

MAT A = B * C

we can cause the matrix called B to be multiplied by the matrix C in order to obtain the matrix A. This is only available on some versions of BASIC and certainly not on most other common high-level languages. An example is shown in Fig. 4.9.

Most versions of BASIC do not allow arrays of more than two dimensions. On the other hand a language such as FORTRAN does allow an array to have many dimensions so that we could have an array element such as

$$A(1, 4, 3, 2, 5)$$

4.6 STRINGS

The final topic in this chapter refers to the ability of BASIC to handle *strings* of characters, denoted in BASIC by a $ sign after the variable name. A string variable is written, for example, as A$, F$, Z$, and so on. The contents of a string variable are distinguished from other variables in that they are enclosed in quotation marks, just as *literals* are in a PRINT statement. In fact the print statement

300 PRINT "THIS IS THE END"

is instructing the computer to print out the string of characters which is enclosed in the quotes. We can write statements such as

10 A$ = "DEMONSTRATION"

or

10 A$ = "A"

but we must not write

10 A$ = A

since BASIC would be fooled into thinking that we were trying to assign the value of a numeric variable, called A, to a string variable called A$. This is not allowed, largely because of the different ways in which characters and numbers are stored, hence the use of quotation marks in order to make our intentions clear and unambiguous. If we write

Fig 4.8

```
5 REM***THIS PROGRAM ILLUSTRATES THE USEOF NESTED LOOPS IN BASIC***
10 INPUT "HOW MANY ROWS IN FIRST MATRIX ?";X
20 INPUT "HOW MANY COLUMNS IN FIRST MATRIX ?";Y
30 INPUT "HOW MANY ROWS IN SECOND MATRIX ?";P
40 INPUT "HOW MANY COLUMNS IN SECOND MATRIX ?";Q
50 IF Y=P THEN 80
60 PRINT "CAN'T DO THIS ONE"
70 STOP
80 DIM A(X,Y),B(P,Q)
85 REM***START OF FIRST NESTED LOOP***
90 PRINT "ENTER THE";X*Y;"ELEMENTS OF THE FIRST MATRIX"
100 FOR I=1 TO X
110 FOR J=1 TO Y
120 INPUT A(I,J)
130 NEXT J
140 NEXT I
145 REM***END OF FIRST NESTED LOOP***
150 PRINT
155 REM***START OF SECOND NESTED LOOP***
160 FOR I=1 TO X
170 FOR J=1 TO Y
180 PRINT A(I,J);
190 NEXT J
200 PRINT
210 NEXT I
215 REM***END OF SECOND NESTED LOOP***
220 PRINT "NOW THE";P*Q;"ELEMENTS OF THE SECOND MATRIX"
225 REM***START OF THIRD NESTED LOOP***
230 FOR I=1 TO P
240 FOR J=1 TO Q
250 INPUT B(I,J)
260 NEXT J
270 NEXT I
275 REM***END OF THIRD NESTED LOOP***
280 PRINT
285 REM***START OF FOURTH NESTED LOOP***
290 FOR I=1 TO P
300 FOR J=1 TO Q
310 PRINT B(I,J);
320 NEXT J
330 PRINT
340 NEXT I
345 REM***END OF FOURTH NESTED LOOP***
350 PRINT
360 PRINT "THEIR PRODUCT IS :-"
370 PRINT
375 REM***START OF FIFTH NESTED LOOP - 3 LOOPS, ONE INSIDE THE OTHER***
380 FOR I=1 TO X
390 FOR K=1 TO Q
400 FOR J=1 TO Y
410 S=S+A(I,J)*B(J,K)
420 NEXT J
430 PRINT S;
440 S=0
450 NEXT K
460 PRINT
470 NEXT I
475 REM***END OF FIFTH NESTED LOOP***
480 STOP
```

*Program outline: The first few lines of this program establish the sizes of
the two matrices to be multiplied and line 80 uses the values of X, Y, P
and Q to dimension the arrays A and B which will contain the two
matrices—this is known as 'dynamically setting up the arrays' so that the*

dimensioning is done as the program is actually running. Then the elements of the matrix A are entered by using a loop bracketed by lines 100 and 140 with another loop inside it, bracketed by lines 110 and 130. What this does is to set the value of I to 1 and then the value of J to 1. While I stays constant J goes from 1 to whatever Y may be set at. This means that the numbers are allocated to the array A in the order A (1, 1), A (1,2), A(1,3), etc., until the loop finishes with the set of values from 1 to Y. Then the NEXT I is executed and I increases by 1 to 2 and the inner loop starts again at 1 and goes through to Y again, that is, A (2, 1), A (2, 2), A (2, 3), etc. The I increases by 1 and J is reset to 1 and goes through its set of values again to give us A (3, 1), A (3, 2), etc. Only when I has reached its target value of X and J its target value of Y will line 150 be executed. Then, in a similar manner to the lines 100 to 140 will the array A be printed out. Notice that there is a semicolon at the end of line 180 to enable the values to be printed across the page. However, in order to start the printing of the following row in the proper place there is PRINT on line 200 to bring the printing head of the teleprinter back to the start of the line. The same procedure is adopted for the input and printing of the matrix called B. The multiplication of the two matrices is done in lines 380 to 470 where there is a set of three loops nested inside one another. To describe the mathematical technique involved here is outside the scope of this book, but anyone who knows about matrices will see what is being done. If the reader does not know sufficient mathematics to appreciate the niceties, suffice it to say that these last few lines exhibit the use of loops nested inside one another.

Fig 4.9

```
5 REM***THIS PROGRAM ILLUSTRATES THE USE OF MATRIX OPERATIONS IN BASIC**
*
10 INPUT "NUMBER OF ROWS IN 1st MATRIX ";X
20 INPUT "NUMBER OF COLUMNS IN 1st MATRIX ";Y
30 INPUT "NUMBER OF ROWS IN 2nd MATRIX ";P
40 INPUT "NUMBER OF COLUMNS IN 2nd MATRIX ";Q
50 DIM B(X,Y),C(P,Q)
60 DIM A(X,Q)
65 REM***THIS LINE ALLOWS ALL THE ELEMENTS IN THE MATRIX TO BE INPUT ONE
 AT A TIME***
70 MAT INPUT B
75 REM***THIS LINEPRINTS OUT THE MATRIX ROW BY ROW***
80 MAT PRINT B
90 PRINT
100 MAT INPUT C
110 MAT PRINT C
120 PRINT
125 REM***THIS LINE PERFORMS ALL THE MATRIX MULIPLICATION***
126 REM***OF MATRIX B BY MATRIX C AND ASSIGNS THE PRODUCT TO MATRIX A***
130 MAT A=B*C
140 MAT PRINT A
150 STOP
```

Program outline: This is exactly the same program as Fig. 4.8 but the particular version of BASIC used here allows us to condense the whole of lines 100 to 140 into line 70, lines 160 to 210 into line 80, lines 230 to 270 into line 100, lines 290 to 340 into line 110. Finally lines 380 to 470 are condensed into lines 130 and 140.

10 A$ = "MACMILLAN"

then the nine characters which go to make up the word are stored in successive bytes of memory, 1 byte per character. Now here comes a problem. In most minicomputer versions of BASIC the use of a string variable implies that there is to be a *list* of characters stored one after the other starting at the base address of the list. Two characters are stored in each computer word, since one character per 8 bits means that a 16 bit word can contain two characters. Hence the storage would be like this, starting from, say, a base address of 500, as shown in Table 4.3.

Table 4.3

Address	Contents
500	MA
501	CM
502	IL
503	LA
504	N

Since lists require DIMension statements we must provide one for each string variable (see Fig. 4.10). In this example a pair of strings are input and the only operation available on strings is performed. That operation is called *concatenation*. This is the amalgamation of two or more strings into

Fig 4.10

```
10 DIM A$(20),B$(20),C$(40)
20 INPUT A$
30 INPUT B$
40 C$=A$,B$
50 PRINT C$
60 C$=A$," ",B$
70 PRINT C$
80 STOP
RUN

? UNITED
? STATES
UNITEDSTATES
UNITED STATES

STOP AT 80
```

Program outline: Line 10 states that there are to be three strings of charac-
ters used in the program. A$ is to contain a maximum of 20 characters,
B$ is to contain a maximum of 20 and C$ is to contain a maximum of 40
characters. Lines 20 and 30 allow us to input characters into the strings
A$ and B$ and line 40 creates a new string, C$, by concatenating A$ and
B$ into a single string. Line 60 produces another version of the string C$
by concatenating the strings containing A$, a blank and B$ into a new
string. The output from the program shows the result.

one. Concatenation is usually denoted by a comma (,) or a plus sign (+) so
that we could write

  50 A$ = B$, C$

or

  50 A$ = B$ + C$

depending on the version of BASIC we are using. Most microBASICs use
the + sign. A concatenation program is shown in Fig. 4.11.

Fig 4.11

```
10 CLEAR 80
20 INPUT A$
30 INPUT B$
40 C$=A$+B$
50 PRINT C$
60 C$=A$+" "+B$
70 PRINT C$
80 STOP
```

Program outline: This is a version of the previous program rewritten in a
version of BASIC suitable for running on a microcomputer. Line 10 con-
tains an instruction to clear sufficient space in memory for 80 characters
to be stored. DIMensioning of strings to reserve space for the characters
is not normally required for this type of BASIC. The rest of the pro-
gram is the same as the previous one except that + is used for the con-
catenation operation.

There is a major inconsistency here between the way we write programs
using miniBASICs and the way we write them using micro BASICs. In
microBASICs we use the statement CLEAR or STRING to reserve string
space so that

  10 CLEAR 200

means that 200 bytes of memory are to be reserved for strings in the programs. This seems a little confusing at first since microBASICs also use DIM statements for strings as well. This is because they allow the use of lists of strings and arrays of strings, a feature not found in most mini-BASICs. The DIMension statement when applied to strings when most microBASICs are being used reserve space for a list of strings or an array of strings. For example

10 DIM A$(10)

means that there is going to be a list of strings called A$ where A$(1) might be "GEORGE", A$(2) might be "FRED", and so on. Fig. 4.12 is a program which uses this feature in order to sort a list of names into order. In fact, it uses the same technique as the program shown earlier in Fig. 4.5, which performed a bubble sort on numbers. The DIM statement in this program refers to the list of names and the program requires the CLEAR statement as well as the DIM.

Fig 4.12

```
5 REM***THIS PROGRAM WILL SORT A LIST OF NAMES INTO ALPHABETICAL ORDER**
*
12 REM***THIS WILL CLEAR 200 BYTES OF MEMORY FOR STRING STORAGE***
10 CLEAR 200
15 REM***THIS DIMENSIONS A LIST OF 20 NAMES***
20 DIM N$(20)
25 REM***THIS INPUTS THE LIST OF 20 NAMES***
30 FOR I= 1 TO 20
40 INPUT N$(I)
50 NEXT I
60 F=0
65 REM*x*THIS SCANS THE LIST SWAPPING PAIRS INTO ASCENDING ORDER***
70 FOR I=1 TO 19
80 IF N$(I)>>N$(I+1) THEN 160
90 NEXT I
95 REM***THIS TESTS TO SEE IF ANY SWAPS HAVE BEEN MADE***
100 IF F=0 THEN 120
110 GOTO 60
115 REM***THIS PRINTS THE SORTED LIST OF NAMES·****
120 FOR I=1 TO 20
130 PRINT N$(I);" ";
140 NEXT I
150 STOP
155 REM***THIS IS THE SWAPPING ROUTINE***
160 T$=N$(I)
170 N$(I+1)=N$(I)
180 N$(I+1)=T$
190 F=1
200 GOTO 90
```

Program outline: This program uses the bubble sort technique used to sort a list of numbers as shown in Fig. 4.5. It is written for use on a micro-computer, hence the CLEAR 200 instruction on line 10. This will allocate 200 bytes of memory for string storage. The instruction on line 20 states that there are to be 20 strings of characters in a list called N$. The loop bracketed by lines 30 to 50 allows 20 strings of characters to be input as *items of this list. If by chance the space in memory allocated to string storage is used up before the end of the loop is reached an error message which says*

OUT OF STRING SPACE IN 40

will indicate this. An increase in the number of bytes cleared in line 10 will be the only way out of this problem. The rest of the program follows the same pattern as the sort program for numbers. It might be noted that the test in line 80 is quite reasonable and logical. For example the string "AAAB" is deemed to be greater than the string "AAAA" and the string "JONES" is greater than the string "JOHNSON".

4.7 SUBSTRINGS

Substrings are parts of strings and in most miniBASICs are denoted by doubly subscripted string variables. Thus

A$(3, 6)

refers to that part of the string A$ starting at the third character and continuing to the sixth character. The program illustrated in Fig. 4.13 uses this convention.

One simple use of this concept of substrings is shown in Fig. 4.14 where a word can be analysed for the number of vowels it contains. A$(I, I) denotes the single Ith character of the string called A$.

Again, here is an area where microBASICs differ from miniBASICs in that substrings are referred to by the keywords

LEFT$
RIGHT$
MID$

Fig 4.13

```
10 DIM S$(30)
20 INPUT S$
30 PRINT S$
35 PRINT"THE STRING CONTAINS ";LEN(S$);"CHARACTERS"
40 INPUT A,B
50 IF A>B THEN 100
60 PRINT S$(A,B)
70 PRINT S$(A,A)
80 PRINT S$(B,B)
90 END
100 PRINT "THE FIRST NUMBER MUST NOT EXCEED THE SECOND"
110 GOTO 40
```

Program outline: Line 10 reserves space for a string called S$ which can contain up to 30 characters. Then the string is input and printed out. Line

35 uses the LEN function to tell us how many characters the string contained. Line 40 asks us to input a pair of numbers, in which the first should not exceed the second, in order to pick out some of the substrings contained within S$. Thus if S$ was the set of characters "LONDON" and A was set to 2 and B to 4 the output from line 60 would be "OND", from line 70 "O" and from line 80 "D".

Fig 4.14

```
10 DIM V$(5),S$(72)
20 V$="AEIOU"
30 INPUT"TYPE IN A WORD ",S$
40 FOR I=1 TO LEN(S$)
50 FOR J=1 TO 5
60 IF S$(I,I)=V$(J,J) THEN V=V+1
70 NEXT J
80 NEXT I
90 PRINT S$;"CONTAINS ";V;"VOWELS"
100 END
```

Program outline: This program searches for vowels in a word using the loop enclosed by lines 40 to 80 with an inner loop enclosed by lines 50 to 70. The outer loop takes each character in the string in turn and then uses the inner loop to test that character against the characters held in the string V$ which contains the vowels. If any one of the vowels matches a character in the string S$, then the vowel count, V, is increased by one. The whole string has been tested when the end of the string is reached—when I reaches the value of LEN(S$). Then the value of V is printed.

where LEFT$(A$, 3) refers to the three left-most characters in the string A$. RIGHT$(A$, 6) will refer to the last six characters of the string called A$. MID$(A$, 4, 2) will refer to the substring of the string A$ consisting of the two characters starting at character number 4. To compare and contrast the two versions let us take the string which contains the characters "MACMILLAN", as shown in Table 4.4.

Table 4.4

MiniBASIC	MicroBASIC	Substring
A$(1, 4)	LEFT$(A$, 4)	"MACM"
A$(5, 9)	RIGHT$(A$, 5)	"ILLAN"
A$(2, 4)	MID$(A$, 2, 3)	"ACM"
A$(5, 5)	MID$(A$, 5, 1)	"I"

Thank goodness there is one consistent feature of the way the two mainstreams of the BASIC language handle strings. This in the use of the LEN function which counts the number of characters in a string. For example if we write

20 P\$ = "DEMONSTRATION"
30 L = LEN(P\$)

then L will be assigned the value 13, there being that number of characters in the string. Fig. 4.15 shows a program written in a microBASIC which does the same thing as the program in Fig. 4.14, which is in a mini-BASIC. Notice the way the different versions handle strings, substrings in particular.

Fig 4.15

```
10 CLEAR 100
20 V$="AEIOU"
30 INPUT "TYPE IN A WORD ";S$
40 FOR I=1 TO LEN(S$)
50 FOR J=1 TO 5
60 IF MID$(S$,I,1)=MID$(V$,J,1) THEN V=V+1
70 NEXT J
80 NEXT I
90 PRINT S$;"CONTAINS";V;"VOWELS"
100 STOP
```

Program outline: This follows exactly the same pattern as the previous program except that it is in a microcomputer version of BASIC using CLEAR instead of DIM and the MID\$ function for defining substrings.

CHAPTER 5

THE ELECTRONIC FILING CABINET

5.1 INTRODUCTION

Much of the power of a computer system comes from its ability to store and retrieve large quantities of data. The dusty books and ledgers of the old-fashioned office are now quite outmoded since all the information they contain can be stored on magnetic tape or magnetic discs taking up a very small amount of space. Of course, the stored data has to be converted into special codes which are technically necessary for the transcription on to a magnetic medium. Luckily, the computer software will handle this encoding and all the programmer has to do is to decide what data is to be placed on what computer file. This is similar to the storage of music and speech on a gramophone or recording tape, for in that case we do not need to be more than vaguely aware of the technology of the stereo disc or cassette tape in order to use them. So long as we appreciate the advantages and disadvantages of the various types of storage media, then that is enough. The storage of computer data has many parallels with audio technology. Both discs and tape are used and each has specific and very good reasons for being used in the way it is. In fact, some of the hardware used in both computers and audio is identical since microcomputers often use audio cassette tapes for storing programs and files of data. The discs used on computers are not the same as the vinyl gramophone discs but more like, if such a thing were possible, a flat piece of recording tape. Computer discs are reusable, but gramophone records are not, except as flower pots! The advantage of using discs for the storage of data is that any piece of data can easily and quickly be retrieved by setting the reading head over the location of that data on the disc. Reading data stored on tape is very different since reading can only take place in sequence starting at the beginning of the tape. This is why a disc is essentially a *random access* device but a tape is a *serial access* device. Each system has its own merits. A tape has to be wound on past the reading head until the required piece of data, or piece of music, is found. This can take a very significant time especially if what is required is near the end of the tape. The reading of the required data from a disc, however, is far faster than from a tape since all that is required is for the correct track on the disk to be selected and the only time lag is in waiting for the correct part of that track to appear under the reading head.

Most computers need one or more magnetic discs in order to work efficiently. The smallest microcomputer will have a *mini-floppy* disc of $5\frac{1}{4}$ inches diameter, and this can store a few thousand bytes of data (see Fig. 5.1). A small minicomputer can have one or more *hard* discs capable of storing maybe 20 million bytes each (see Fig. 5.2). A large mainframe computer will have perhaps 20 or more disc drives each containing multi-platter discs which can store hundreds of millions of bytes of data (see Fig. 5.3). Magnetic tape is not so commonly used in the day-to-day running of a computer. Tape drives (see Fig. 5.4) are usually used for the longterm backing-up of data files by taking copies from the more expensive and delicate discs.

5.2 SERIAL FILES

Most computer systems actually hold both serial files and direct access files on disc. Serial files are easier for the beginner to deal with and understand. Special techniques have to be used when handling direct access files in practice, so only simple applications will be dealt with in this book.

Disc or tape storage can be used to retain files of program instructions over long periods and the computer software is used for this purpose. If one writes a program which is to be used more than once, then after it has been tested and found error-free it can be saved for future use by a single command such as

SAVE "PROGNAME"

where the name of the program is displayed, often within quotation marks as shown above. The name must be unique to that program.

The SAVE command enables a copy of the program currently in memory to be transferred to the backing store. The name of the program is automatically entered into a directory of names on that disc. This enables the software to keep track of all the program files stored on that disc so that they can be located whenever they are required.

To retrieve a program file from disc the command

LOAD "PROGNAME"

is used. The software examines the disc directory to establish that a file of that name actually does exist. Having done that the location of that file on

Fig 5.1 *microcomputer systems with 5¼ inch floppy discs (Photos: Stukeley Computer Services and Research Machines Ltd)*

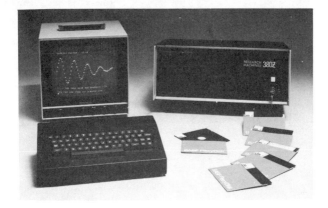

Fig 5.2

Fig 5.3

Fig 5.4

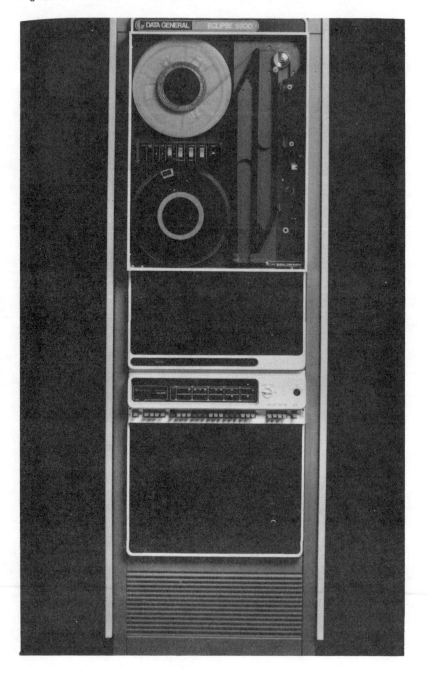

the disc is discovered and a copy of the program file is loaded into memory. The program is now in memory and ready to be run just as if it had been typed in laboriously at the keyboard.

You may notice that the words *program file* are used. This is because a program is simply a collection of characters which have no life of their own until they are presented to BASIC by the RUN command (see Fig. 5.5 for an example of a program being SAVEd, LOADed and run). Remember, a

Fig 5.5

```
* NEW
* 10 INPUT A,B,C
* 20 M=(A+B+C)/3
* 30 PRINT"THE AVERAGE OF THE 3 NUMBERS IS ";M
* 40 END
* SAVE"AVERAGE"
* LIST
10 INPUT A,B,C
20 M=(A+B+C)/3
30 PRINT"THE AVERAGE OF THE 3 NUMBERS IS ";M
40 END
READY
* NEW
* LIST
* READY
* LOAD"AVERAGE"
* RUN
? 3,7,8
THE AVERAGE OF THE 3 NUMBERS IS 6

END IN 40
READY
```

Program outline: The first line in the illustration is the command NEW, typed in by the programmer. This clears any lines of program from the memory. Then the program is typed in line by line, a simple program to input three numbers and calculate and print their average. The command SAVE "AVERAGE" will cause a copy of the current program to be saved on the backing store. At that point there exist two versions of the same program: one in memory ready for execution if need be and one on the backing store under the name "AVERAGE". As proof that the copy does exist in memory the command LIST causes a list of the program instructions to be printed at the programmer's terminal. Having printed the program the computer types the word READY which indicates that it is awaiting further instructions. The programmer types NEW which clears all the program instructions out of memory. This is demonstrated by the effect of the LIST command. All that happens is that the word READY is typed immediately after the command has been issued showing that there are now no program instructions in memory. The programmer types LOAD "AVERAGE" which causes the instructions which are stored under that name on backing store to be copied into memory. The original set of

instructions have now been restored to memory from backing store and
the command RUN causes them to be executed and the program asks for
three numbers, computes their average and prints the answer according to
the instructions contained in the program called "AVERAGE".

program in memory is only there while the computer is switched on and until you type NEW or LOAD another program. A program on backing store is there permanently until someone deliberately destroys it with a DELETE or KILL command. Fig. 5.6 shows a copy of a disc directory, where the extension ·BAS indicates that a file is a BASIC program file, ·DAT indicates a data file and ·TXT is a text file.

Fig 5.6

```
A>DIR B:
B: JPFUN      BAS
B: PIP        COM
B: STAT       COM
B: DBASS      COM
B: AWARI      BAS
B: NABEST     BAS
B: JHNUTS     BAS
B: CTS1       BAS
B: XYZPQRST   BAS
B: NORMAL     BAS
```

When dealing with data files, as opposed to program files, there are three operations which must be mastered.

(1) Putting data into a file for permanent storage.

(2) Copying the data stores in a file on to some display device such as a printer or a video screen.

(3) Amending the data stored in a data file.

A good example of putting these operations to good use would be the setting up, maintenance and printing of a mailing list of names and addresses stored away on a disc file. First of all, a program has to be written which will accept names and addresses from some input device, usually a keyboard at a terminal, and to place them in some sort of order on to a disc file. Next, there must be a program which will read these names and addresses from the file and print them on to sticky labels ready to be affixed to envelopes. The format of the output is shown in Fig. 5.7. A moment's thought will show that this is not quite as easy as it seems at first sight since printers print one line across a page at a time — hence the term *line printer* — so that four names are printed across the page and then the four addresses line by line across the page; not a trivial task.

Finally, a program is needed which will maintain the name and address file and keep it up to date. This means that it must be capable of deleting out-of-date entries and modifying addresses when people who remain on the file move house or when incorrect addresses are on the file.

5.3 USE OF FILES IN PROGRAMS

The first type of program — writing data to a file — requires that the programmer first of all asks for space to be made ready on the disc to receive the data. This is the operation of OPENing a file, which must bear a unique name, entering its name in the disc directory and making it ready for data to be written to it. Such a program statement might be

OPEN FILE (0, 1), "STOCKFILE"

where the first of the two numbers in brackets is called the *logical file number*. It is by this number that the file will be referred to throughout the current program. The second number indicates the *mode* of the file, in this case it is the *write* mode, that is, that data is going to be recorded on to the file.

The next thing to do is to tell the computer which pieces of data are to be put on to each *record* of the file. A file record is a single set of data and a file is made up of a collection of records. If the data on each record consists of a part number, description and number in stock then an INPUT instruction would place that data in memory, having been typed in at the keyboard, by the instruction

INPUT N$, D$, N

The instruction to record this data on the file would be of the form

WRITE FILE (0), N$, D$, N

This has the effect of copying the data held in the memory locations named N$, D$ and N on to the next record of the file. The computer would then be instructed to request a further set of data which would then be transferred to the following record and so on.

A program such as this would look as shown in Fig. 5.8. Note that line 40 allows the user to break out of the loop and so transfer control to line 70 at which line the instruction to close off the file is given. Not all computer languages require that a file be CLOSEd after use by a program instruction, but it is quite common practice. In some versions of BASIC, for example, any files which have been OPENed will automatically be CLOSEd when the program stops. A run of the program in Fig. 5.8 is shown in Fig. 5.9. Now we have a file containing data. We now require another program, quite separate from the first to read the data from the file and print it out.

A file-reading program must have its OPEN statement, but it will first of all check to see whether there is, in fact, a file of that name actually in

Fig 5.7

MR.J.SMITH
12 THE PARK
CHELTENHAM
GLOUCESTERSHIRE

MR.JOHN WATSON
PEABODY BUILDINGS
STREATHAM
LONDON

MR.D.KNIGHT
WAVERLEY COURT
UPPER NORWOOD
LONDON

THE EDITOR
DAILY TELEGRAPH
FLEET STREET
LONDON
E.C.

THE EDITOR
PAGE 3
THE SUN
FLEET STREET
LONDON E.C.

THE EDITOR - CHILDREN'S PAGE
THE MORTICIAN'S WEEKLY
AND EMBALMERS' GAZETTE
NEASDEN
SURREY

DIRECTOR GENERAL
B.B.C.
BROADCASTING HOUSE
LONDON
W1A 4WW

THE EDITOR
DAILY TELEGRAPH
FLEET STREET
LONDON
E.C.

Fig 5.8

```
5  REM***THIS PROGRAM LOADS DATA RECORD BY RECORD INTO "STOCKFILE"***
10 DIM N$(10),D$(30)
20 OPEN FILE(0,1),"STOCKFILE"
30 INPUT N$,D$,N
40 IF N$="LAST"THEN 70
50 WRITE FILE(0),N$,D$,N
60 GOTO 30
70 CLOSE FILE(0)
80 STOP
90 END
```

Program outline: The first line of the program declares that there are to be two strings used, the first of these—N$—will consist of not more than 10 characters. N$ will, in fact, store the number of a stock item, that is, its code number. The 30 character string D$ will be used to hold a description of the item. Line 20 is an instruction to open a file called "STOCK-FILE" in mode 1 (write mode) and specifies that the file is to be referred to throughout the program as file number 0. Any number could have been chosen and there is no deep significance in choosing this number. At line 30 the code number N$, description, D$, and the number of items of that description which are to be placed on the file are requested. After this line has been executed the values assigned to these variables will be in memory. Line 40 tests to see if N$ has been assigned the value "LAST", since this will act as a trigger by causing the program to jump to line 70. Line 50 is the instruction which causes a copy of each of the three variables—N$, D$ and N—currently in memory to be placed on to the next record of the file numbered 0—"STOCKFILE" in fact. Line 60 causes a jump back to line 30 to input the next set of three variables into N$, D$ and N. Then these are placed in the file, on the next record in sequence. Notice that the values assigned to the three variables constantly change as new values are read in replacing what was already there. Copies of them are stored on the file in the order in which they were presented to the computer. When the test in line 40 succeeds, no further data items are transferred to the file, which is then closed and the program stops.

A sample run of this program is shown in Fig. 5.9. Notice that the values of, for example, the variable N will be 345, 456, 432, 654, 450, 569, 67, 45 and 0. The last value is not, however, written on to file. N and D$ have to be given values since line 30 requires it. So they are given dummy values of zero and it is only the value of N$ which is of any significance. The next program, Fig. 5.10, is a program which copies out the contents of the file written to it by this program.

Fig 5.9

```
* RUN
? 12341, BOLTS-2BA, 345
? 12352, BOLTS-4BA, 456
? 12456, NUTS-2BA, 432
? 12476, NUTS-4BA, 654
? 12567, WASHERS SIZE 1, 450
? 12568, WASHERS SIZE 2, 569
? 43256, PAINT(WHITE GLOSS) LITRES, 67
? 43266, PAINT(WHITE U'COAT) LITRES, 45
? LAST, 0, 0

STOP AT 0080
```

existence. If the file does exist then it can be opened for reading by a statement such as

OPEN FILE (0, 3), "STOCKFILE"

Again, the logical number is 0, but any number would do. This is because the program you are running has no knowledge of any previous programs and it is only the file name which is stored in the directory not its number. The mode in this case is 3, the READ mode.

The records will be transferred from the file into memory by means of a READ FILE instruction

READ FILE (0), N$, D$, N

which will transfer the data items from the file into memory locations named N$, D$, N. A simple PRINT instruction will then copy these variables on to some appropriate output device. Notice that this process deals with only one record at a time. BASIC keeps track of the records by means of a *pointer*. Each READ FILE instruction moves the pointer on to the next record in sequence, hence the serial nature of the file. The same use is made of a pointer when writing to a file. Fig. 5.10 shows a program which reads from our file and Fig. 5.11 shows the program in action. Line 40 contains a special test which is used to see if the file pointer is pointing to a record which contains no data. If the program tries to read beyond the last record in the file then an *end-of-file marker* is detected (E.O.F. = END

Fig 5.10

```
5 REM***THIS PROGRAM PRINTS OUT THE CONTENTS OF "STOCKFILE"***
10 DIM N$(10), D$(30)
20 OPEN FILE(0,3), "STOCKFILE"
30 READ FILE(0), N$, D$, N
40 ON EOF(0) THEN 70
50 PRINT N$, D$, N
60 GOTO 30
70 CLOSE FILE(0)
80 STOP
90 END
```

Program outline: The first program line dimensions the two character strings just as in Fig. 5.8. Line 20 opens the file "STOCKFILE" but now in a different mode, mode 3, since we wish to read the data contained in it rather than write data to it as in the first program. Again the file is allotted the number 0. The program assumes that "STOCKFILE" actually exists and if the program were to be run but for some reason the file could not be found, then an error message such as

FILE NOT FOUND

would be printed and the program would come to a halt. Line 30 is the instruction to copy the three pieces of data from the next record on the file into memory where they are called, as before, N$, D$ and N. The instruction on line 50 will copy the values of the variables from memory to the programmer's terminal and then the instruction on line 60 returns the program to line 30 to read the contents of the next record. Line 40 is very important as it is the instruction which says what the program must do if it cannot read data from the next record of the file. If what is called an 'end-of-file' marker is read rather than the data which is on all the previous records, the program must jump to line 70, close the file and then stop. If a program is written without the test in line 40 then at the point where the end-of-file marker is read there will be an error message saying

END OF FILE FOUND

and the program will stop.

Fig 5.11

```
* RUN

12341        BOLTS-2BA         345
12352        BOLTS-4BA         456
12456        NUTS-2BA          432
12476        NUTS-4BA          654
12567        WASHERS SIZE 1                450
12568        WASHERS SIZE 2                569
43256        PAINT(WHITE GLOSS) LITRES     67
43266        PAINT(WHITE U'COAT) LITRES    45

STOP AT 0080
```

OF FILE) and says, 'if you have reached the end of file number 0 then go to line number 70'.

A variation of the program which will interrogate the file and print out some piece of data contained on it is shown in Fig. 5.12. It is used to discover the current stock position of a particular item on the file. Line 60 checks to see if the part number typed in corresponds with the one read from the current record. If the two numbers do not match then the next

Fig 5.12

```
5 REM***THIS PROGRAM SEARCHES FOR A PART IN "STOCKFILE"***
6 REM***AND PRINTS OUT THE CURRENT STOCK OF THAT PART***
10 DIM N$(10),D$(30),N1$(10)
20 OPEN FILE(0,3),"STOCKFILE"
30 INPUT "PART NO ? ",N1$
40 READ FILE(0),N$,D$,N
50 ON EOF(0) THEN 120
60 IF N1$=N$ THEN 80
70 GOTO 40
80 PRINT "PART NO:";N$
90 PRINT N;" IN STOCK"
100 CLOSE FILE(0)
110 STOP
120 PRINT"PART NUMBER NOT ON FILE"
130 GOTO 100
```

Program outline: This program uses "STOCKFILE" in a different way from the previous program. After the dimensioning of strings and the opening of the file in read mode there is a request for a part number at line 30. The number input is held in the string N1$ and then successive records on the file are read one by one and the instruction on line 60 causes a test to be made of each value of the string N$ against the value of N1$ which is held in memory. If the test fails and the part numbers fail to match then the next file record is read. Should the part numbers match then a jump is made to line 80 when the value of N, the number in stock of that part, is printed, the file is closed and the program stops. If the end-of-file marker be reached before a match has been found then the message on line 120 is printed to the effect that the part has not been found, the file is closed and the program stops. Notice that whenever a record is read every piece of data on it is read and placed in memory even though only part of the data is used—the variable D$ is ignored.

record is read and its data checked, and so on. If the whole file is read without a match being found, line 50, then the message on line 110 is printed. On matching the number input with the one on the current record the relevant data is printed out as instructed on line 80. Notice that the entire record has to be read each time even though all its data is not required by this program. Fig. 5.13 shows the program in use.

A program which modifies the contents of a file tends to be more complicated than the ones demonstrated previously. Such a program requires the use of two files since the technique is to copy all the records up to the one to be modified on to another file, then the modification is placed on the next record of the new file and finally the rest of the original file is copied across record by record. A program which does this is shown in Fig. 5.14 and Fig. 5.15 shows the amendments which need to be made to

Fig 5.13

```
        RUN
        PART NO ?  12476
        PART NO: 12476
         654  IN STOCK

        STOP AT 0110
        * RUN
        PART NO ?  43266
        PART NO: 43266
         45  IN STOCK

        STOP AT 0110
        * RUN
        PART NO ?  43276
        PART NUMBER NOT ON FILE

        STOP AT 0110
```

Fig 5.14

```
5 REM***THIS PROGRAM ADDS NEW STOCK TO A RECORD ON THE FILE***
6 REM***CALLED "STCKFILE" AND CREATES A NEW UPDATED FILE***
7 REM***CALLED "NEWSTOCK"***
10 DIM N$(10),D$(30),N1$(10)
20 OPEN FILE(0,3),"STOCKFILE"
30 OPEN FILE(1,1),"NEWSTOCK"
40 INPUT "PART NO ? ",N1$
50 INPUT "HOW MANY ADDITIONAL STOCK ITEMS ? ",K
55 F=0
60 READ FILE(0),N$,D$,N
65 ON EOF(0) THEN 100
70 IF N$=N1$ THEN N=N+K
75 IF N$=N1$ THEN F=1
80 WRITE FILE(1),N$,D$,N
90 GOTO 60
100 IF F=0 THEN PRINT "PART NO. NOT FOUND"
110 CLOSE FILE(0)
120 CLOSE FILE(1)
130 STOP


    RUN
PART NO ? 12455
HOW MANY ADDITIONAL STOCK ITEMS ? 50
PART NO. NOT FOUND

STOP AT 0130
* RUN
PART NO ? 12567
HOW MANY ADDITIONAL STOCK ITEMS ? 50

STOP AT 0130
*
```

*Program outline: Here two files are opened. The first is "STOCKFILE"
which is opened in read mode and is allocated the number 0 and the other
is "NEWSTOCK" which is a file to which data is going to be written,
hence the mode is write mode, and that is given the number 1. Then the
part number whose stock is to be amended and the number of additional
stock items are requested and held in the variables N1$ and K in memory.*

The variable F in line 55 is used as a flag to indicate whether or not the part number has been found. Initially it is set to 0 and only if there is a match between N1$ and a part number read from "STOCKFILE" is it changed to 1. The searching for the part number is done in the same way as the previous program but as each record is read it is copied on to a corresponding record on "NEWSTOCK". If a match is found then the value of N, the number in stock, is increased by K and the new value written to "NEWSTOCK". Then the rest of the file is copied over to "NEWSTOCK" until the end of the file is reached. Only if there has been no match between N$ and N1$ will the flag F stay at 0 in which case the message on line 100 is printed. We now have two files each containing the same number of records and with the stock position of one stock item updated and on the new file.

Fig 5.15

```
5 REM***THIS PROGRAM PRINTS THE CONTENTS OF A NAMED FILE***
10 DIM N$(10),D$(30),A$(10)
15 INPUT"FILENAME ? ",A$
20 OPEN FILE(0,3),A$
30 READ FILE(0),N$,D$,N
40 ON EOF(0) THEN 70
50 PRINT N$,D$,N
60 GOTO 30
70 CLOSE FILE(0)
80 STOP
90 END
```

Program outline: This program asks for a string input, which is then used as a file name in line 20 when the file is opened and the contents of that file read and printed in sequence, as the printout in Fig. 5.16 shows. The procedure is exactly the same as that of the program in Fig. 5.10. If by any chance a file name is input which does not exist then after an attempt to open the (non-existent) file in line 20 there will be a message printed which says

FILE NOT FOUND

and the program will stop. If, however, a file name is input for the wrong file then it will be opened satisfactorily but should its data not be in the same format as the file actually required then another error will be noted by a message such as

FILE DATA ERROR IN LINE 30

and the program will again stop. This will be because the file is expected to have each record containing data in the form of two strings followed by a number. If the file actually read has, for example, each record containing *four numbers followed by a string then the program will fail to read the record. In other words a line such as*

> READ FILE (0), N$, D$, N

cannot read data arranged as

> 3.456, 45672, 2134, 45.60, TAPE

Fig 5.16

```
* RUN
FILENAME ? STOCKFILE
12341          BOLTS-2BA         345
12352          BOLTS-4BA         456
12456          NUTS-2BA          432
12476          NUTS-4BA          654
12567          WASHERS SIZE 1              450
12568          WASHERS SIZE 2              569
43256          PAINT(WHITE GLOSS) LITRES   67
43266          PAINT(WHITE U'COAT) LITRES  45

STOP AT 0080
*
```

```
   RUN
FILENAME ? NEWSTOCK
12341          BOLTS-2BA         345
12352          BOLTS-4BA         456
12456          NUTS-2BA          432
12476          NUTS-4BA          654
12567          WASHERS SIZE 1              500
12568          WASHERS SIZE 2              569
43256          PAINT(WHITE GLOSS) LITRES   67
43266          PAINT(WHITE U'COAT) LITRES  45

STOP AT 0080
*
```

the program in Fig. 5.10 so that the contents of either file can be read. Fig. 5.16 shows the program running giving the contents of both "STOCK-FILE" and "NEWSTOCK".

5.4 FILES IN DATA PROCESSING

The kind of data processing for which a serial file would be used would be in the updating of a stock file, a simple example of which was shown in Fig. 5.13. The usual way of doing this task, however, would not be to amend one record at a time, as in the example, but would be to amend a whole series of records. These amendments would be batched together into a file and the amendments file merged with the existing file in order to produce a new updated file. In practice this is very useful method of operation since a hierarchy of files is created forming a 'grandparent', 'parent' and 'child' set of files. The procedure of creating a new updated file is shown in flowchart form in Fig. 5.17. By following this sequence of events the carried-forward file for this week becomes the brought-forward file for next week, and so on. By having this hierarchy of files it is possible to recreate a file by re-running the update progam should any failure take place. It is for this reason that there is a need for librarians to take charge of the disc and tape files in a large computer centre.

The procedure adopted to update, say, a stock file is first of all to collect the changes which are to be made to the file (that is, the issues of stock, arrival of new stock and the insertion of new stock items into the file). The data relating to all of these will arrive during, say, a week and in

Fig 5.17

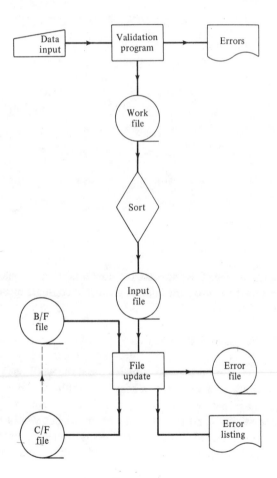

a haphazard order. This data is then collected into a file and validated in order to prevent any unacceptable data being processed. For example, invalid dates such as 31 February would be rejected. In addition, part numbers are often made up in such a way as to contain inbuilt checks as in the Standard Book Number allocated to every book published. These numbers all have to be checked. (Remember GIGO.) Thus checks are made for every possible type of error in the data in order to prevent the program trying to process rubbish. Once the data has been validated it needs to be sorted into some sort of order. This order is dictated by the order of the data on the file being updated. If the main file is in part-number order then the data used to amend it must also be in part-number order. The two files can then be merged and a new updated file created. Even at the merging process errors can be detected. These are known as *reconciliation* errors. These errors occur when additional stock is bought for a part which is not yet on the file, or when stock of a discontinued line has apparently been issued. The retention of the original stock file and the new, updated, file is obviously important so that these reconciliation errors can be put right.

A flowchart for the merging of two sorted files is shown in Fig. 5.18 and the program which will effect this is shown in Fig. 5.19. The files are already sorted into key order, where the key is the first number in each record. Notice that when the program discovers that the end of each file has been reached the key is set to 99999. Fig. 5.20 shows two files and the result of merging them by the program shown in Fig. 5.19.

5.5 RANDOM ACCESS FILES

Finally a word about random access files, or direct access files as they are sometimes called. With files of this type it is only necessary to specify the number of a record within the file for it to be accessed directly instead of having all the records preceding it read first. This is because when a record is written in to a random file not only are the contents of the record specified but also the number of the record. In other words it is rather like saying 'put this data on page 34 of the ledger' rather than 'Put this data on the next available page of the ledger'.

A serial file write instruction looks like this

WRITE FILE (1), A$, B$, C, D

but a random file instruction will be of this form

WRITE FILE (1, 34), A$, B$, C, D

where the program instructs that the data is to be written into record number 34 of the file.

104

Fig 5.18

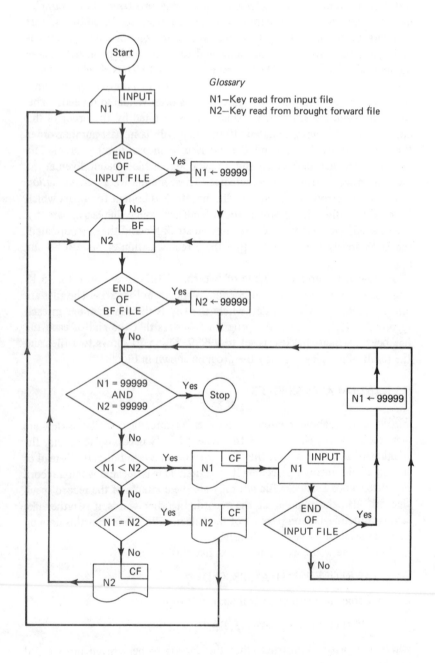

Glossary

N1—Key read from input file
N2—Key read from brought forward file

Fig 5.19

```
  5 DIM A$(20),B$(20)
 10 OPEN FILE(1,3),"INPUT"
 20 PRINT "CONTENTS OF INPUT FILE"
 30 PRINT
 40 READ FILE(1),X,A$
 50 IF EOF(1) THEN 80
 60 PRINT X;A$
 70 GOTO 40
 80 CLOSE FILE(1)
 90 PRINT
100 OPEN FILE(2,3),"BF"
110 PRINT"CONTENTS OF B/F FILE"
120 PRINT
130 READ FILE(2),X,A$
140 IF EOF(2) THEN 170
150 PRINT X;A$
160 GOTO 130
170 CLOSE FILE(2)
180 PRINT
190 OPEN FILE(1,3),"INPUT"
200 OPEN FILE(2,3),"BF"
210 OPEN FILE(3,1),"CF"
220 READ FILE(1),N1,A$
230 IF EOF(1) THEN N1=99999
240 READ FILE(2),N2,B$
250 IF EOF(2) THEN N2=99999
260 IF N1=99999 THEN IF N2=99999 THEN 370
270 IF N1<N2 THEN 310
280 IF N1=N2 THEN 350
290 WRITE FILE(3),N2,B$
300 GOTO 240
310 WRITE FILE(3),N1,A$
320 READ FILE(1),N1,A$
330 IF EOF(1) THEN N1=99999
340 GOTO 260
350 WRITE FILE(3),N2,B$
360 GOTO 220
370 CLOSE FILE(1)
380 CLOSE FILE(2)
390 CLOSE FILE(3)
400 PRINT"CONTENTS OF C/F FILE"
410 PRINT
420 OPEN FILE(3,3),"CF"
430 READ FILE(3),X,A$
440 IF EOF(3) THEN 470
450 PRINT X;A$
460 GOTO 430
470 CLOSE FILE(3)
480 END
```

As a general rule it should be noted that if a file is opened as a serial file it can only be accessed as a serial file. A file opened as a random access file must always be treated as a random file. The example shown in Fig. 5.21 shows how we can compute the record number from the numeric key. in this case a telephone number. The technique is that of *hash coding* where the record number to be allocated to a particular record is found by some arithmetic operation performed on the key to that record. In this example the first two digits of the key are divided by 2. This gives the record number for that record. If there is already data stored in the record with that number then the next in order is used. If that is occupied the next is

Fig 5.20

```
CONTENTS OF INPUT FILE

2341  P.JONES
2546  J.SMITH
3345  H.JOHNSON
3458  K.WILLIAMS
4421  L.POPPLE
4567  W.WINN
5501  T.SERGEANT
5678  Q.PEASGOOD
5782  O.ROBSON
6671  D.WARD
6672  P.WATSON
7708  D.KNIGHT

CONTENTS OF B/F FILE

2314  H.BROWN
2455  T.WATSON
3321  J.HUNT
3451  P.WILLIAMS
3555  H.PYM
3675  M.THATCHER
4091  M.FOOT
4213  P.SCOTT
4561  T.JACKSON
5467  F.BOGG
5568  H.SECOMBE
5789  S.MILLIGAN
6601  R.TWELVETREE
6608  T.HOOD
7701  T.COPPLE

CONTENTS OF C/F FILE

2314  H.BROWN
2341  P.JONES
2455  T.WATSON
2546  J.SMITH
3321  J.HUNT
3345  H.JOHNSON
3451  P.WILLIAMS
3458  K.WILLIAMS
3555  H.PYM
3675  M.THATCHER
4091  M.FOOT
4213  P.SCOTT
4421  L.POPPLE
4561  T.JACKSON
4567  W.WINN
5467  F.BOGG
5501  T.SERGEANT
5568  H.SECOMBE
5678  Q.PEASGOOD
5782  O.ROBSON
5789  S.MILLIGAN
6601  R.TWELVETREE
6608  T.HOOD
6671  D.WARD
6672  P.WATSON
7701  T.COPPLE
7708  D.KNIGHT
```

Fig 5.21

```
5 REM***THIS PROGRAM PLACES RECORDS INTO A RANDOM FILE BY USING A 'HASH'
  CODING TECHNIQUE***
10 DIM A$(20),A1$(20),N$(4),N1$(4)
20 OPEN FILE (1,0),"NOFILE"
25 REM***THIS SETS UP AN EMPTY FILE***
30 FOR I=1 TO 50
40 WRITE FILE (1,I),"-1","0"
50 NEXT I
60 FOR J=1 TO 50
70 INPUT N1$,A1$
75 REM***USING A 'HASH' CALCULATION TO DETERMINE RECORD NUMBER***
80 LET K=VAL(N1$(1,2))
90 LET K=INT(K/2)
95 REM***READS FILE RECORD K - DETERMINES IF IT CONTAINS A RECORD***
100 READ FILE (1,K),N$,A$
110 IF N$="-1" THEN WRITE FILE (1,K),N1$,A1$
115 IF N$="-1" THEN 150
115 REM***PREPARES TO LOOK AT NEXT RECORD***
120 LET K=K+1
130 IF K>50 THEN LET K=1
140 GOTO 100
150 NEXT J
170 CLOSE FILE(1)
180 END
```

Program outline: After dimensioning the strings to be used in the program we open the file "NOFILE" in mode 0, which is random access mode so that we can read from and write to any record in the file as we wish and in any order. The lines 30 to 50 fill the first 50 records of the file with the pair of dummy pieces of data −1 and 0. Then 50 pairs of numbers, $N1\$$, and names, $A1\$$, are placed on the file according to a rule which is derived from examination of $N1\$$. Line 80 takes the first two characters of the number, $N1\$(1, 2)$, converts these from a string into a number by using VAL and assigning this number to K. Then K is divided by 2 and the whole number part extracted from the answer using INT. For example if $N1\$$ was "4531" then $N1\$(1, 2)$ is "45" and $VAL(N1\$(1, 2))$ is 45. Hence K is 45. $INT(K/2)$ is 22. This calculation establishes that this record is to be placed into record number 22, provided nothing else has been placed there already. This is done by line 110 which finds out if the first of the two data strings in the record is "−1". If it is, we can write our complete record on to the file at that point. If the record already contains a number and a name then K is increased by 1 and the next record in turn is examined. This carries on until record 50 is reached. If record 50 contains real, as opposed to dummy, data then we go to record number 1, lines 120 to 140. Eventually every one of the 50 records has a number and a name assigned to it and the program stops.

tried, and so on. The formula for calculating the record number must bear some relation to the number of records likely to be placed on the file. In this case, for practicability, only 50 records were used.

The program in Fig. 5.22 shows how any record is found in the file by recalculating the record number to be searched for from its key. The amount

Fig 5.22

```
5 REM***SEARCHES FILE FOR RECORD USING SAME 'HASH' METHOD AS PREVIOUS EX
AMPLE***
10 DIM A$(20),A1$(20),N$(4),N1$(4)
20 OPEN FILE (1,0),"NOFILE"
30 INPUT "NUMBER TO BE SEARCHED FOR ? ",N1$
40 LET R=0
50 IF N1$="END" THEN 160
55 REM***CALCULATION OF 'HASH' NUMBER TO DETERMINE FIRST RECORD TO EXAMI
NE***
60 LET K=VAL(N1$(1,2))
70 LET K=INT(K/2)
80 READ FILE (1,K),N$,A$
90 LET R=R+1
95 REM***TESTS TO SEE IF RECORD IS FOUND***
100 IF N$=N1$ THEN PRINT N$,A$
110 IF N$=N1$ THEN 30
115 REM***PREPARES TO LOOK AT NEXT RECORD FOR A MATCH***
120 LET K=K+1
130 IF R=50 THEN 180
135 REM***IF END OF FILE IS REACHED GO BACK TO FIRST RECORD***
136 REM***AND START SEARCHING FROM THERE***
140 IF K>50 THEN LET K=1
150 GOTO 80
160 CLOSE FILE(1)
170 STOP
180 PRINT "RECORD NOT FOUND"
190 GOTO 30
```

Program outline: This program will search for a record in the file called "NOFILE" using the same technique to search for the record using a number as a key as when the data was placed on the file in Fig. 5.21. After the file has been opened in random access mode the number to be used as a key is requested. The variable R is used as a flag to tell the program how many records have been tested. As there are only 50 records in the file the test in line 130 tells the program that every record has been tried and no number found which matches the one input in line 30. If the number 1679 is input then lines 60 and 70 convert this into the number 8 and it will be on record 8 that the first test is made. If you look at the list of the file in Fig. 5.23 you will see that record number 8 does, in fact, contain the number 1679, so a match is found and line 100 will be executed to print out the complete contents of the record. If the number 7890 had been input at line 30 then K would have been calculated as 39. Record 39 fails to produce a match, but not 40. Record 40 provides us with the data required.

of searching through the file is minimised by this method, so all that is needed is to type in the telephone number and the name associated with that number is quickly found. Fig. 5.23 shows the list of the contents of the file. Some more programs which use random files are shown in Chapter 8.

Fig 5.23

```
RUN
RECORD NO     TELE   NAME
-----------   ----   ------
         1    9901   J.FINCH
         2    9821   R.MAYWOOD
         3    8852   H.LOCKWOOD
         4    9021   J.ROCHESTER
         5    1111   A.WALL
         6    8832   J.CRACKNELL
         7    9055   U.BYTON
         8    1679   M.WALTERS
         9    8875   D.COON
        10    2134   H.MORTON
        11    2345   J.SMITH
        12    2223   A.THOMSON
        13    2345   F.BROADWAY
        14    2233   H.STEWART
        15    2154   T.KNOWLES
        16    3343   S.SUMMERS
        17    3289   C.CLARKE
        18    2174   P.SHEEN
        19    3962   G.TAYLOR
        20    3215   H.HOWES
        21    4356   I.JONES
        22    4531   T.HEATH
        23    4444   D.HEALEY
        24    3254   P.GOSLING
        25    3341   M.THATCHER
        26    5254   C.WOOD
        27    5468   B.DUCKWORTH
        28    5590   R.WOODCOCK
        29    5591   M.HINDMARCH
        30    5555   G.EYRE
        31    2288   A.LINCOLN
        32    5571   R.WATERMAN
        33    6657   R.BENNETT
        34    6678   N.HOWES
        35    6139   R.SUMMERS
        36    6690   M.SUNDERLAND
        37    9021   K.PADGET
        38    7756   R.JONES
        39    7762   D.ASH
        40    7890   R.GREEN
        41    7788   A.SUMNER
        42    7773   R.CLARKE
        43    8765   G.LONG
        44    8976   J.GREEN
        45    8890   M.FOOT
        46    9087   D.EVANS
        47    8976   J.HEATH
        48    8897   J.SIMPSON
        49    9876   R.BOND
        50    9915   G.CAPES

END AT 0090
*
```

CHAPTER 6

SUBROUTINES

6.1 A MUSICAL DIGRESSION

The first Noël: A Christmas Carol

The first Noël the angels did say
was to certain poor shepherds in fields where they lay.
In fields where they lay keeping their sheep
on a cold winter's night that was so deep.

GOTO CHORUS

They looked up and saw a star
shining in the East beyond them far.
And to the Earth it gave great light
and so it continued both day and night.

GOTO CHORUS

The star it shone from the North-West
O'er Bethlehem it took its rest.
And there it did both stop and stay
right over the place where Jesus lay.

GOTO CHORUS

And by the light of that same star
three wise men came from countries far.
To seek for a King was their intent
And to follow the star wherever it went.

GOTO CHORUS

STOP

CHORUS

Noël, Noël, Noël, Noël. Born is the King of Israel.

RETURN

Soldier, Soldier Won't you marry me?: American/English Folk Song

Soldier, soldier won't you marry me,
With your musket, fife and drum?
How can I marry such a pretty maid, when I have
no shows to put on?

GOTO CHORUS (Cobbler's)

Soldier, soldier won't you marry me,
With your musket, fife and drum?
How can I marry such a pretty maid, when I have
no socks to put on?

GOTO CHORUS (Draper's)

Soldier, soldier won't you marry me,
With your musket, fife and drum?
How can I marry such a pretty maid, when I have
no pants to put on?

GOTO CHORUS (Tailor's)

Soldier, soldier won't you marry me
With your musket, fife and drum?
How can I marry such a pretty maid, when I've a
wife and baby at home?

STOP

CHORUS (*shop*)

Off to the *shop* she did go as fast as she could run.
Brought back the finest was there and the soldier
put them on.

RETURN

It might seem incongruous at first sight to include a Christmas carol and a folk song in a book on computer programming. However, close inspection of the words of the songs shows that they are not quite written in the conventional manner. Look at the way the choruses are written down. In the carol we see that GO TO CHORUS is printed and at the end of the chorus, which is printed separately from the main body of the carol, the word RETURN appears. The chorus of the song is, in fact, a common use of what in computing is known as a *subroutine*. A subroutine is a temporary deviation from the main theme of what is going on in the (in this case) song with a return to the point where the deviation took place. In the first case we have a chorus repeated in exactly the same way each time. In the second example, the folk song, the main body of the chorus remains the same but a different word is inserted into the space provided for it. The first time the chorus is sung we put the word 'cobbler's' in. The second time round we insert the word 'draper's' and so on. This means that although the main part of the chorus is the same each time its meaning is altered by the inclusion of a particular word. That word is specified at the appropriate point in the verse when the chorus is brought in, thus adding to the narrative of the song.

6.2 DOWN TO BUSINESS

A subroutine in a computer program is very like the chorus of a song. When the time is right we leave the main body of the program and go to a subordinate part of the program which performs some frequently required function. As with the song chorus we need only to write this subordinate part out once and refer to it whenever necessary. Most subroutines work in the way that the chorus of the folk song works. We hand over a number, or a set of numbers, to the subroutine so that it can process them in its own way and then hand back control to the main program. A very simple example of this has already been used when, in a BASIC program, we need to calculate the square root of a number. We do not need to tell the computer every time how to perform the calculation. All that is needed is to use the keyword SQR followed by whatever variable we wish to have rooted and then leave it alone. The computer software contains a special square root subprogram which handles the calculation and hands the answer back to the program which has called for it. The actual calculation performed will be very similar to that shown in Fig. 3.6. If we write a program which starts off with the lines

```
10 INPUT X
20 Y = SQR(X)
30 PRINT Y
```

then at line 20 the calculation of the square root is handed over to a software routine which will work out the square root of the number known as X and then hand back the answer to the program ready to have this number allocated to the variable Y.

There are a number of these functions available in all the versions of BASIC and a list of some of them is to be found on p. 45. They are all characterised by having a single variable name enclosed in brackets following the function name. This variable is known as the *argument* so that if an attempt is made to evaluate the square root of a negative number then a message such as

ERROR–INVALID ARGUMENT

will be sent to the programmer indicating that the subroutine cannot cope with the number handed over to it.

Some additional functions not listed on p. 45 are

VAL–used in Fig. 5.21; it returns the numeric value of the string
TAB–used in Fig. 2.11; it positions the printing head.

Any reader who wishes to use BASIC seriously should consult the manufacturer's manual for a full list of the functions available for that particular version of the language.

6.3 HOME-MADE FUNCTIONS

BASIC allows the programmer to write his own one-line functions by defining them at the start of the program by using

DEF FNa(X)

where a is any letter of the alphabet and X is the subroutine argument. For example

$$10 \text{ DEF FNA}(X) = 3 * X \uparrow 2 + 2 * X - 3$$

means that the function subroutine defined above will always refer to the value $3x^2 + 2x - 3$ whenever FNA is used in the program. An example of the use of a home-made function (two, in fact) is found in the program shown in Fig. 6.1. This program is used to line up numbers so that they are printed with the decimal points lying under one another, something which BASIC does not do very well without help. Notice also the number of other functions used in this program.

Fig 6.1

```
5 REM***PROGRAM USING FN FUNCTIONS TO ALIGN DECIMAL POINTS FOR COLUMNS
6 REM***OF NUMBERS***
10 DEF FNT(N)=INT(LOG(ABS(N))/LOG(10))
20 DEF FNS(N)=INT(LOG(0.1+ABS(N))/LOG(10))
25 REM***READ IS USED INSTEAD OF INPUT TO SAVE TYPEING IN SETS***
26 REM***OF NUMBERS WHEN PROGRAM TESTING***
30 READ N
40 IF N=1.0E50 THEN 140
50 T=10
60 IF ABS(N)<0.1 THEN 90
70 PRINT TAB(T-FNT(N));N
80 GOTO 30
90 PRINT TAB(T-FNS(N));N
100 GOTO 30
105 REM***THIS DATA IS READ ONE ITEM AT A TIME EACH TIME LINE 30 IS
106 REM***EXECUTED***
110 DATA 3.45,56.7,789.05,-67.8,800.54,-1.00005,45.567,-45.567
120 DATA 0.3,-0.008,45,467.89,.1,.99999,2,3,-.1
125 REM***THIS IS THE DATA ITEM WHICH CAUSES THE PROGRAM TO STOP***
130 DATA 1.0E50
140 END
```

```
RUN
        3.45
       56.7
      789.05
      -67.8
      800.54
       -1.00005
       45.567
      -45.567
        .3
       -.008
      45
     467.89
        .1
        .99999
      2
      3
       -.1

END AT 0140
*
```

For the non-mathematical, the exact calculations performed by the functions defined in lines 10 and 20 will not be analysed. Suffice it to say that two fairly complicated mathematical calculations are defined by the two functions called FNT and FNS, and these are called on in lines 70 and 90. Line 30 is an alternative to INPUT and sends the program to seek for data on special DATA lines, lines 110, 120 and 130 in this case. The first time line 10 is executed N is assigned the value of 3.45, then this number is processed and printed in the appropriate position across the page by either line 70 or line 90. Line 100 sends the program back to line 30 where the next number on the DATA line is assigned to N, 56.7 this time. This loop continues until N is assigned the last value in the DATA list which is 1.0E50 which acts as a trigger and is tested in line 40. Should there be no *test of the sort we have in line 40 the program will try to READ data, which does not exist and this would cause an error message saying*

> OUT OF DATA IN LINE 30

and the program would stop.

6.4 BASIC SUBROUTINES

If subroutines longer than one line are required by a BASIC program then the words GOSUB and RETURN are used. In this case the subroutine is a special part of the BASIC program containing the code that constitutes the subroutine and this is entered by writing

> GOSUB 2000

This instructs the program to go immediately to line 2000 and continue from that point until the instruction

> RETURN

is encountered. This signifies the end of the subroutine and the program jumps back to the line immediately following the GOSUB last executed. A very simple example of this in action is shown in Fig. 6.2. A far more meaningful use of a subroutine is shown in Fig. 6.3 where the subroutine

Fig 6.2

```
10 PRINT"START OF PROGRAM"
20 GOSUB 100
30 PRINT"I'M AT LINE 30"
40 GOSUB 200
50 PRINT"I'M AT LINE 50"
60 GOSUB 100
70 PRINT"THIS IS THE END"
80 STOP
100 REM****SUBROUTINE NO.1****
110 PRINT"I'M IN THE FIRST SUBROUTINE"
120 PRINT"AT LINE 120"
130 RETURN
200 REM****SUBROUTINE NO.2****
210 PRINT"I'M IN THE SECOND SUBROUTINE NOW"
220 PRINT"AT LINE 220"
230 RETURN
240 END
```

Program outline: The first line will print the heading "START OF PRO—GRAM" then line 20 will cause a jump to line 100 so that lines 110 and 120 are executed. The instruction on line 130 will send the program back to the line immediately following the instruction which sent the program off to the subroutine, line 30. Then line 30 is executed and line 40 sends the program off to the subroutine which starts at line 200. Then lines 210 and 220 are executed and line 230 sends the program back to line 60.

116

Then the first subroutine is executed again but this time the return is to line 70. Then the program stops. The sequence of line numbers executed by this program will therefore be 10, 20, 100, 110, 120, 130, 30, 40, 200, 210, 220, 230, 50, 60, 100, 110, 120, 130, 70, 80.

Fig 6.3

```
5 REM***PART OF A BOOK ISSUING SYSTEM***
10 DIM D$(6),A$(30),B$(10),I$(10)
15 OPEN FILE(1,2),"WORKFILE"
20 INPUT "DATE - DAY ",D;
30 INPUT "MONTH ",M;
40 INPUT "YEAR ",Y
45 REM***FORMS THE DATE INTO A 6 DIGIT STRING - I.E. 12/5/82 BECOMES***
46 REM***THE STRING "820512".  THIS ENABLES DATES TO BE SORTED INTO***
47 REM***ORDER VERY EASILY***
50 D$(1,2)=STR$(Y)
60 IF M<10 THEN 110
70 D$(3,4)=STR$(M)
80 IF D<10 THEN 140
90 D$(5,6) = STR$(D)
100 GOTO 160
110 D$(3,3)="0"
120 D$(4,4)=STR$(D)
130 GOTO 80
140 D$(5,5)="0"
150 D$(6,6)=STR$(D)
160 INPUT "BOOK NO: ",B$
165 IF B$="9999" THEN 2000
170 GOSUB 1000
175 IF F=1 THEN 160
180 INPUT "RETURN/ISSUE ",K$
190 IF K$(1,3)="RET" THEN C=2
195 IF K$(1,3)="ISS" THEN C=1
200 WRITE FILE(1),D$,B$,C
210 GOTO 160
999 REM***SUBROUTINE FOR CHECKING S.B.N.***
1000 F=0
1010 I$=B$
1020 IF LEN(I$)<>10 THEN 1100
1025 T=0
1030 K=10
1040 FOR I=1 TO 10
1050 A=VAL(I$(I,I))
1060 T=A*K+T
1070 K=K-1
1080 NEXT I
1090 IF T/11 = INT(T/11) THEN 1120
1100 PRINT "ERROR - INVALID S.B.N."
1110 F=1
1120 RETURN
2000 CLOSE FILE(1)
2010 STOP
```

Program outline: After the strings used in the program have been dimensioned a file called "WORKFILE" is opened in what is known as 'append' mode, mode 2. This enables data to be written on to a file already in existence and any records written to this file will be placed after the last record placed there by a previous program. The first part of the program, lines 20 to 50, convert a date into a six-character string of the form

YYMMDD. STR$(Y) in line 50 converts the number assigned to Y into a string character. At line 160 the book number is input as a string and, unless the number is 9999, the subroutine to test for a valid book number is executed. What this subroutine does is to examine the book number first of all to see if it contains 10 characters. If it does not there must be an error as all book numbers must have 10 characters, the flag F is set to 1 and a further number requested. If the test at line 1020 is successful then the characters which make up the number must follow a simple rule: multiply the first character by 10, the second by 9, the third by 8 and so on. Add these numbers up and the answer should be exactly divisible by 11. The loop contained by lines 1040 to 1080 calculates the sum—VAL converts the string character into a number—and line 1090 tests for divisibility by 11. This will work for a book number of, say, 0 860 681150 5, but if by error a non-numeric character, say @ was included, this would pass the test at line 1020 but be picked up on line 1050 where VAL (@) cannot be determined. This will produce an error message such as

INVALID STRING CONVERSION

since VAL can only be applied to the combinations of the digits 1, 2, 3, 4, 5, 6, 7, 8, 9, 0.

is used to check the validity of a book number. Only part of the complete program is shown as it is a section of a book-issuing system for a library. The validity of a book number must be checked before the details of its issue are placed on to file. Notice another software routine which is used in this program, that of the STR$ function which converts a number into a string.

6.5 CALLED SUBROUTINES

All versions of BASIC allow subroutines to be incorporated into a program as shown in a previous section. This does not make BASIC an economical language to use. These subroutines tend to make conventional BASIC programs rather lengthy and complicated, and hence difficult to follow. All the other high-level languages we meet in later chapters will allow us to create subroutines as separate entities which are called on whenever required, just like the chorus of a song. Luckily there is one version of BASIC that does allow the use of this type of CALLed subroutines so that the point can be illustrated without a drastic change of language at this point. This version of BASIC was created by the Open University and a program which illustrates its subroutine capabilities is one that does the simple task of arranging three numbers in ascending order of size. The object of the example is to show how, by using subroutines in this way, programming can be performed in a *modular* manner with a main program which does little else but call in subroutines at appropriate times. The program uses two subroutines called SWAP and PRINT. They are written and then saved on backing store. The main program (Fig. 6.4) starts with a statement of which subroutines it intends to use by means of the LIB keyword. Whenever the main program requires one of the subroutines to be executed it issues a CALL to that subroutine, following the name of the subroutine with the names of the variables it wishes to hand over for processing. The subroutine SWAP which is shown in Fig. 6.5 starts with the declaration that it is a subroutine and follows its name with a

Fig 6.4

```
10 LIB SWAP,PRINT
20 INPUT A,B,C
30 CALL SWAP(A,B)
40 CALL SWAP(B,C)
50 CALL SWAP(A,B)
60 CALL PRINT(A,B,C)
70 END
```

Program outline: Line 10 declares that this program will use programs called "SWAP" and "PRINT" which must have been SAVEd on backing store by the time the program is run. Line 20 calls for three numbers to be input. Line 30 directs the program to execute the subroutine called "SWAP" and handing over to it the values of the variables A and B. Similarly lines 40 and 50 hand over the values of B and C and then A and B again to be processed by "SWAP". Line 60 asks for the values of the variables A, B and C to be handed over to the subroutine called "PRINT" and then the program ends.

Fig 6.5

```
10 SUB SWAP(X,Y)
20 IF X<Y THEN 60
30 T=X
40 X=Y
50 Y=T
60 EXIT
70 END
```

Program outline: Line 10 announces that this is a subroutine and its name is "SWAP". The variable names in brackets are the variables whose values it expects to be handed over by some other program. Whatever the names given to these variables in the main program this program will refer to them as X and Y. Lines 30 to 50 of this program perform the exchange of values between X and Y and line 60 returns control to the calling program. What this has done, therefore, is to have taken a pair of numbers specified by a calling program and exchanged them for another pair of numbers returning these altered values to the original locations.

list of variables to be passed between it and the main program. These are called the subroutine *parameters*. The first time SWAP is used it is the values of A and B which are allocated to the *local* variables of the subroutine called X and Y. On the second occasion it is the values of B and C which are passed between them, and so on. The subroutine PRINT is listed in Fig. 6.6 and the run of the whole program is shown in Fig. 6.7. Notice that these subroutines use EXIT rather than RETURN. If the program were written using the more common BASIC subroutine structure then it would have to look as shown in Fig. 6.8. Notice how more untidy and clumsy the program now is since there are sections where the variables

Fig 6.6

```
10 SUB PRINT(X,Y,Z)
20 PRINT "THE NUMBERS IN ORDER ARE";X;Y;Z
30 EXIT
40 END
```

Program outline: This short subroutine has three numbers transmitted to it, prints them and returns control to the program which called it.

Fig 6.7

```
RUN
SORT
?100,50,3
THE NUMBERS IN ORDER ARE 3          50        100

DONE
RUN
SORT
?1,5,9
THE NUMBERS IN ORDER ARE 1          5          9

DONE
RUN
SORT
?5,7,3
THE NUMBERS IN ORDER ARE 3          3          7

DONE
```

are renamed both before and after the subroutine is executed. This may not be the best way of carrying out this simple sort, but it illustrates the problems created by subroutines in BASIC.

Another example of the use of subroutines in BASIC is in the following examples in which two lists or sorted numbers are merged into a third list containing the joint lists arranged in order. The program, shown in Fig. 6.9, uses two subroutines called GETNEXT and ADD respectively. The first of these gets the next number from one of the original lists, A and B. The subroutine ADD adds the appropriate number into its proper place into the final list C. The program is written in the conventional form of BASIC but

Fig 6.8

```
10 INPUT A,B,C
20 IF A>B THEN 70
30 IF B>C THEN 130
40 IF A>B THEN 190
50 PRINT"THE NUMBERS IN ORDER ARE";A;B;C
60 STOP
70 X=A
80 Y=B
90 GOSUB 250
100 A=X
110 B=Y
120 GOTO 30
130 X=B
140 Y=C
150 GOSUB 250
160 B=X
170 C=Y
180 GOTO 40
190 X=A
200 Y=B
210 GOSUB 250
220 A=X
230 B=Y
240 GOTO 50
250 REM***SWAP SUBROUTINE***
260 T=X
270 X=Y
280 Y=T
290 RETURN
300 END
```

Program outline: This program combines the three programs of Figs 6.4, 6.5 and 6.6 into one single BASIC program. The tests of pairs of numbers are in lines 20 to 40 and line 50 prints the answer. The subroutine which effects the exchanges is in lines 250 to 290. However, before the sub-routine can be executed values have to be assigned to X and Y and then after it has been executed the revised values are reassigned, lines 70 and 80 and then lines 100 and 110 for the first swap for example. These four assignment statements have to bracket each subroutine call.

Fig 6.9

```
10 DIM A(100),B(100),C(200),X(200)
20 INPUT"LIST A - HOW MANY NUMBERS ? ",N1
30 FOR I = 1 TO N1
40 INPUT A(I)
50 NEXT I
60 INPUT"LIST B - HOW MANY NUMBERS ? ",N2
70 FOR I = 1 TO N2
80 INPUT B(I)
90 NEXT I
100 P=A(1)
110 Q=B(1)
120 L=2
130 K=1
140 J=2
150 IF P<Q THEN 350
160 H=Q
170 GOSUB 660
180 M=J
190 X(M)=B(M)
200 N=N2
210 GOSUB 580
```

```
220 Q=H
230 J=M
240 IF E<>1 THEN 150
250 H=P
260 GOSUB 660
270 M=L
280 X(M)=A(M)
290 N=N1
300 GOSUB 580
310 P=H
320 L=M
330 IF E=1 THEN 540
340 GOTO 256
350 H=P
360 GOSUB 660
370 M=L
380 X(M)=A(M)
390 N=N1
400 GOSUB 580
410 P=H
420 L=M
430 IF E<>1 THEN 150
440 H=Q
450 GOSUB 660
460 M=J
470 X(M)=B(M)
480 N=N2
490 GOSUB 580
500 J=M
510 Q=H
520 IF E=1 THEN 540
530 GOTO 440
540 FOR I= 1 TO K-1
550 PRINT C(I);
560 NEXT I
570 STOP
580 REM***GETNEXT***
590 E=0
600 IF M>N THEN 640
610 H=X(M)
620 M=M+1
630 GOTO 650
640 E=1
650 RETURN
660 REM***ADD***
670 C(K)=H
680 K=K+1
690 RETURN
700 END
```

Program outline: First of all the numbers in the lists A and B are input. They must be in ascending numerical order otherwise the program will not work. The final list containing the merged list in ascending order is the list C. The next thing to happen is that the first item in A is assigned to the variable P and the first item in B is assigned to the variable Q—lines 100 and 110. The variables L and J keep track of the next item to be read from the lists A and B respectively. The variable K keeps track of the number of the next item to be written into the list C. This means that by the time line 150 has been reached the next items to be read from lists A and B are the second in each case and the first item has yet to be written to list C. If the value of P is less than the value of Q then it is P which is to be written into list C thus calling for the ADD subroutine which will make P the Kth element of that list and increases K by 1. After ADD has been executed we have to get the next element from list A, which is what the GETNEXT subroutine is for, and allocate that value of P. Then we go back to line 150 again. The variable E is a flag which tells the program that the end of one of the lists has been reached. This will cause all that remains of the other list to be copied into C until that produces another flag to denote the end of that list. Finally the list C is printed out and the program stops.

an example of the same process will be shown later, written in FORTRAN, which does allow the use of properly called subroutines.

To end this chapter an example now follows of a subroutine which calls itself a *recursive* subroutine. The program in Fig. 6.10 is such a subroutine which is used to calculate factorials. For the non-mathematical reader the expression factorial 6, written as 6! is equal to $6 \times 5 \times 4 \times 3 \times 2 \times 1 = 720$ and factorial 4, written as 4! is equal to $4 \times 3 \times 2 \times 1 = 24$.

Fig 6.10

```
GET-FACT
LIST
FACT

10    SUB FACT(N,F)
20    IF N#1 THEN 50
30    F=1
40    EXIT
50    CALL FACT(N-1,F)
60    F=F*N
70    EXIT
80    END
GET-PROG
LIST
PROG
```

this is the subroutine, saved on the backing store ready to be called by any program that wishes to use it

```
10    LIB FACT    ◄──────
20    INPUT N
30    CALL FACT(N,F)
40    PRINT F
50    END
RUN
PROG
```

this line takes the name of the subroutine that the program wishes to call

This is the main program which calls the S/R FACT

```
?1
 1

DONE
RUN
PROG

?2
 2

DONE
RUN
PROG

?3
 6

DONE
RUN
PROG

?4
 24

DONE
RUN
PROG

?5
 120

DONE
```

CHAPTER 7

SUMMARY OF BASIC

7.1 INTRODUCTION

Fig. 7.1 is a summary of the features of a typical version of the BASIC language. However, BASIC exists in an ever increasing number of variations or dialects, each with its own particular advantages and disadvantages, and this chapter will attempt to highlight some important features which the potential programmer in this popular language should look out for.

Fig 7.1 *summary of BASIC operators*

Arithmetic

+ Addition − Subtraction * Multiplication / Division ↑ Exponentiation

Relational

= equals < less than > greater than < = less than or equal to
> = greater than or equal to # or < > not equal to

Logical

AND   OR   NOT

The order of precedence of the arithmetic operators is

        ↑
        unary minus (for example, −4)
      * /
      + −

Statements

All statements mube prefixed by a line number Statements are executed
in order of line number when the RUN command is given.

Name	Example
LET	100 LET C = 4 * A + B (The use of LET is optional)
INPUT	200 INPUT X, Y, F
PRINT	300 PRINT "THE ANSWERS ARE:"; A1, C$
READ	400 READ A1,A2,A3 (Must be used in conjunction with DATA)
DATA	500 DATA 5.8,9.7,4.668
GOTO	600 GOTO 125
IF . . . THEN.	700 IF B + C = 0 THEN (any executable statement)
GOSUB	800 GOSUB 8000
RETURN	900 RETURN
STOP	111 STOP
DIM	345 DIM A (25), B (50), C$ (80)
END	999 END
FOR . . . NEXT.	875 900 NEXT I FOR I = 1 TO 50 STEP .5
REM	654 REM (Any text)
DEF FNn	987 DEF FNC(K) = K * 3.5 + 5.678

Functions

ABS(X)	Absolute value of X
ATN(X)	Angle in radians whose tangent is X
COS(X)	Cosine of angle X (in radians)
EXP(X)	Exponential function of X
INT(X)	Largest integer less than or equal to X
LEN(A$)	Current length of string variable A$
RND(X)	Random number in range zero to 1
SGN(X)	1, X greater than zero. 0, X equal to zero. −1, X less than zero.
SIN(X)	Sine of angle X (in radians)
SQR(X)	Positive square root of X
TAB(X); Y	Tabs to position X and prints value of Y
TAN(X)	Tangent of angle X (in radians)

Strings

String variables are denoted by a letter or a letter followed by a digit
followed by the $ sign (for example, A$, D3$). A string can usually contain
from 1 to 255 characters enclosed in quotation marks. Strings longer than
10 characters must be dimensioned by a DIM statement.

Name	Example
DIM	300 DIM D$(80)
LET	400 LET F$ = "THE MEAN =" (The use of LET is optional)
INPUT	500 INPUT C$ (Quotation marks are optional unless the string commences with blanks.)

Comparisons can be made between strings using the same relational tests as used on arithmetic variables.

Concatenation of strings

400 C$ = "MR", " ", "AND", " ", "MRS" results in C$ containing the string "MR AND MRS"

Substrings

If A$ contains the string "LONDON TOWN" substrings are denoted by subscripted variables, for example: A$(4,6) is "DON", A$(2,2) is "O", and A$(8) is "TOWN".

Files

Files are opened by means of the OPEN statement which is of the form

        300 OPEN FILE(n,m), "FILENAME"

where n is the logical file number and m is the mode: m = 0 (random file), m = 1 (serial write), m = 2 (serial append), m = 3 (serial read). After use files are closed using

        600 CLOSE FILE(n)

File read

        400 READ FILE(3), A, B, C

reads next record in sequence from a serial file.

        500 READ FILE(2,K), X, Y, Z

reads the contents of record number K from a random file.
File write

        700 WRITE FILE(6), P, Q, R$

writes to the next record in sequence of a serial file.

        900 WRITE FILE(5, J), A$, H1, G

writes data to record number J of a random file.

End of file test

        ON EOF (2) THEN . . .

placed after a serial file read directs the program to the next statement
to be executed after the last record of the file has been read.

Commands

RUN	Begins execution of the current program.
LOAD "PROGNAME"	Copies the named program into memory.
SAVE "PROGNAME"	Saves a copy of the current program in memory on backing store.
NEW	Deletes the current program from memory.
LIST	Lists all the program statements of the program currently in memory.
LIST n	Lists line number n of the program currently in memory.
LIST n, m	Lists the program statements numbered n to m.
RENUMBER	Renumbers the program currently in memory starting at line 10 and numbering in increments of 10.
n	Deletes program line number n.
n, m	Deletes program lines from number n to number m.

The most elementary forms of BASIC are known as *integer* BASICs
where the only arithmetic possible is in whole numbers (integers). This can
produce some strange results when, for example, division is attempted: the
division of the integer 5 by the integer 2 will produce an integer answer of
2. The earliest version of the electricity bill program was written in ACE
which is an integer language. The program in Fig. 1.11 overcomes the
integer division problem by extracting the pounds and the pence separately.
Only a very few functions are available in integer BASICs and certainly
none of those which involve the calculation of square roots or sines, for
example. Integer BASICs are available on very small microcomputers with
very limited amounts of RAM (random access memory).

Very few versions of BASIC these days insist on the use of the word
LET in assignment statements and it is for this reason that most of the
examples quoted in this book omit this keyword. Once the concept of
what an assignment statement does is appreciated, the use of LET becomes
redundant.

Major variations within the language probably start with the variable names which are allowed. The original version of BASIC allowed only single letters to stand for variables or single letters followed by a single digit. However, in the more elegant microcomputer versions of the language we are allowed to use whole words for variables so that it is quite legal to write

10 TOTAL = TOTAL + X

But beware of using this facility without reading the manual. It is quite possible for the programmer to use whole words as variable names but the first two characters of the name are the only ones of significance. In other words, two variables might be called MEAN and MEDIAN but BASIC will be fooled into thinking that they are the same variable because they both start with the letters ME. Hence, they both share the same location in memory.

We have already met the concept of the string variable, where the $ sign is placed after the name in order to distinguish a string from a numeric variable. The rest of the naming convention will follow the pattern of the particular dialect of BASIC, so that it is possible to have string variables such as

ADDRESS$

or

NAME$

Some versions of the language allow the use of the % sign after a variable name to indicate that the variable is to be treated as an integer, not a floating point number. The most common versions of BASIC treat all numbers as floating point numbers and this sometimes leads to problems.

In general, but not always (since it depends on the precision with which the computer carries out its calculations), we say that

(1) A floating point number occupies 4 bytes (32 bits) of memory space and gives 6 significant-digit accuracy.
(2) An integer occupies 2 bytes (16 bits) of memory space and will allow integers in the range -32768 to $+32767$ to be used.
(3) Each character of a string variable occupies 1 byte (8 bits) of memory space. Typically a string variable can contain up to 255 characters.

7.2 DECISION STATEMENTS

All BASICs use the IF ... THEN ... and GOTO jump instructions but some restrict the first of these to the form

IF (Assertion) THEN *nnnn*

where *nnnn* is a line number in the program. More commonly the THEN can be followed by any valid BASIC statement so that it is generally legal to write

IF X = 21 THEN X = 0

or

IF X = 0 THEN PRINT FILE (1), P, Q, R

or

IF P < Q THEN GOSUB 500

A very useful, and increasingly more common addition to the IF statement is in the use of the word ELSE so that we can write

IF ... THEN ... ELSE ...

By this means a more compact form of coding is available so that a program which might look like this

```
10 INPUT X
20 Y = X/2
30 IF Y = INT(Y) THEN 60
40 PRINT "ODD"
50 STOP
60 PRINT "EVEN"
70 STOP
```

could be condensed to become

```
10 INPUT X
20 Y = X/2
30 IF Y = INT(Y) THEN PRINT "EVEN" ELSE PRINT "ODD"
40 STOP
```

which is not only shorter to write but easier to understand. We shall meet this concept later when the Pascal language is described.

Another useful extension to decision statements is in the use of logical conjections, AND and OR. A program using these is shown in Fig. 7.2 which tests numbers to see if they lie within certain limits. A statement such as

IF 0 < X < 1 THEN ...

might appear at first sight to be quite satisfactory BASIC as it is easy to understand and appears to say that if the value of the variable X lies between 0 and 1 then the assertion is true and everything is fine. Unfortunately it is not. Some BASICs might actually accept the statement, but

Fig 7.2

```
5 REM***TESTS FOR VALID DATA USING THE 'AND' CONJUNCTION***
10 T=C=0
20 INPUT X
30 IF X=-1 THEN 80
40 IF X=INT(X) AND X>= 1 AND X<=10 THEN 70
50 PRINT X;"REJECTED"
60 GOTO 20
70 T=T+X
71 C=C+1
72 GOTO 20
75 REM***TESTS TO SEE IF THERE WERE ANY VALID NUMBERS ACCEPTED***
80 IF C=0 THEN 110
90 PRINT "AVERAGE OF ";C;"VALID NUMBERS IS ";T/C
100 STOP
110 PRINT "NO VALID DATA"
120 STOP
130 END
```

Program outline: Line 10 sets the variables T and C to zero. Then a number, X, is input. A trigger of −1 senses the end of the input and causes lines 80 onwards to be executed. Note that the program tests to see if C has stayed at zero in which case there is no point in trying to perform the division by C in line 90. In fact, an attempt to do this will result in an error message such as

ATTEMPT TO DIVIDE BY ZERO IN LINE 90

and the program will stop. The tests in line 40 ensure that only numbers which are simultaneously whole numbers—$X = INT(X)$—greater than or equal to 1—$X >= 1$—and less than or equal to 10—$X <= 10$. If all three conditions are satisfied then a jump is made to line 70 where the total T is increased by X and C, the number of valid numbers processed, is increased by 1.

most will reject it. Those that do accept the statement will unfortunately produce some very strange results. What should be written is

IF $0 < X$ AND $X < 1$ THEN ...

or possibly

IF $0 < X$ THEN IF $X < 1$ THEN ...

since this ties in with the convention of following a BASIC assertion with another valid statement, which itself could be another assertion.

A program which uses the OR conjunction is shown in Fig. 7.3 and Fig. 7.4 shows the way to write code which allows for the OR situation if OR is not available.

Fig 7.3

```
5 REM***TESTS FOR INVALID DATA USING THE 'OR' CONJUNCTION***
10 T=C=0
20 INPUT X
30 IF X=-1 THEN 80
40 IF X<>INT(X) OR X<1 OR X>10 THEN 50
41 GOTO 70
50 PRINT X; "REJECTED"
60 GOTO 20
70 T=T+X
71 C=C+1
72 GOTO 20
80 IF C=0 THEN 110
90 PRINT "AVERAGE OF ";C;"VALID NUMBERS IS ";T/C
100 STOP
110 PRINT "NO VALID DATA"
120 STOP
130 END
```

*Program outline: This follows exactly the same pattern as the previous
program except that the test in line 40 is altered so that if any one of the
conditions hold the number is rejected. These are that X is not a whole
number—X < > INT (X)—or X less than 1—X < 1—or X greater than
10—X > 10.*

Fig 7.4

```
5 REM***TESTS FOR VALID DATA USING THREE SEPARATE TESTS***
6 REM***BECAUSE 'OR' AND 'AND' ARE NOTAVAILABLE***
10 T=0
11 C=0
20 INPUT X
30 IF X=-1 THEN 80
40 IF X<>INT(X) THEN 50
41 IF X<1 THEN 50
42 IF X>10 THEN 50
43 GOTO 70
50 PRINT X; "REJECTED"
51 GOTO 20
70 T=T+X
71 C=C+1
72 GOTO 20
80 IF C=0 THEN 110
90 PRINT "AVERAGE OF ";C;"VALID NUMBERS IS ";T/C
100 STOP
110 PRINT "NO VALID DATA"
120 STOP
130 END
```

*Program outline: This follows the same pattern as the previous two pro-
grams except that the OR conjunction has not been used. This means that
the tests which previously could be written on one line have had to be
spread over three lines—lines 40, 41, 42.*

7.3 COMPUTED GOTO AND GOSUB

Many programs offer the facilities of executing certain sections of themselves according to the value of some key number, in particular, programs which offer a *menu* from which to choose. An example of this is shown in Fig. 7.5 where the selection of the required part of the program is made in line 10. Line 20 acts as a switch depending on the value of the variable K. If K has the value 1 then the first of the list of line numbers is executed. If K has the value 2 then the second of the line numbers is chosen, and so on. There are two standard ways of writing this. It can be either

$$ON\ K\ GOTO\ n_1, n_2, n_3, \ldots$$

or

$$GOTO\ K\ OF\ n_1, n_2, n_3, \ldots$$

Fig 7.5

```
10 INPUT K
20 ON K THEN GOTO 50, 70, 90
30 PRINT "K MUST 1,2 OR 3"
40 GOTO 10
50 PRINT "I'M AT LINE 50"
60 STOP
70 PRINT "I'M AT LINE 70"
80 STOP
90 PRINT "I'M AT LINE 90"
100 STOP
```

Program outline: At line 10 a number is input. If its value is 1 then line 20 causes a jump to be made to line 50. A value of 2 causes a jump to line 70 and a value of 3 causes a jump to line 90. If any other value of K is input then we go to line 30 which prints a gentle reprehension and sends the program back to line 10 again. The line numbers jumped to depend solely on the value of K: if K is 1 it is the first in the list, if K is 2 it is the second in the list, and so on.

Subroutines can be chosen in the same way by writing either

$$ON\ K\ GOSUB\ n_1, n_2, n_3, \ldots$$

or

$$GOSUB\ K\ OF\ n_1, n_2, n_3, \ldots$$

Consultation of the manufacturer's manual will show you which is the version applicable to your dialect of BASIC.

7.4 MULTIPLE STATEMENTS

Very often the start of a program consists of setting a series of variables to some starting value, usually zero. This can be done, if your version of the language allows it, by writing statements such as either

$$10\ T = C = N = 0$$

or

$$10\ T, C, N = 0$$

This avoids a series of very short, almost identical lines of code and will almost certainly save on storage space for the program.

Another way of saving on the number of lines of code is to write more than one statement on a line. Again, if your version of the language allows it you can do it by separating statements on the same line by colons (:). For example, instead of

```
10 INPUT X
20 Y = 4 * X ↑ 2
30 PRINT Y
40 STOP
```

We could write

$$10\ INPUT\ X : Y = 4 * X \uparrow 2 : PRINT\ Y : STOP$$

This is not possible, however, if one has to jump to a statement in the middle of a multiple line.

7.5 STRINGS

The major variations in the way BASIC can be made to handle strings have been dealt with in Chapter 4.

7.6 FILES

All versions of BASIC that are available for computers which have backing store in the form of magnetic discs or tape, provide file handling facilities and the reader is again referred to the manuals to discover the precise form of the coding needed to effect the following file operations. They can vary widely as you will see.

(1) Opening a file for reading.
(2) Opening a file for writing.
(3) Opening a random file for reading and/or writing.
(4) Closing a file.

(5) Reading the next record from a serial file.

(6) Reading a record from a random file.

(7) Writing the next record to a serial file.

(8) Writing a record to a random file.

(9) Testing for the physical end of a serial file.

The last of these can be tricky since some versions of BASIC require the end of file test to be placed immediately after a record bas been read and some require it to be placed at the start of the program. What the first of these is saying is, 'If you have just read an end of file marker then do this . . .' The second is saying, 'Whenever you come across an end of file mark you must do this . . . ' A variation of the second one of these tests is the one where you have to place the end of file test immediately before the file reading takes place and says, 'If the next thing you read is an end of file mark then . . . '

Figs 7.6, 7.7 and 7.8 show three variations of the same program. The programs all look different but all write a series of records into a serial file and then print the contents of the file.

Fig 7.6

```
10 OPEN "O",1,"B:FILE1"
20 INPUT X,Y,B$
30 IF X=0 THEN 60
40 PRINT#1,X,Y,B$
50 GOTO 20
60 CLOSE 1
70 OPEN "I",1,"B:FILE1"
80 IF EOF(1) THEN 120
90 INPUT#1,X,Y,B$
100 PRINT X,Y,B$
110 GOTO 80
120 CLOSE 1
130 END
```

Fig 7.7

```
10 STRING=0
20 OPEN #1,FILE1
30 INPUT X,Y,B$
40 IF X=0 THEN 70
50 WRITE #1,X,Y,B$
60 GOTO 30
70 CLOSE #1
80 OPEN #1,FILE1
90 READ #1,X,Y,B$
100 IF EOF(1)=1 THEN 130
110 PRINT X,Y,B$
120 GOTO 90
130 CLOSE #1
```

Fig 7.8

```
10 OPEN FILE (1,1), "FILE1"
20 INPUT X,Y,B$
30 IF X=0 THEN 60
40 WRITE FILE (1),X,Y,B$
50 GOTO 20
60 CLOSE FILE (1)
70 OPEN FILE (1,3), "FILE1"
80 READ FILE (1),X,Y,B$
90 ON EOF(1) THEN 120
100 PRINT X,Y,B$
110 GOTO 80
120 CLOSE FILE (1)
130 STOP
```

7.7 RUNNING BASIC PROGRAMS

The final examples in this chapter are of BASIC programs which do not need line numbers. The first of these performs the same function as the previous three examples. The difference between this program and all the others is that apart from the fact that it uses words for variable names and labels which are not line numbers it is not written in *interactive* BASIC. An interactive language is one where there is a constant dialogue between the programmer and BASIC. This, the most common form of the language, makes writing programs, their amendment and their execution very easy. Its disadvantage is that the time taken for execution of the finished program is unnecessarily long. This is because most of the conversion of the BASIC instructions into machine instructions takes place at run time. So what you gain in ease of preparation and debugging of programs is rather lost in the time taken in running it. This would be particularly noticeable if large and complex programs were run in BASIC. A computer program needs to work as efficiently as possible and programs written in interactive BASIC are just not efficient. The examples in Figs 7.9 and 7.10 are written in what is called a *compiled* BASIC. More details of compiled languages will be given in Chapter 11 but at this stage all that need be appreciated is that the program is written and then submitted to a program called a *compiler* which has the task of converting the original program into the efficient machine code which is actually executed by the computer. It is this final *object* code which is stored away and executed whenever the program is run. In fact, the original BASIC code can be discarded once the compilation process has taken place.

Finally, it should be emphasised that writing programs in BASIC, or any other language for that matter, requires you to consult the manufacturer's manual to see what is and is not, available on the computer you are using. All that this chapter has attempted to do is to point the way

Fig 7.9

```
EXAMPLE PROGRAM NUMBER 1 WRITTEN FOR THE ALPHA MICRO COMPUTER

          OPEN £1,"FILE1.DAT",OUTPUT     ! OPEN FILE FOR OUTPUT
NEXTREC:                                 ! LABEL FOR NEXT RECORD
          INPUT "X  ",X                  ! GET VALUE OF X
          IF X=0 GOTO ENDINPUT           ! END IF X=0
          INPUT "Y  ";Y                  ! GET VALUE OF Y
          INPUT "B$ ";B$                 ! GET VALUE OF B$
          PRINT £1,X,Y,B$                ! OUTPUT TO FILE
          GOTO NEXTREC                   ! GO FOR NEXT RECORD
ENDINPUT:                                ! LABEL FOR OUTPUT FILE CLOSING
          CLOSE £1                       ! CLOSE OUTPUT FILE
          OPEN £1,"FILE1.DAT",INPUT      ! OPEN FILE FOR INPUT
READNEXT:                                ! LABEL FOR GETTING NET RECORD FROM FILE
          INPUT £1,X,Y,B$                ! GET NEXT RECORD FROM FILE
          IF EOF(1) GOTO FINISH          ! IF NO MORE GOTO FINISH
          PRINT X,Y,B$                   ! DISPLAY ON V.D.U.
          GOTO READNEXT                  ! GO TO GET NEXT RECORD FROM FILE
FINISH:                                  ! FINISH LABEL
          CLOSE £1                       ! CLOSE INPUT FILE
          END                            ! END PROGRAM
```

Fig 7.10

```
     INPUT NO'OF'UNITS
     IF NO'OF'UNITS <=150 GOTO UNIT'COST ELSE GOTO EXCESS'UNITS
UNIT'COST:
     COST=NO'OF'UNITS * 0.07
     IF COST<3.64 GOTO MIN'CHARGE ELSE GOTO STANDING'CHARGE
MIN'CHARGE:
     COST=3.64
STANDING'CHARGE:
     COST=COST+3.25
     COST=COST*1.15
     PRINT "£";COST
     STOP
EXCESS'UNITS:
     COST=COST-150
     COST=COST*0.05+10.5
     GOTO STANDING'CHARGE
```

towards some of the inconsistencies which lie in wait for the unwary.
When in doubt, try it out and see what happens. BASIC is very forgiving
and will tell you, although not always very clearly, if you have made a
mistake and what it is likely to be. Then the detective work starts!

CHAPTER 8

PUTTING PROGRAMMING TO WORK

8.1 INTRODUCTION

This chapter is largely about the birth, and its pangs, of a computer program written in BASIC. It has been said that programming is essentially a creative process and in some cases is akin to an art form. The latter statement is debatable, but the former is certainly true. A program usually starts with an idea, often in the form of a problem to be solved. In the case of professional programming it could be the result of the analysis of a system, say an invoicing or a stock control system, and the production of a program specification. Such a specification would consist of a clear description of the type of data to be input to the program for processing and the information to be output by the computer system. The programmer is thus presented with a clear indication of what his program is required to do. The task is fairly clear cut and straightforward. After the programmer has written and tested the program it is handed over to other people to use.

Now that there is an ever-increasing number of microcomputer systems being introduced into smaller and smaller organisations the tasks of systems analyst, programmer and operator are tending to be merged into one. It is now quite common for a single person to specify the requirements of the program, write it and then use it. This is why there is an ever-growing requirement for people who are technically expert in some field who additionally need to learn and practise the skills of computer programming.

8.2 GETTING STARTED

The example to be used in this section is in itself quite trivial, but an attempt has been made to be as general as possible so that readers from all specialisms can relate to the ideas involved. The starting point is that of designing a simple computer game in which the computer chooses a num-

Fig 8.1

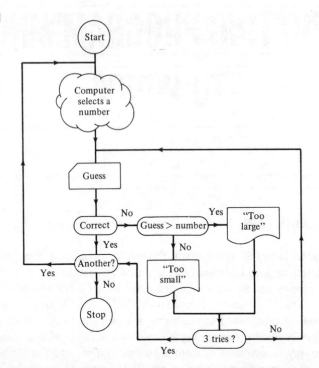

ber and the human player attempts to guess it. Initially the form of the program can be drawn in an *outline flowchart* as shown in Fig. 8.1. The 'clouds' in a flowchart represent operations which have to take place, but with no specific steps detailed in these clouds. The details begin to emerge in the first detailed flowchart, Fig. 8.2, where the shapes of the boxes follow a convention, which indicates the kind of operation taking place at that point. The most common of these are

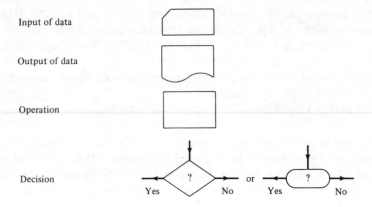

Fig 8.2

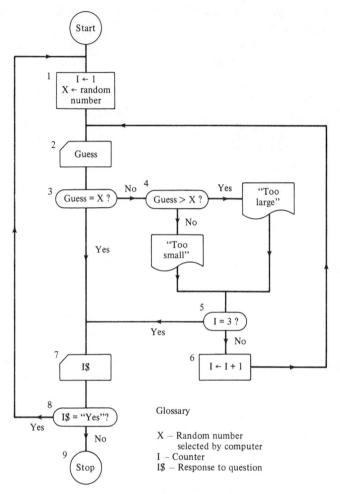

There are two things to be noticed about the detailed flowcharts. One is that we use the ← sign, which means 'takes the value of'. We keep the = sign for decisions. The other is that the flowchart does not, as far as possible, contain statements in any particular language. The glossary which accompanies the flowchart is most important because it explains what each of the variable names used in the chart stand for. Having drawn out a flowchart and tested it by following the path of specimen data through it, a so-called *dry run*, the next job is to convert it into some suitable language, in this case, BASIC. If we number the boxes it becomes very easy to convert these into program line numbers. In order to avoid too many GOTO statments it is good practice to make the NO exit from a decision box go to the next number in sequence. Fig. 8.3 shows the BASIC program from the flowchart.

Fig 8.3

```
 1 RANDOMIZE
10 I=1
11 X=INT(RND(0)*10)+1
20 INPUT G
30 IF G=X THEN 70
40 IF G>X THEN PRINT "TOO LARGE" ELSE PRINT "TOO SMALL"
50 IF I=3 THEN 70
60 I=I+1
65 GOTO 20
70 INPUT I$
80 IF I$="YES"THEN 10
90 STOP
```

8.3 FILLING IN THE DETAILS

By the time we have reached this stage we should have a program that works. In our case we may not have a very exciting program, but at least it does work. However, because it has been designed to run in an inter-active system, hence the choice of BASIC as the programming language, it appears a little 'cold' to a user who may not be familiar with the program. A simple ? with no indication of what is expected in the way of a response is not very 'user friendly' and is certainly no way to inspire confidence or sympathy with the computer. The addition of a few PRINT statements makes the program much more attractive. The flowchart now amended is shown in Fig. 8.4 with the corresponding program and a run in Fig. 8.5.

The game can now be developed into one which is more sophisticated. In this a four-digit number is generated by the computer and the human player is asked what it is. This time the computer tells the contestant if he has made any correct guesses (bulls) of digits in their correct places in the number, or a correct digit chosen but in the wrong place in the number (cows). An outline flowchart for this is shown in Fig. 8.6.

Fig. 8.7 is an expansion of section A of the previous flowchart. The three-part box is a good way of showing a loop in a flowchart, in fact it uses a more 'structured' approach to programming by hinting at the FOR . . . NEXT . . . type of loop. The top left-hand corner of the box shows the starting point of the loop with the initial value of the starting variable called I. The bottom left-hand box shows the amount by which I is incremented each time the loop is traversed. The right-hand side of the block is really saying 'while' the index I is less than or equal to 4 the path from the bottom of the box is taken. When the test finally fails the right-hand exit

Fig 8.4

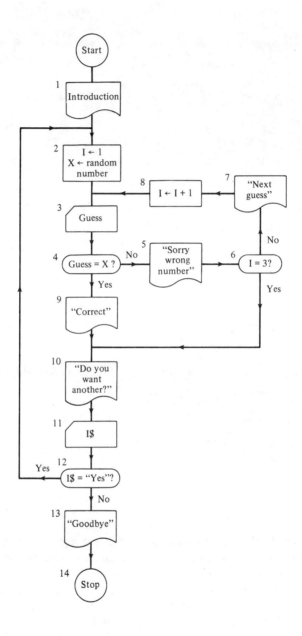

Fig 8.5

```
0001 RANDOMIZE
0010 PRINT "I SHALL CHOOSE A NUMBER BETWEEN 1 AND 10, YOU HAVE THREE GUESSES
0020 LET I=1
0021 LET X=INT(RND(0)*10)+1
0030 INPUT G
0040 IF G=X THEN GOTO 0090
0050 PRINT "SORRY WRONG NUMBER"
0060 IF I=3 THEN GOTO 0100
0070 PRINT "NEXT GUESS"
0080 LET I=I+1
0081 GOTO 0030
0090 PRINT "CORRECT"
0100 PRINT "DO YOU WANT ANOTHER";
0110 INPUT I$
0120 IF I$="YES" THEN GOTO 0001
0130 PRINT "GOODBYE"
0140 STOP
* RUN
I SHALL CHOOSE A NUMBER BETWEEN 1 AND 10, YOU HAVE THREE GUESSES
 ? 5
SORRY WRONG NUMBER
NEXT GUESS
 ? 3
CORRECT
DO YOU WANT ANOTHER ? YES
I SHALL CHOOSE A NUMBER BETWEEN 1 AND 10, YOU HAVE THREE GUESSES
 ? 7
SORRY WRONG NUMBER
NEXT GUESS
 ? 2
SORRY WRONG NUMBER
NEXT GUESS
 ? 6
CORRECT
DO YOU WANT ANOTHER ? YES
I SHALL CHOOSE A NUMBER BETWEEN 1 AND 10, YOU HAVE THREE GUESSES
 ? 9
SORRY WRONG NUMBER
NEXT GUESS
 ? 2
SORRY WRONG NUMBER
NEXT GUESS
 ? 5
SORRY WRONG NUMBER
DO YOU WANT ANOTHER ? NO
GOODBYE

STOP AT 0140
*
```

is taken. In this part of the program the first digit of the guess is tested against the first digit of the computer's number. Then the pair of second digits are compared and so on. The score of 'bulls' is kept in the variable B.

Fig. 8.8 is an attempt to expand section B of Fig. 8.6. At first sight the loop within a loop seems quite satisfactory for finding if any digits in the guess, G$, exists anywhere in the string of four digits called N$. But what if there are two occurrences of, say, the digit 4 in N$ and only one in G$? In order to overcome this problem the two program segments need to be amended by the introduction of a new string variable called Z$. At the

Fig 8.6

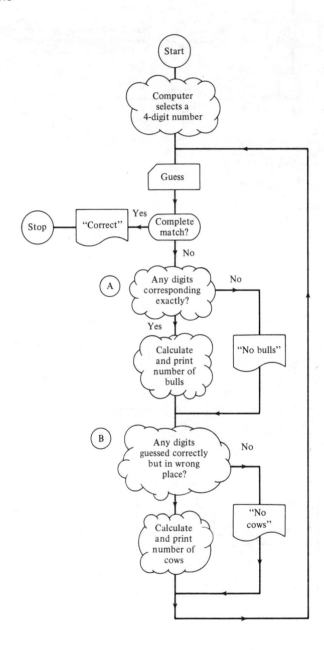

Fig 8.7

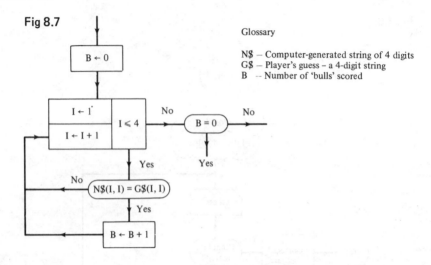

Glossary

N\$ — Computer-generated string of 4 digits
G\$ — Player's guess – a 4-digit string
B — Number of 'bulls' scored

Fig 8.8

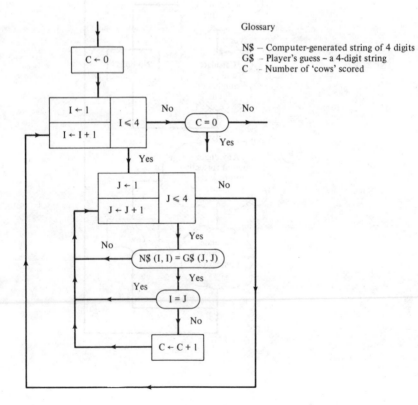

Glossary

N\$ — Computer-generated string of 4 digits
G\$ – Player's guess – a 4-digit string
C — Number of 'cows' scored

start of section A, Z$ is set to contain the characters "****" and if identical digits occur in both G$ and N$ then Z$ has that digit placed in the appropriate position. For example, if G$ is "4376" and N$ is "4697" then at the exit from the segment Z$ will become "4***" and B has the value of 1. Fig. 8.9 shows the amended version. In Fig. 8.10 the other segment is shown in its new form so that use is made of the newly introduced Z$. Finally a complete flowchart, Fig. 10.11, can be put together. The BASIC program derived from this final flowchart is shown in Fig. 8.12.

Fig 8.9

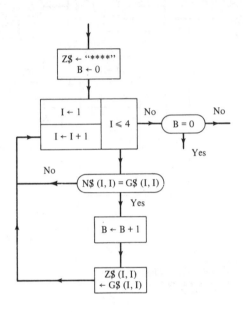

Glossary

Z$ — Reference string
N$ — Computer-generated string of 4 digits
G$ — Player's guess – a 4-digit string
B — Number of 'bulls' scored

Although at this stage the task of writing the program could be thought as being complete, this is true only so long as it is left running under the particular version of BASIC it was designed for. If, on the other hand, it is intended to make it possible for the program to be run under as many versions of BASIC as possible, then a few notes about possible variations would be helpful. Also, the original author may not be around when someone wants to start making changes to the program. A set of useful notes about the program is shown in Fig. 8.13.

Fig 8.10

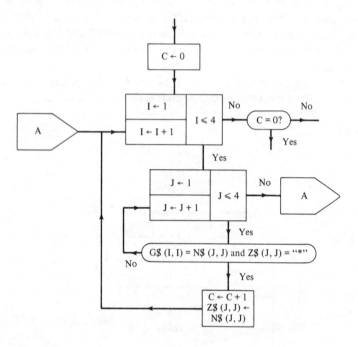

Glossary

Z\$ – Reference string
N\$ – Computer-generated string of 4 digits
G\$ – Player's guess – a 4-digit string
C – Number of 'cows' scored

The notes on a program are part of the documentation associated with it and should be kept for reference together with other details about the program such as

(1) Program name
(2) Author
(3) Date written
(4) Specification of program requirements
(5) General description of the program and its operation
(6) Flowcharts or any other recognised program structure charts
(7) Input/output requirements
(8) Tape or disc file and record formats
(9) Specification of storage and the use of peripherals

(10) Coding sheets and/or program listings

(11) Data preparation requirements and operating instructions

(12) Program development documentation

(13) Any modifications made to the program during its life.

Fig. 8.14 shows a sample of the kind of information given about the bulls and cows program.

It is often useful to include, for quick reference, remarks or comments within the program itself. All high-level languages provide the facility to do this and a good example of this is shown in the Pascal program of Fig. 10.12. Fig. 8.15 shows our demonstration program complete and containing useful remarks.

8.4 SOME USEFUL PROGRAMS

Many of the programs illustrated so far have demonstrated specific aspects of programming techniques. The rest of this chapter will be devoted to examples of these techniques put to work on some practical tasks. Two of these, in particular, are searching and sorting. Data, once it has been stored in the computer's memory, very often needs to be sorted into some sort of order; numerical data often needs to be sorted into numerical order and alphabetical data (names and addresses for example) needs to be sorted into alphabetical order. Several programs of this type have already been shown in Figs 4.3, 4.4, 4.5 and 4.6, but although they illustrate the programming techniques well enough they are a little divorced from real data processing. This is because they deal with data which is stored in memory and sorting which takes place in memory, a so-called 'in-core' sort is not used very often. This is because it is not possible to store very large quantities of data in main memory.

Backing store is the proper place for large quantities of data. Data which consists perhaps of thousands of records will be stored on magnetic discs or tape and it is via these media that practical sorting of data should take place. Data held in files can be stored in a number of different ways. Some of these rely on the use of serial files held on magnetic tape and others use random access files. It is the latter type that the following examples are going to describe.

The first example is a simple one using a version of the bubble sort. When using this method records are moved about within the files until successive records in the file hold the data in the correct order. The data used in this example is the same as that used in the example shown in Fig. 5.20. Fig. 8.16a shows the file sorted into numerical order of telephone numbers together with the program which executes it. Fig. 8.16b

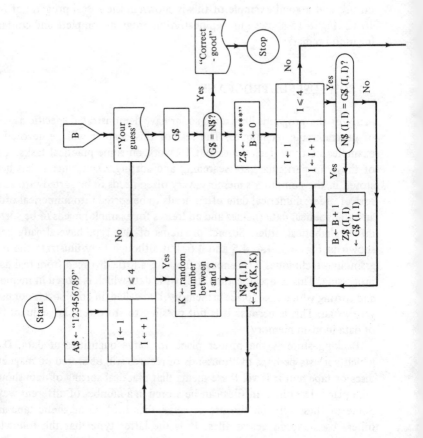

Fig 8.11

149

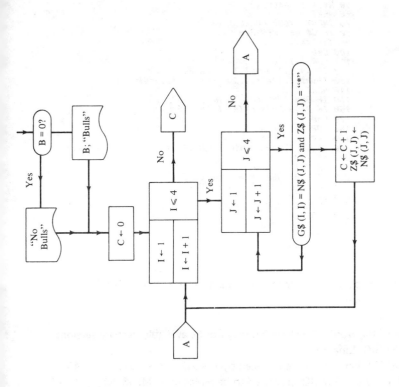

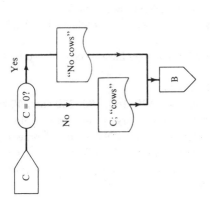

Glossary

A\$ – String of digits > 1 to 9
N\$ – Computer-generated 4-digit string
G\$ – Player's guess – 4-digit string
Z\$ – Reference string
I, J, K – Indexes to individual characters in string
B – Number of 'bulls'
C – Number of 'cows'

Fig 8.12

```
10 A$="123456789"
20 RANDOMIZE
30 FOR I=1 TO 4
40 K=INT(RND(0)*8)+1
50 N$(I,I)=A$(K,K)
60 NEXT I
70 INPUT "YOUR GUESS ";G$
80 IF G$=N$ THEN 260
90 Z$="****"
100 B=0
110 FOR I=1 TO 4
120 IF N$(I,I)=G$(I,I) THEN B=B+1
130 IF N$(I,I)=G$(I,I) THEN Z$(I,I)=G$(I,I)
140 NEXT I
150 IF B=0 THEN PRINT "NO BULLS"
160 IF B<>0 THEN PRINT B;"BULLS"
170 C=0
180 FOR I=1 TO 4
190 FOR J=1 TO 4
200 IF G$(I,I)=N$(J,J) THEN IF Z$(J,J)="*" THEN 280
210 NEXT J
220 NEXT I
230 IF C=0 THEN PRINT "NO COWS"
240 IF C<>0 THEN PRINT C;"COWS"
250 GOTO 70
260 PRINT "CORRECT - GOOD"
270 STOP
280 Z$(J,J)=N$(J,J)
290 C=C+1
300 GOTO 220
```

Fig 8.13 *Notes on the variations on the BASIC used in the BANDC program*

(1) Use of the word RANDOMIZE may not be available in some versions of BASIC. Line 20.
(2) RND(O) may have to be replaced by RND(X) or RND(1). Line 40.
(3) N$(I,I) and A$(K,K) may need to be replaced by MID$(N$, I,1) and MID$(A$,K,1). Line 50.
(4) The ; may have to be replaced by ,. Line 70.
(5) N$(I,I) and G$(I,I) may have to be replaced by MID$(N$, I,1) and MID$(G$, I,1). Line 120.
(6) As for note 5 and Z$(I,I) may have to be replaced by MID$(Z$,I,1). Line 130.
(7) As for note 6. Line 200.
(8) It may be that lines 120, 130, 150, 160, 230 and 240 have to be changed as the facility that every IF test can be followed by an executable statement such as PRINT or an assignment may not be available. In this case additional GOTO statements will be needed.
(9) THEN IF may have to be replaced by AND. Line 200. To test the program insert an extra line, line 65,

   65 PRINT N$

and then run the program. A typical run is shown below.

```
      LOAD"BANDC"
    * 65 PRINT N$
    * RUN
    1314
    YOUR GUESS 3141
    NO BULLS
     4 COWS
    YOUR GUESS 1331
     2 BULLS
     1 COWS
    YOUR GUESS 3311
     2 BULLS
     1 COWS
    YOUR GUESS 1314
    CORRECT - GOOD

    STOP AT 0270
    * RUN
    5123
    YOUR GUESS 5555
     1 BULLS
    NO COWS
    YOUR GUESS 1234
    NO BULLS
     3 COWS
    YOUR GUESS 1235
    NO BULLS
     4 COWS
    YOUR GUESS 5132
     2 BULLS
     2 COWS
    YOUR GUESS 5132
     2 BULLS
     2 COWS
    YOUR GUESS 5123
    CORRECT - GOOD

    STOP AT 0270
```

Fig 8.14

PROGRAM: BANDC (Game of Bulls and Cows).
WRITTEN BY: P. E. GOSLING
DATE: 21st January 1981
Written for ABC NADIR MK. 2 microcomputer with 32 K bytes
of memory.
Version 1.2 of BESTBASIC
Runs on any teletype or teletype compatible terminal.

Fig 8.15

```
1 REM*****************************************************************
2 REM***                 PROGRAM BANDC                            ***
3 REM***                                                          ***
4 REM***             WRITTEN BY P.E.GOSLING                       ***
5 REM***                21ST JANUARY 1981                         ***
6 REM***       WRITTEN IN BESTBASIC 1.2 FOR ABC NADIR MK3 COMPUTER ***
7 REM***                 VERSION 1.0                              ***
8 REM*****************************************************************
10 A$="123456789"
20 RANDOMIZE
30 FOR I=1 TO 4
35 REM***SELECTS A SET OF FOUR DIGITS AT RANDOM FROM THE STRING A$****
40 K=INT(RND(0)*8)+1
45 REM***BUILDS UP COMPUTER'S STRING OF DIGITS IN N$****
50 N$(I,I)=A$(K,K)
60 NEXT I
65 REM***ACCEPTS PLAYER'S GUESS IN FOUR DIGIT STRING G$****
70 INPUT "YOUR GUESS ";G$
75 REM***TESTS FOR CORRECT GUESS***
80 IF G$=N$ THEN 260
95 REM***SETS UP REFERENCE STRING Z$****
90 Z$="****"
95 REM***SETS NUMBER OF 'BULLS' TO ZERO***
100 B=0
105 REM***CHECKS FOR 'BULLS' AND PLACES CORRECT GUESS IN Z$****
110 FOR I=1 TO 4
115 REM***TEST FOR DIGITS IN THE CORRECT PLACE IN THE COMPUTER'S STRING*
   **
120 IF N$(I,I)=G$(I,I) THEN B=B+1
125 REM***PLACES CORRECT GUESSES IN REFERENCE STRING***
130 IF N$(I,I)=G$(I,I) THEN Z$(I,I)=G$(I,I)
140 NEXT I
150 IF B=0 THEN PRINT "NO BULLS"
160 IF B<>0 THEN PRINT B;"BULLS"
165 REM***ZEROS THE COUNT OF 'COWS'***
170 C=0
180 FOR I=1 TO 4
190 FOR J=1 TO 4
175 REM***TESTS TO SEE IF CHOSEN DIGITS EXIST IN COMPUTER'S STRING***
200 IF G$(I,I)=N$(J,J) THEN IF Z$(J,J)="*" THEN 280
210 NEXT J
220 NEXT I
230 IF C=0 THEN PRINT "NO COWS"
240 IF C<>0 THEN PRINT C;"COWS"
250 GOTO 70
260 PRINT "CORRECT - GOOD"
270 STOP
275 REM***ADDS SELECTED DIGITS TO REFERENCE STRING TO ACCOUNT FOR REPEAT
   ED DIGITS***
280 Z$(J,J)=N$(J,J)
290 C=C+1
300 GOTO 220
```

shows the program amended to sort the same file into name order. Notice that in this program there has to be a search for the start of each surname, hence a test for the part of the string which follows the full stop after the initial.

This method of sorting is all right if there are only a small number of records to be sorted. With large numbers of records on the file the method becomes far too slow and unwieldy and here a better scheme is to structure

Fig 8.16a

```
0005 REM***SORTS RANDOM ACCESS FILE INTO ORDER BASED ON CONTENTS OF FIRST VARIAB
LE IN EACH RECORD***
0010 DIM A$(20),B$(20)
0020 DIM A1$(20),B1$(20)
0030 OPEN FILE (2,0),"NEWFILE"
0035 LET K=0
0040 FOR I=1 TO 49
0050    READ FILE (2,I),A$,B$
0060    READ FILE (2,I+1),A1$,B1$
0070    IF A$>A1$ THEN GOTO 0110
0080 NEXT I
0090 IF K=1 THEN GOTO 0035
0100 FOR I=1 TO 50
0101    READ FILE (2,I),A$,B$
0102    PRINT A$,B$
0103 NEXT I
0104 CLOSE
0105 STOP
0107 REM***WRITES DATA BACK INTO RECORDS IN REVERSE ORDER OF RECORDS***
0110 WRITE FILE (2,I+1),A$,B$
0120 WRITE FILE (2,I),A1$,B1$
0130 LET K=1
0131 GOTO 0080
*
```

```
RUN
1111          A.WALL
1679          M.WALTERS
2134          H.MORTON
2154          T.KNOWLES
2174          P.SHEEN
2223          A.THOMSON
2233          H.STEWART
2288          A.LINCOLN
2345          F.BROADWAY
2345          J.SMITH
3215          H.HOWES
3254          P.GOSLING
3289          C.CLARKE
3341          M.THATCHER
3343          S.SUMMERS
3962          G.TAYLOR
4444          D.HEALY
4531          T.HEATH
5254          C.WOOD
5468          B.DUCKWORTH
5555          G.EYRE
5555          G.EYRE
5571          R.WATERMAN
5590          R.WOODCOCK
5591          M.HINDMARCH
6139          R.SUMMERS
6657          R.BENNETT
6678          N.HOWES
6690          M.SUNDERLAND
7756          R.JONES
7762          D.ASH
7773          R.CLARKE
7788          A.SUMNER
7890          R.GREEN
8765          G.LONG
8832          J.CRACKNELL
8852          H.LOCKWOOD
8875          D.COON
8890          M.FOOT
8897          J.SIMPSON
```

```
8976        J.GREEN
8976        J.HEATH
9021        K.PADGET
9021        J.ROCHESTER
9055        U.BLYTON
9087        D.EVANS
9821        R.MAYWOOD
9876        R.BOND
9901        J.FINCH
9915        G.CAPES

STOP AT 0105
*
```

Program outline: This program opens the random access file called "NEW-FILE" on line 30. Each record of that file contains a pair of strings. Pairs of these are read in turn starting with records number 1 and 2 and finishing with records 49 and 50—that is why I goes from 1 to 49 and not from 1 to 50. The first set of string characters from each record are tested and if A\$ from the first record exceeds A1\$ from the second record then contents of the records are written back, but the other way round. That is, the contents of Record 5 are written to Record 4 and the contents of Record 4 are written on to Record 5 for example. Again as with other sorting programs a flag, called K this time, is used to indicate whether the file has been scanned without any interchanges having been made. If this is so then the contents of the file are printed out in order and the program stops—lines 100 to 105.

Fig. 8.16b

```
0005 REM***SORTS A FILE INTO ORDER BY MOVING RECORDS***
0010 DIM A$(20),B$(20)
0020 DIM A1$(20),B1$(20)
0025 REM***OPENS FILE TO BE SORTED - MUST BE A RANDOM ACCESS FILE***
0030 OPEN FILE (2,0),"NEWFILE"
0035 LET K=0
0040 FOR I=1 TO 49
0050     READ FILE (2,I),A$,B$
0060     READ FILE (2,I+1),A1$,B1$
0065     REM***TESTS SURNAME ONLY OMITTING INITIAL***
0070     IF B$(3,LEN(B$))>B1$(3,LEN(B1$)) THEN GOTO 0110
0080 NEXT I
0090 IF K=1 THEN GOTO 0035
0100 FOR I=1 TO 50
0101     READ FILE (2,I),A$,B$
0102     PRINT A$,B$
0103 NEXT I
0104 CLOSE
0105 STOP
0107 REM***WRITES DATA BACK TO FILE IN REVERSE ORDER OF RECORDS***
0110 WRITE FILE (2,I+1),A$,B$
0120 WRITE FILE (2,I),A1$,B1$
0130 LET K=1
0131 GOTO 0080
*
```

```
7762        D.ASH
6657        R.BENNETT
9055        U.BLYTON
9876        R.BOND
2345        F.BROADWAY
9915        G.CAPES
3289        C.CLARKE
7773        R.CLARKE
8875        D.COON
8832        J.CRACKNELL
5468        B.DUCKWORTH
9087        D.EVANS
5555        G.EYRE
5555        G.EYRE
9901        J.FINCH
8890        M.FOOT
3254        P.GOSLING
7890        R.GREEN
8976        J.GREEN
4444        D.HEALY
4531        T.HEATH
8976        J.HEATH
5591        M.HINDMARCH
3215        H.HOWES
6678        N.HOWES
7756        R.JONES
2154        T.KNOWLES
2288        A.LINCOLN
8852        H.LOCKWOOD
8765        G.LONG
9821        R.MAYWOOD
2134        H.MORTON
9021        K.PADGET
9021        J.ROCHESTER
2174        P.SHEEN
8897        J.SIMPSON
2345        J.SMITH
2233        H.STEWART
3343        S.SUMMERS
6139        R.SUMMERS
7788        A.SUMNER
6690        M.SUNDERLAND
3962        G.TAYLOR
3341        M.THATCHER
2223        A.THOMSON
1111        A.WALL
1679        M.WALTERS
5571        R.WATERMAN
5254        C.WOOD
5590        R.WOODCOCK

STOP AT 0105
```

Program outline: This follows exactly the same form as the previous pro-gram except that names are used as the sorting key. Because all the names start with one initial followed by a full stop we use the substring B$(3, LEN(B$)) to isolate the surname.

the data as it is put on to the file in the first place. This is done by setting up the file with a 'linked' structure so that each record contains a 'pointer' to the next record in the file which will follow it in order. In other words, we start with a completely empty file. As each record is written to the file Record 1 is filled first, then Record 2, Record 3, and so on. However, as

the record is written to the file, part of that record will contain the data
we wish to store and another part will contain the record number of the
next record in sequence. In other words a form of sorting takes place as
the records are read in. The unfilled records are held in a 'free storage list'
and a note must be made of the record number of the record at the head
of this list together with the record number of the first record in the
sorted sequence. This may sound complicated but fig. 8.17 shows a program which does this.

Fig 8.17

```
5 REM***CREATES A LINKED FILE AND ADDS NEW RECORDS TO IT***
10 DIM A$(20),X$(20),L$(20),Y$(20),Z$(20),P$(20),M$(20)
20 OPEN FILE (1,0),"LNKFL"
30 INPUT "ARE YOU STARTING A NEW FILE ?";Y$
40 IF Y$="YES" THEN GOSUB 450
50 PRINT "DO YOU WANT TO INSERT,LIST THE FILE OR STOP ?"
60 INPUT "TYPE INSERT,LIST OR STOP ";P$
70 IF P$="LIST" THEN 510
80 IF P$="INSERT" THEN 120
90 IF P$="STOP" THEN CLOSE FILE (1)
100 IF P$="STOP" THEN STOP
110 GOTO 60
120 INPUT A$
130 READ FILE (1,0),L,M
140 IF L=0 THEN 720
150 READ FILE (1,L),L1,L$
155 REM***TESTS FOR FIRST RECORD BEING ONLY RECORD IN FILE***
160 IF L=1 THEN IF L1=-1 THEN L1=1
170 K=L
180 IF L$>A$ THEN 320
190 X=L
200 READ FILE (1,X),X1,X$
210 IF X$<A$ THEN 400
220 Z=M
230 READ FILE (1,Z),Z1,Z$
240 M=Z1
250 Z1=X
260 Z$=A$
270 Y1=Z
280 WRITE FILE (1,0),L,M
290 WRITE FILE (1,Z),Z1,Z$
300 WRITE FILE (1,Y),Y1,Y$
310 GOTO 60
320 READ FILE (1,M),M1,M$
330 L1=K
340 L$=A$
350 L=M
360 M=M1
370 WRITE FILE (1,0),L,M
380 WRITE FILE (1,L),L1,L$
390 GOTO 60
400 Y=X
410 X=X1
420 Y$=X$
430 IF X=-1 THEN 220
440 GOTO 200
450 WRITE FILE (1,0),0,1
455 REM***CREATES FILE WITH DUMMY RECORDS***
460 FOR I=1 TO 20
470 WRITE FILE (1,I),I+1,"XXXX"
480 NEXT I
490 WRITE FILE (1,20),-1,"XXXX"
```

```
500 RETURN
505 REM***PRINTS CONTENTS OF FILE IN ORDER***
510 PRINT "LINKED LIST FILE"
520 READ FILE (1,0),L,M
530 PRINT
540 PRINT "RECORD NO"; TAB(15);"LINK"; TAB(25)"DATA"
550 IF L=0 THEN 640
560 L2=L
570 READ FILE (1,L2),L1,L$
580 IF L1=-1 THEN 620
590 PRINT   TAB(5);L2; TAB(16);L1; TAB(25);L$
600 L2=L1
610 GOTO 570
620 PRINT   TAB(5);L2; TAB(16);L1; TAB(25);L$
630 PRINT
640 M2=M
650 READ FILE (1,M2),M1,M$
660 IF M1=-1 THEN 700
670 PRINT   TAB(5);M2; TAB(16);M1; TAB(25);M$
680 M2=M1
690 GOTO 650
700 PRINT   TAB(5);M2; TAB(16);M1; TAB(25);M$
710 GOTO 60
720 WRITE FILE (1,1),-1,A$
730 WRITE FILE (1,0),1,2
740 GOTO 60
```

```
ARE YOU STARTING A NEW FILE ?YES
DO YOU WANT TO INSERT,LIST THE FILE OR STOP ?
TYPE INSERT,LIST OR STOP INSERT
 ? BLAKE
TYPE INSERT,LIST OR STOP INSERT
 ? ADAMS
TYPE INSERT,LIST OR STOP INSERT
 ? DAWSON
TYPE INSERT,LIST OR STOP INSERT
 ? HOWARD
TYPE INSERT,LIST OR STOP ROBEY
TYPE INSERT,LIST OR STOP INSERT
 ? ROBEY
TYPE INSERT,LIST OR STOP INSERT
 ? GEORGE
TYPE INSERT,LIST OR STOP INSERT
 ? ROBERTS
TYPE INSERT,LIST OR STOP LIST
LINKED LIST FILE
```

RECORD NO	LINK	DATA
2	1	ADAMS
1	3	BLAKE
3	6	DAWSON
6	4	GEORGE
4	7	HOWARD
7	5	ROBERTS
5	-1	ROBEY
8	9	XXXX
9	10	XXXX
10	11	XXXX
11	12	XXXX
12	13	XXXX
13	14	XXXX
14	15	XXXX
15	16	XXXX
16	17	XXXX
17	18	XXXX
18	19	XXXX
19	20	XXXX
20	-1	XXXX

```
TYPE INSERT,LIST OR STOP INSERT
 ? THATCHER
TYPE INSERT,LIST OR STOP LIST
LINKED LIST FILE

RECORD NO     LINK        DATA
    2          1          ADAMS
    1          3          BLAKE
    3          6          DAWSON
    6          4          GEORGE
    4          7          HOWARD
    7          5          ROBERTS
    5          8          ROBEY
    8         -1          THATCHER

    9         10          XXXX
   10         11          XXXX
   11         12          XXXX
   12         13          XXXX
   13         14          XXXX
   14         15          XXXX
   15         16          XXXX
   16         17          XXXX
   17         18          XXXX
   18         19          XXXX
   19         20          XXXX
   20         -1          XXXX
TYPE INSERT,LIST OR STOP STOP
```

Program outline: This program arranges that records placed into successive locations of a random access file are in fact organised in such a way that we can read the records out and print them in ascending order of their key, and in this example this is a name. Each record in the file contains this name and number, called a link, which is the record number of the next higher key in the file. In other words, it points to the logical successor of the record. The first record in the file is numbered zero and contains two numbers. The first of these, called L, is the record number of the logically first record in the list. The second number, M, is the first available free record into which a new piece of data can be placed. Initially the file only contains 20 records, say, and when the file is first set up the set of program instructions in lines 450 to 500 are carried out. This fills all the records with dummy data, "XXXX" and a link to the next record. Record 1 will have a link to Record 2, Record 2 to Record 3 and so on. The last record, Record 20, has the number −1 as its link. This is an indication that it is the last record in the file. Thus by reading each record, as in line 230, the first piece of data, Z1 in this case, gives the record number of the next record in order after record number Z. Z$ is the data, a name only in this case, which the record stores. As each new record is added to the file at line 120 the first action of the program is to read record 0 in order to find the record number of the lowest-keyed record. In addition the value of M gives the number of the record where the new data is to be stored. The section of program from line 200 to line 400 handles the organisation of the links so that the new record is going to be linked for-

wards to the one that must logically follow it and backwards from the one that must logically precede it. The section from line 150 to line 190 ensures that the situation when there is only one record in the file is dealt with. The test on line 140 handles the other special situation when the file has no data in it and has to be 'seeded' with a record, which is not only the first but also the last. The sequence of lines from 510 to 710 arranges for the printing of the two parts of the file in link order. The first part of the file is that which contains the data and the second part is the list of free records which have yet to be filled up. Hence, as the following figure shows, as the first of these sets of records grows, the second shrinks.

The first record is numbered 0 and holds the record numbers of the head of the free storage list and the logical first record in the file. Initially the entire file will be empty and this is denoted by data "XXXX" in each record. The last record in the file has nothing to point to and has −1 as its pointer in the link field. The links thus enable the file to be read out in its proper order despite the fact that the records have been placed in the file in random order. The beauty of this method is that no movement of records takes place at all. The only movement is that of the disc head as it follows the trail indicated by the links contained within each record. The example only shows records being added to the file and how the contents of the file are printed in order. Fig. 8.18 shows a program which will delete a record from a linked list file and also how the contents of a particular record can be retrieved and displayed.

Fig 8.18

```
5 REM***DELETES RECORDS FROM A LINKED FILE***
10 DIM A$(20),X$(20),L$(20),Y$(20),Z$(20)
20 DIM F$(20),M$(20)
30 OPEN FILE (1,0),"LNKFL"
40 INPUT "TYPE DELETE,LIST OR STOP ";P$
50 IF P$="DELETE" THEN GOSUB 140
60 IF Z=1 THEN 110
70 IF P$="LIST" THEN 390
80 IF P$="STOP" THEN CLOSE FILE (1)
90 IF P$="STOP" THEN STOP
100 GOTO 40
110 PRINT "DATA ITEM NOT FOUND"
120 Z=0
130 GOTO 40
140 INPUT A$
150 READ FILE (1,0),L,M
160 X=L
170 READ FILE (1,X),X1,X$
175 REM***RECORD FOUND***
180 IF X$=A$ THEN 250
190 Y=X
```

```
200 X=X1
205 REM***END OF FILE REACHED WITHOUT RECORD BEING FOUND***
210 IF X=-1 THEN 360
220 READ FILE (1,X),X1,X$
230 IF X$=A$ THEN 270
240 GOTO 190
250 L=X1
260 GOTO 300
270 READ FILE (1,Y),Y1,Y$
280 Y1=X1
290 WRITE FILE (1,Y),Y1,Y$
300 Z=0
310 X1=M
320 M=X
330 WRITE FILE (1,X),X1,X$
335 REM***POINTERS TO HEAD OF FILE AND FREE STORAGE LIST AMENDED***
340 WRITE FILE (1,0),L,M
350 RETURN
360 Z=1
370 WRITE FILE (1,0),L,M
380 RETURN
385 REM***PRINTING OF FILE CONTENTS IN ORDER***
390 PRINT "LINKED LIST FILE"
400 PRINT
410 PRINT "RECORD NO"; TAB(15);"LINK"; TAB(25);"DATA"
420 READ FILE (1,0),L,M
430 IF L=0 THEN 520
440 L2=L
450 READ FILE (1,L2),L1,L$
460 IF L1=-1 THEN 500
470 PRINT  TAB(5);L2; TAB(16);L1; TAB(25);L$
480 L2=L1
490 GOTO 450
500 PRINT  TAB(5);L2; TAB(16);L1; TAB(25);L$
510 PRINT
520 M2=M
530 READ FILE (1,M2),M1,M$
540 IF M1=-1 THEN 580
550 PRINT  TAB(5);M2; TAB(16);M1; TAB(25);M$
560 M2=M1
570 GOTO 530
580 PRINT  TAB(5);M2; TAB(16);M1; TAB(25);M$
590 GOTO 40
```

```
TYPE DELETE,LIST OR STOP DELETE
 ? GEORGE
TYPE DELETE,LIST OR STOP LIST
LINKED LIST FILE
```

RECORD NO	LINK	DATA
2	1	ADAMS
1	3	BLAKE
3	4	DAWSON
4	7	HOWARD
7	5	ROBERTS
5	8	ROBEY
8	-1	THATCHER
6	9	GEORGE
9	10	XXXX
10	11	XXXX
11	12	XXXX
12	13	XXXX
13	14	XXXX
14	15	XXXX
15	16	XXXX
16	17	XXXX
17	18	XXXX
18	19	XXXX
19	20	XXXX
20	-1	XXXX

```
TYPE DELETE,LIST OR STOP DELETE
 ? BLAKE
TYPE DELETE,LIST OR STOP DELETE
 ? HOWERD
DATA ITEM NOT FOUND
TYPE DELETE,LIST OR STOP DELETE
 ? HOWARD
TYPE DELETE,LIST OR STOP LIST
LINKED LIST FILE

RECORD NO      LINK        DATA
     2           3         ADAMS
     3           7         DAWSON
     7           5         ROBERTS
     5           8         ROBEY
     8          -1         THATCHER

     4           1         HOWARD
     1           6         BLAKE
     6           9         GEORGE
     9          10         XXXX
    10          11         XXXX
    11          12         XXXX
    12          13         XXXX
    13          14         XXXX
    14          15         XXXX
    15          16         XXXX
    16          17         XXXX
    17          18         XXXX
    18          19         XXXX
    19          20         XXXX
    20          -1         XXXX
TYPE DELETE,LIST OR STOP STOP
```

Program outline: This program follows a very similar pattern to the pre-vious one but it deletes records from "LNKFL". As a record is deleted it is placed at the head of the free storage list of records. In order to delete a record from the file the first operation is to locate its position. This is done by searching through the file and this is done in lines 140 to 350. The variable Z is used as a flag, which is initially set to zero and changes to 1 if the entire file is read without the record being found. Once the record is found—line 230— then the lines 270 to 340 are executed in order to change the links so that the deleted record no longer forms a part of the file and it is placed in the free storage list—lines 310 to 340. The section of program which prints the file is exactly the same as in the previous program.

The program illustrated in Fig. 8.19 is another which searches for infor-mation, again using random files. In this case it represents a simple airline booking system where the data held in each record consists of a flight number, the number of seats available on that flight and the number of the next flight to that destination. The data is held in order of flight numbers and is searched for using the binary search technique. Once the flight number has been found the number of seats available is compared with the number required on that flight. If seats are available a suitable message is displayed and the contents of the record amended. If there are not enough seats available then the next flight to that destination is examined. A next flight number of 999 indicates that there are no more flights to that destination that day.

Fig 8.19

```
5 REM***FLIGHT BOOKING SIMULATION PROGRAM***
10 OPEN FILE (1,0),"FLIGHT"
20 INPUT "FLIGHT NO. - TYPE ZERO TO FINISH ";N
30 IF N=0 THEN 230
40 INPUT "HOW MANY SEATS ? ";S
45 M1=0
46 REM***SETS UP BINARY SEARCH FOR FLIGHT
50 H=21
60 L=1
70 M=INT((H+L)/2)
75 IF M1=M THEN 180
80 READ FILE (1,M),X,Y,Z
90 IF X=N THEN 130
100 IF X<N THEN L=M
110 IF X>N THEN H=M
115 M1=M
120 GOTO 70
130 IF S<=Y THEN 200
140 IF Z=999 THEN 320
150 PRINT "NOT ENOUGH SEATS ON FLIGHT NO. ";X;"NEXT FLIGHT IS NO. ";Z
160 N=Z
170 GOTO 50
180 PRINT "FLIGHT NOT FOUND"
190 GOTO 20
200 PRINT S;" SEATS BOOKED ON FLIGHT NO.";X
205 REM***AMENDS RECORD BY DEDUCTION OF NUMBER OF SEATS BOOKED***
210 WRITE FILE (1,M),X,Y-S,Z
220 GOTO 20
230 PRINT "FLIGHT NO.  SEATS AVAILABLE NEXT FLIGHT NO."
240 PRINT "---------------------------------------------"
250 PRINT
260 FOR I=1 TO 20
270 READ FILE (1,I),X,Y,Z
280 PRINT X,Y,Z
290 NEXT I
300 CLOSE FILE (1)
310 STOP
320 PRINT "NO MORE FLIGHTS TO THAT DESTINATION TODAY"
330 GOTO 20
```

Program outline: This program uses a random access file called "FLIGHT" which has already been set up by another program. Each record on the file contains three numbers. The first of these is a flight number, the second is the number of seats available on that flight and the third is the number of the next flight to the same destination. This data is stored on a random access file for a number of reasons. One of these is that because an airline booking system has to work in what is called 'real time', that is, the records have to be capable of being amended immediately a booking is made. Only by use of a random access file is it possible to read the contents of a particular record and amend it then and there. If a serial file had been used, all reads and writes would have to take place from the start of the file and this will be far too slow for this type of operation. This leads to the other good reason for using a file of the random (sometimes called direct) access type. Since a search always has to be made for the records associated with a flight of a particular number, there has to be a better way than starting at the first record of the file and reading them all in sequence until the record with the appropriate flight number is found. The flight required in this example is found using a binary search *technique which is a very fast way of locating a particular number in a previously sorted list. In our example there are only 20 possible flights stored on the file and the flight number is input at line 20. Then the search starts. At line 70 the file is divided into two parts and the flight number of the record which lies at the middle point of the file is examined—line 80. Lines 100 and 110 establish whether the required flight number lies in the top or bottom half of the file, unless M has happened to give the correct flight number straight away—line 90. When we know which half of the file our record lies in, M is recalculated and we try again. Eventually by continual division of the file into halves time and again the required flight record is found. Then the value of Y, the number of seats available, is tested against S, the number of seats required. Should there not be enough seats on that flight, Z will tell us which flight number will need to be examined next. If Z has the value of 999 then there is no further flight to that destination and an appropriate message is printed on line 320 and the program returns to line 20. Should there be enough seats available on the flight then line 210 writes the amended data back to the record, since the number of seats available has been reduced by the number stored in S.*

If, on a return to line 20, a list of the current state of flights is required then an input of zero will cause the loop from lines 260 to 290 to read the contents of the file in order and print them out. Then the program stops.

The term 'user friendly' has been used quite often so far and it describes programs which are designed to help the user along, especially when that user is not a computer person. One way of achieving this is by the 'menu' approach. This also has the advantage of allowing the programmer to develop his program in a modular way. This means that the program is written as a series of linked programs possibly by members of a programming team. These separate programs are held together by one main 'driver' program. The example which follows is of a simple mailing list package of programs which has a program called "MAIL". It is designed to be run at a video terminal and "MAIL" provides the menu from which the rest of the suite of programs is called. Fig. 8.20 shows the program and Fig. 8.21 shows what the video screen will look like when the program starts up.

Fig 8.20

```
10 PRINT "T H E   M A S T E R P L A N   C O M P U T I N G   S E R V I C E"
20 PRINT
30 PRINT "                    MAILING LIST PACKAGE"
40 PRINT "                    ====================="
50 PRINT
60 PRINT
70 PRINT "THIS PROGRAM MAINTAINS A MAILING LIST OF ADDRESSES"
80 PRINT "IT PROVIDES FACILITIES AS FOLLOWS :"
90 PRINT "(1)........ADDITION OF NEW NAMES AND ADDRESSES TO THE LIST"
100 PRINT "(2)........AMENDMENT OR DELETION OF ENTRIES IN THE LIST"
110 PRINT "(3)........PRINTING OF THE LABELS OR A LIST OF ENTRIES IN THE
LIST"
120 PRINT "(4)........SORTS AN ADDRESS FILE INTO ALPHABETICAL ORDER"
130 PRINT "EACH ENTRY IN THE MAILING LIST HAS A PRINTING KEY WHICH ENABL
ES"
140 PRINT "SELECTION OF PARTS OF THE LIST TO BE PRINTED"
150 INPUT "FACILITY REQUIRED - TYPE 1,2,3 OR 4 - 0 STOPS PROGRAM :",N
160 IF N=0 THEN STOP
170 ON N THEN GOTO 180, 190, 200, 210
180 CHAIN "ADDRLIST"
190 CHAIN "ADDRAMEND"
200 CHAIN "ADDR"
210 CHAIN "SURNAME"
220 GOTO 50
```

*Program outline: The majority of this program consists of printing the
'menu' of options available to the user. The option required is selected
on line 170 where lines 180, 190, 200 or 210 are executed depending
of the value of N being 1, 2, 3 or 4. If for example N was set to 3 then a
jump would be made to line 200 and the program known as "ADDR"
would be loaded into memory and executed. The existing program would
be deleted from memory and can only be reinstated by another "CHAIN"
command being issued by the program currently running.*

Fig 8.21

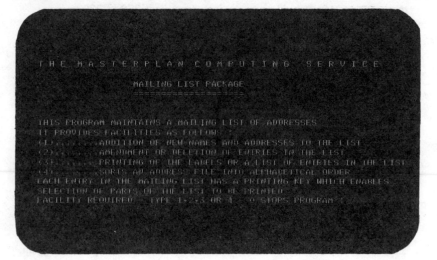

On completion of the required feature offered by the package a technique known as 'chaining' is used. If the printing selection is made then the program which handles the printing of the mailing list is called into action. CHAIN is equivalent to LOAD followed by RUN. At the completion of the printing program it takes the user back to the main program by the CHAIN "MAIL" instruction.

If packages of programs are written in this modular fashion not only does it mean that several people can get on with the programming at once but it also means that programs, which would otherwise be too large to fit into memory, can be run since they are split up into smaller sections which do fit into the available memory space. Figure 8.22 shows one of the subprograms of the mailing list package. Note the CHAIN "MAIL" instruction at the end which returns control to the main program.

So much for some of the how and why of programming. The next chapter deals with making programs work in the way you want them to work and finding out why your programs sometimes fail.

Fig 8.22

```
10 REM****ADDRLIST***ADDS ADDRESSES TO THE LIST***
20 DIM A$(30),B$(30),C$(30),D$(30),E$(30)
30 DIM N$(10)
40 INPUT "FILENAME ?";N$
50 OPEN FILE (1,2),N$
60 PRINT "        END = END OF INPUT"
70 INPUT A$
80 IF A$="END" THEN 180
90 INPUT B$
100 INPUT C$
110 INPUT D$
120 INPUT E$
130 INPUT "PRINTING KEY: ";K
140 PRINT
150 PRINT
160 WRITE FILE (1),K,A$,B$,C$,D$,E$
170 GOTO 70
180 CLOSE FILE (1)
190 CHAIN "MAIL"
```

Program outline: This program adds new names and addresses to the address file being used—its name being specified in line 40—and this is the reason for the file being opened in mode 2 (the append mode), which allows data to be added to data which already exists on the file. The result is that every time this program is used the file becomes larger and larger as more names and addresses are added. The use of the printing key, K, as part of the record as well as the name and address is because very often a file needs to be subdivided into sections so that only parts of the file are printed out. For example the mailing list may be to schools but by an appropriate use of a key, K, they can be subdivided into primary, junior, comprehensive, grammar, and so on. The final instruction on line 190 takes us back to the main menu program.

CHAPTER 9

BUG HUNTING,
OR WHY MY PROGRAM
NEVER WORKS FIRST TIME

9.1 INTRODUCTION

This section applies to debugging programs written in BASIC, but the general ideas are applicable to all languages.

It is almost a law of Nature that no program of more than four lines ever works first time. The reasons for this are manifold but they can usually be put down, in many cases, to very simple errors of typing or the use of the computer language itself. Errors in computer programs are called *bugs* and the various ways of debugging a program form the basis of this chapter. An attempt is made to itemise the various types of errors but it is often a combination of several of these which will cause a program to fail.

9.2 TYPING ERRORS

This type of error is sometimes difficult to spot since it is a human failing to see what we want to see, particularly when checking a program listing. We strike the wrong key and produce an error which fools us and the BASIC interpreter as well. For example, one program the author wrote consistently failed to work properly and eventually the error was tracked down to a line which should have read

        215 LET T = 10

having been mistyped as

        215 LEY T = 10

Now it is true to say that LEY is not a BASIC instruction but the BASIC interpreter being used at the time allowed variable names to be longer than one letter, or one letter followed by a digit. Not only that but the LET, as is usual, was optional and so the value 10 was allocated to a variable called

LEY T, spaces being allowable in names as well, instead of the variable T. This of course is a good argument for not using LET. The moral of this is to check program listings very carefully.

9.3 WRONGLY LABELLED INSTRUCTIONS

An error caused by wrongly labelled instructions, line numbers in the case of BASIC, is often difficult to track down. This is because the fault is shown up by an error message which says that a jump cannot be made to a label that does not exist. The problem then becomes one of finding where the jump ought to have been made to in the first place. If it is not possible, a good way to detect this type of error is to issue the RENUMBER command. This will attempt to renumber the lines of the program and any unresolved GOTOs will cause an error message to be printed. Very often the BASIC interpreter will cause unresolved GOTOs to be listed as GOTO 0000. In this case the detective work has to start to find where the jump should have been to. Once the inconsistency has been sorted out the program can be test run again. Luckily, compiled languages issue messages at the compilation stage if this situation occurs.

9.4 WRONGLY NESTED LOOPS

If one loop lies within another then it must lie wholly within it. A program may have a section such as

```
┌──FOR I = ...
│ ┌─FOR J = ...
│ │
│ │
│ └─NEXT J
└── NEXT I
```

which is fine. But to have an arrangement such as

```
┌──FOR I = ...
│ ┌─FOR J = ...
│ │
│ │
│ └─NEXT I
└─NEXT J
```

is illegal and will cause messages such as

NEXT WITHOUT FOR

or

FOR WITHOUT NEXT

to be output at run time.

9.5 HARD LOOPS

At its worst this error is typified by a program statement such as

45 GOTO 45

This error is usually observed when there is apparently nothing happening when some form of output is expected. If this is observed then it is often a good idea to stop the execution of the program (you may have a RUN STOP or BREAK key), and the program will halt and the line at which this takes place is printed on the screen. CONT or CON will usually continue the program and after this has been done a few times it is usually fairly clear what the program is doing and where it is looping. If you are in doubt about the path of the program then insert a few extra PRINT statements which indicate where the program is at any time. If the values of the relevant variables are printed at regular intervals then the result can be very revealing. Remember that microcomputers do not perform some calculations very quickly and what appears to be a hard loop is in fact a perfectly correct, but lengthy, set of calculations.

9.6 PROBLEMS WITH LOOPS

This type of error can be very frustrating to search for and is due to the fact that not all loops work in the same way. The simple program shown below illustrates the point. Try it on your system and see the result:

```
10 INPUT A, B, C
20 FOR I = A TO B STEP C
30 PRINT I;
40 NEXT I
50 PRINT "EXIT VALUE OF I"; I
60 END
```

Use values of A, B, C of 1, 10, 1, then 1, 1, 1 and finally 5, 1, 1 and compare the outputs with those shown in Fig. 9.1. This shows the results of running the program on several versions of BASIC. The differences occur because of the different points in the loop where the index variable, I, is updated. Also note that it is possible to traverse a loop even though the target value is smaller than the initial value of I with a positive step size.

Fig 9.1

```
10    INPUT A,B,C
20    FOR I=A TO B STEP C
30       PRINT I;
40    NEXT I
50    PRINT "EXIT VALUE OF I IS ";I
60    END
RUN


?1,10,1
  1       2       3       4       5       6       7       8       9       10
EXIT VALUE OF I IS   11

DONE
RUN


?1,1,1
  1       EXIT VALUE OF I IS   2

DONE
RUN


?5,1,1
EXIT VALUE OF I IS   5

DONE
```

```
10 INPUT A,B,C
20 FOR I=A TO B STEP C
30 PRINT I;
40 NEXT I
50 PRINT"EXIT VALUE OF I ";I
60 END
RUN
? 1,10,1
 1  2  3  4  5  6  7  8  9  10 EXIT VALUE OF I  11

>READY
RUN
? 1,1,1
 1 EXIT VALUE OF I  2

>READY
RUN
? 5,1,1
 5 EXIT VALUE OF I  6

>READY
```

```
  10 INPUT A,B,C
* 20 FOR I=A TO B STEP C
* 30 PRINT I;
* 40 NEXT I
* 50 PRINT"EXIT VALUE OF I ";I
* 60 END
* RUN
 ? 1,10,1
 1  2  3  4  5  6  7  8  9  10 EXIT VALUE OF I  10

END AT 0060
* RUN
 ? 1,1,1
 1 EXIT VALUE OF I  1

END AT 0060
* RUN
 ? 5,1,1
EXIT VALUE OF I  5

END AT 0060
*
```

9.7 **INTERPRETER ERRORS**

These are errors discovered by BASIC on an attempt to run a program when using a microcomputer. As has been already mentioned, when a program is typed in line by line the lines are placed in memory and are not interpreted until the RUN command is issued. When BASIC finds an error the program halts and only when the line has been corrected will BASIC be able to get past that line. Unless a command such as

RUN 70

can be issued—RUN from line 70—RUN will always cause execution to start from the lowest numbered line in the program. It is therefore very important to test each program thoroughly by making sure that every possible jump is made so that no incorrect lines are left lurking about in the background ready to stop the program when an unexpected piece of data is processed. The most common errors will usually be indentified by error messages such as

UNMATCHED PARENTHESES

(unequal number of left- and right-hand brackets);

UNDEFINED VARIABLE

(a variable is used whose value has not been assigned previously);

OVERFLOW

(an attempt has been made to divide by zero);

SUBSCRIPT OUT OF BOUNDS

(an attempt has been made to use a value of a subscript larger than allowed for in the DIM statement); and

FUNCTION ARGUMENT

(an attempt has been made, for example, to find the square root of a negative number).

The most common error issued by any language is

SYNTAX ERROR

which means that the language has not been used correctly. This can cover a multitude of errors. The most common are where words have been misspelt or misused. Typical of these are

```
1Ø PRIMPT X
2Ø OUTPUT X
3Ø WHEN X = 5 THEN 65
4Ø LET Y = X : P
5Ø LET P = 3 (X + Y)
6O END
```

In the last example the letter O has been used instead of the digit Ø, usually written with a slash through it in order to distinguish between the two characters.

9.8 CHOOSING TEST DATA

Many programs contain errors which can be detected before it becomes too late by the use of suitable test data. If the program successfully copes with the test data then it can fairly safely be said that the program is safe to use for the purpose it is intended. For example in Section 9.6 a program which tests how FOR . . . NEXT . . . loops work is described. Three sets of test data were suggested for use at this point. They were (in the cases where the target value of I was greater than the initial value) equal to it and less than it. If a program is written to sort a set of numbers into ascending order then what better than a set of numbers arranged in descending order to test the program? By choosing good test data all parts of a program can be tested. There is nothing worse than having a program containing a section which has never been tested and thus—as has already been mentioned—containing a possible syntax error. This problem is overcome by using compiled languages. But still the use of adequate test data against the possibility of run time errors is important.

9.9 EXPECTING THE COMPUTER TO DO THE IMPOSSIBLE

There are times when the programmer can get carried away with the thrill of writing complicated programs. It is very easy to forget that a machine has only finite resources, such as a fixed amount of memory. An example of this is the program which contains

$$45 \text{ IF } X\% = 10000000 \text{ THEN } 200$$

forgetting that a signed integer in a microcomputer has to be fitted into 2 bytes of memory; 2 bytes, 16 bits, can only store a number smaller than

$$2^{15} = 32768$$

allowing 1 bit for the sign.

A similar mistake is made in the program which contains

        10 DIM A(200, 400)

thus expecting an array to be stored containing 80 000 elements, and that on a machine with only 48 K of memory.

9.10 TRY THIS

If you have access to a computer using BASIC type in and run the following program

            10 FOR I = 1 TO 200
            20 S = S + 0.01
            30 NEXT I
            40 A(1) = 10
            50 A(2) = 100
            60 A(3) = 1000
            70 PRINT A(S)

If you get the answer you expect you will be a lucky programmer!

CHAPTER 10

OTHER PROGRAMMING LANGUAGES

10.1 INTRODUCTION

So far we have gone into a considerable amount of detail describing programming techniques using the BASIC language as a vehicle. There are, as has already been hinted, many other programming languages apart from BASIC, each designed to help solve different types of problems. FORTRAN — FORmula TRANSslator — was designed as a language to be used for the solution of scientific problems as it is high on computational features. COBOL — COmmon Business Orientated Language — is low on computational facilities but high on the ability to handle files of data. PL/1 — Programming Language 1—was designed by the IBM Corporation in an attempt to combine the features of both FORTRAN and COBOL.

A recent newcomer to the ranks of programming languages is *Pascal*, originating in the early 1970s as an attempt to take a lot of the hard labour out of programming. Pascal experts refer to BASIC and FORTRAN as *spaghetti* code programming languages due to the proliferation of GOTO statements and the well-founded criticism that programs written in these languages are often very hard to follow, and hence to debug. Pascal will be discussed more fully later in this chapter.

10.2 FORTRAN

The history of computing is bound up with the punched card. This is because much of the work performed by early computers was taken over from existing mechanical accounting systems which already made use of this type of card. (In fact, the use of these cards dates from the late nineteenth century.) FORTRAN was one of the earliest high-level languages to be made available and so it is not surprising that the format of the language statements owes a lot to the 80-column punched card. FORTRAN statements must not start before column 7 except for comments which must start with a C in column 1. Labels can be placed in columns 2, 3, 4 and 5. An example of a pre-printed FORTRAN progress card is shown in Fig. 10.1. One program statement is punched on one card (for examples of the codes used in punched cards see P. E. Gosling and Q. L. M. Laarhoven *Digital Codes for Computers and Microprocessors*. Macmillan, 1980). FORTRAN programs are best written out on specially printed coding sheets prior to being entered into the computer and an example in this section will be shown in this form.

Fig 10.1

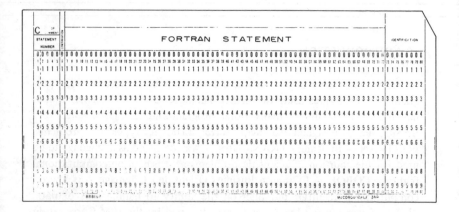

FORTRAN and BASIC have a number of features in common and thus anyone who has had experience of BASIC should not find a simple FORTRAN program difficult to follow. A particular point of similarity is in the arithmetic statements. The same symbols are used with the exception of ** being used instead of ↑ and the word LET is not allowed at all. For example, the statement

$$B = 4 * A + 6 * (C + D)/F$$

is acceptable to both languages. An obvious difference between languages is that FORTRAN names can always consist of more than one character, but this is only an option in some BASICs.

FORTRAN tends to be a far more precise language than BASIC and this is particularly obvious in the way it handles numbers. In chapter 7 it was stated that most versions of BASIC treat all numbers in the same way, that is as floating point numbers. Only some versions of the language allow a differentiation to be made between integers and floating point numbers. FORTRAN has always done this, but not by placing special symbols after the name. All FORTRAN names beginning with the letters I through N are treated as integers and all the others, that is those starting with the letters A through H and M through Z refer to floating point numbers. This convention is easy to remember since I and N are the first two letters of the word INteger. Not only are the names significant in FORTRAN but the way in which a number is written is an indication of its type. Any number without a decimal point is automatically of the integer type. Anything else, which means any number containing a decimal point, is stored as a floating point number, which in FORTRAN is called a REAL number. The same storage is allocated as described in chapter 7 — 4 bytes for a single precision real number, 2 bytes for an integer. Hence the following are integers

$$67, 456, 1 \text{ and } 0$$

whereas the following numbers are valid real numbers

$$45.6, 2.1, 0.0, 9., 0.009 \text{ and } 1.4E+6$$

and notice that 9. and 9 are numbers of two different types. It is important that, unless there is a very good reason for doing otherwise, we must never mix up real numbers and integers. For example

$$I = I + 1$$

and

$$A = A + 1.$$

are perfectly acceptable, but

$$A = A + 1$$

is not advisable since A is a real variable and 1 is an integer constant.

If for some reason we wish to go outside the convention which FORTRAN supplies we can override it by a declaration of the type

REAL ITEM

or

INTEGER XONE, XTWO

thus forcing the numbers to be stored in a form different from that which the names imply.

Another obvious difference, to which it is very easy to adjust, comes with decision statements. In FORTAN we do not use the =, < and > symbols as in BASIC. We use the following instead

.EQ.   equal to
.GT.   greater than

.LE.   less than
.GE.   greater than or equal to
.LE.   less than or equal to
.NE.   not equal to

and the test is put in brackets so that FORTRAN works out the truth value of the contents of the brackets and on the result of this will either carry out the instruction which follows the brackets or proceed to the next instruction in sequence. The word THEN is not used. This results in statements such as

IF (XONE.EQ.XTWO) GOTO 100

or

IF (A.GT.1.) A = 1.

or

IF (MAX.GT.MIN.OR.PONE.EQ.PTWO) STOP

Note that we can use the logical conjunctions .OR. and .AND. in decision statements.

There is a second form of the IF test which in effect allows us a three-way switch. It looks like this

IF (X) n_1, n_2, n_3

If the value of the contents of the brackets is negative the program jumps to the first of the three labels. If the contents of the brackets have zero value then the jump is to the second of the labels. A positive value will cause a jump to the third of the labels. Labels can only be numbers and only labelled statements need any number in front of them, unlike BASIC where every line has a label which is its line number.

The FOR . . . NEXT . . . loop in BASIC becomes a DO loop in FORTRAN and so we get

DO 120 I = 1, 20, 1

which means

Do all the instructions from here up to and including the statement with label 120 for values of I from 1 to 20 in steps of 1.

Loops in FORTRAN are more restrictive than in BASIC. In FORTRAN the starting and finishing values must always be integers and the step size, the last of the three numbers, must always be a positive integer. There is no counting backwards in FORTRAN. Loops often terminate with a CONTINUE statement.

Finally, before giving some examples of programs written in FORTRAN, we must examine, though not in too much detail, the statements which govern input and output (I/O) statements. When data is transferred between the computer and its peripherals the words READ and WRITE are used. The forms in which they are generally used are

READ (m,n) A, B, C, . . .

and

WRITE (m, n) A, B, C, D, . . .

where m is the *channel* number and n is a label attached to a statement which exactly defines the way in which the data is to be handled — a FORMAT statement. Each manufacturer assigns a set of channel numbers to particular devices; for example, the line printer might be channel 12 and the card reader channel 10. The two statements

WRITE (12,200) AMOUNT, IHOURS, RATE
200   FORMAT (1H ,F10.2, I5, F10.2)

will cause the line printer, channel 12, to print the values of the variables AMOUNT and RATE (both real numbers) and the value of the integer variable IHOURS according to the format specified by the statement labelled 200. This format statement specifies that

(1) Printing will start on the next line at the start of that line — 1H , speci-fies that. (Note that it is 1H , not 1H, that is the H must be followed by a space.)
(2) Print a real number in such a way that it occupies 10 spaces with two figures after the decimal point — F10.2 specifies that. The 10 is the *field width* and the 2 is the width of the decimal part of the field. Remember that the decimal point takes up a space so that the output takes the form of XXXXXXX.XX.
(3) Print an integer taking up the next five spaces — I5 specifies that.
(4) Print another real number according to the F10.2 format as described in 2.

The output from such an instruction would look like this

edge of paper →| 42.00   4   10.50

0   5   10   15   20   25

If the format label is omitted as in

WRITE (12) AMOUNT, IHOURS, RATE

then the formatting is left to the computer and we get what is called *free format* so that a number such as 42.0 would probably be output as

0.420000E 2.

Should data be read from files stored on disc then the programmer can allot channel numbers as he wishes.

If data is to be input via the console, which is the 'driving seat' of the computer, then the keyword ACCEPT is used. The word TYPE is used if output is required at the console. FORMAT statements are not associated with either of these statements.

Fig. 10.2 shows a program written in FORTRAN. It is our electricity bill program again, which has already been written in ACE and BASIC. Notice that the program terminates in the word END. All FORTRAN programs must have this word as their final statement.

FORTRAN subroutines are programs written and stored separately from the main program; how they all fit together will be dealt with later. When a subroutine is used by another program it is CALLed, as in

CALL SUBR1 (X, Y, P)

A subroutine cannot be run as a free-standing program. It always has to be CALLed. The variable names in brackets are the subroutine *parameters* and are those variables whose values will be used by the subroutine. The subroutine itself must start with the word SUBROUTINE followed by the name of the subroutine. The names of the parameters passed back and forth between subroutine and main program, if there are any, are listed in brackets after the subroutine name. These parameter names are those by which the variables are known within the subroutine. For example a subroutine called SUBR1 must have as its first line, for example

SUBROUTINE SUBR1 (A, B, C)

where A, B and C are the names of the variables passed between it and the main program. This is in fact exactly the same concept as that mentioned in Chapter 6 on p.118. The next example, Fig. 10.3, is for the same program as is shown in Fig. 6.9 but allowing subroutines in the way FORTRAN uses them.

The example shown in Fig. 10.4 is another FORTRAN program which uses the subroutine called CLEAR. The program plots graphs on the line printer. Note the 'implied DO loop' in the third line from the end of the main program. Here a loop within a loop is executed for J going from 1 to 121 while I goes from 1 to 61 — that is, the values of IG which are printed will be, in order, IG(1,1), IG(1,2) ... IG(1,120), IG(1,121), IG(2,1), IG(2,2) ... IG(2,121) ... IG(61,121).

Fig 10.2

IBM FORTRAN Coding Form

X28-7327-6 U/M 025
Printed in U.K.

PROGRAM Electricity Bill
PROGRAMMER P E Gosling
DATE 1st APRIL '81

PUNCHING INSTRUCTIONS — GRAPHIC / PUNCH
PAGE OF
CARD ELECTRO NUMBER

```
C    ELECTRICITY BILL CALCULATION
     ACCEPT "NO OF UNITS?", E
     IF(E.LE.1Ø.) GOTO 3Ø
     GOTO 9Ø
3Ø   C=E*Ø.Ø7-.Ø7
     IF(C.LT.3.64) GOTO 5Ø
     GOTO 6Ø
5Ø   C=3.64
6Ø   C=C+3.25
     C=C#1.15
     WRITE(12,1ØØ) C
1ØØ  FORMAT(14," COST IS ",F8.2," POUNDS")
     STOP
9Ø   E=E-15Ø.
     C=E*Ø.Ø5+16.5
     GOTO 6Ø
     END
```

*A standard card form. (IBM electro 888157. Is available for punching statements from this form)

Fig 10.3

```
C MERGES TWO LISTS
      DIMENSION A(100),B(100),C(100)
      INTEGER E
      TYPE "LIST A"
      ACCEPT "HOW MANY NUMBERS ? ",N1
      READ(11)(A(I),I=1,N1,1)
      TYPE "LIST B"
      ACCEPT "HOW MANY NUMBERS ?",N2
      READ(11)(B(I),I=1,N2,1)
C   INITIALISE VARIABLES
      P=A(1)
      Q=B(1)
      L=2
      K=1
      J=2
C   MERGE COMMENCES
  300 IF(P.GT.Q) GOTO 500
      CALL ADDUP(P,C,K)
      CALL GNEXT(P,A,L,E,N1)
      IF (E.EQ.1) GOTO 400
      GOTO 300
  400 CALL ADDUP(Q,C,K)
      CALL GNEXT(Q,B,J,E,N2)
      IF (E.EQ.1) GOTO 700
      GOTO 400
  500 CALL ADDUP(Q,C,K)
      CALL GNEXT(Q,B,J,E,N2)
      IF (E.EQ.1) GOTO 600
      GOTO 300
  600 CALL ADDUP(P,C,K)
      CALL GNEXT(P,A,L,E,N1)
      IF (E.EQ.1) GOTO 700
      GOTO 600
  700 WRITE(12)"LIST A"
      WRITE(12)"------:"
      WRITE(12)
      WRITE(12,10)(A(I),I=1,N1,1)
      WRITE(12)
      WRITE(12)"LIST B"
      WRITE(12)"------"
      WRITE(12)
      WRITE(12,10)(B(I),I=1,N2,1)
      WRITE(12)
      WRITE(12)"MERGED LIST C"
      WRITE(12)"-------------"
      WRITE(12)
      N=N1+N2
      WRITE(12,10)(C(I),I=1,N,1)
   10 FORMAT(1H ,10F7.1)
      END



      SUBROUTINE ADDUP(H,CARRAY,KEY)
      DIMENSION CARRAY(100)
      CARRAY(KEY)=H
      KEY=KEY+1
      RETURN
      END
```

```
       SUBROUTINE GNEXT(H,XARRAY,M,F,N)
       DIMENSION XARRAY(100)
       INTEGER F
       F=0
       IF (M.GT.N) GOTO 100
       H=XARRAY(M)
       M=M+1
       GOTO 200
100    F=1
200    RETURN
       END
```

LIST A

3.0	5.0	7.0	8.0	12.0	21.0	33.0	44.0	56.0	60.0
78.0	90.0								

LIST B

1.0	6.0	9.0	10.0	11.0	23.0	24.0	47.0	49.0	57.0

MERGED LIST C

1.0	3.0	5.0	6.0	7.0	8.0	9.0	10.0	11.0	12.0
21.0	23.0	24.0	33.0	44.0	47.0	49.0	56.0	57.0	60.0
78.0	90.0								

10.3 COBOL

Probably the first thing to strike the newcomer to COBOL is that it appears to be a very verbose language. Almost no symbols are used and even simple arithmetic uses words such as ADD, SUBTRACT, MULTIPLY and DIVIDE. However, this does help the legibility of the programs in many ways.

A COBOL program is always divided up into four *divisions*. These are the *Identification Division*, the *Environment Division*, the *Data Division* and the *Procedure Division*.

(1) *The Identification Division* provides the facts about the program identifying who wrote it and when. Any comments about the program are included in this division.

(2) *The Environment Division* specifies the particular computer for which the program was written. It can also contain information regarding the amount of memory required and any special peripheral equipment, such as tape drives, which may be required. This division also contains the *input/output* section which names all the files to be used in the program and the media on which they are stored. For example, this section would contain statements such as

Fig 10.4 *Program outline*

```
      INTEGER BLANK,DOT,EKS,T1,Y1,P,P1
      COMMON EKS,BLANK,DOT,IG(61,121)
      BLANK=" "
      DOT="."
      EKS="*"
      CALL CLEAR
      TYPE "FIRST WAVE"
      ACCEPT "AMPLITUDE - NOT GREATER THAN 1 ",A
      ACCEPT "FREQUENCY - NOT GREATER THAN 10 ",F
      ACCEPT "PHASE ANGLE - DEGREES ",P
      TYPE "SECOND WAVE"
      ACCEPT "AMPLITUDE - NOT GREATER THAN 1 ",A1
      ACCEPT "FREQUENCY - NOT GREATER THAN 10 ",F1
      ACCEPT "PHASE ANGLE - DEGREES ",P1
      WRITE(12,300) A,F,P,A1,F1,P1
300   FORMAT(1H ,"SUMMATION OF A WAVE OF AMPLITUDE",F5.2,",FREQUENCY
     &"OF ",F3.1,"HERTZ AND PHASE ANGLE ",I3,"DEGREES"/" WITH A WAVE OF AMPLITUDE"
     &,F5.2,"FREQUENCY OF ",F3.1,"HERTZ AND PHASE ANGLE ",I3,"DEGREES")
      T=-60
      PI=3.14159
      DO 100 K=1,121,1
      Y=A*SIN(2.*PI*F/250.*T + PI*P/180.)
      Y1=A1*SIN(2.*PI*F1/250.*T + PI*P1/180.)
      T=T+1
      T1=K
      Y=Y+Y1
      Y1=31-Y*15
      IG(Y1,T1)=EKS
100   CONTINUE
      WRITE(12,200)((IG(I,J),J=1,121,1),I=1,61,1)
200   FORMAT(1H ,121A1)
      END

      SUBROUTINE CLEAR
      INTEGER BLANK,DOT,EKS
      COMMON EKS,BLANK,DOT,IG(61,121)
      DO 16 I=1,61,1
10    IG(I,J)=BLANK
      DO 20 I=1,121,1
20    IG(31,I)=DOT
      DO 30 I=1,61,1
30    IG(I,61)=DOT
```

SUMMATION OF A WAVE OF AMPLITUDE 0.70,FREQUENCY OF 4.0HERTZ AND PHASE ANGLE 35DEGREES
WITH A WAVE OF AMPLITUDE 0.40FREQUENCY OF 8.0HERTZ AND PHASE ANGLE 60DEGREES

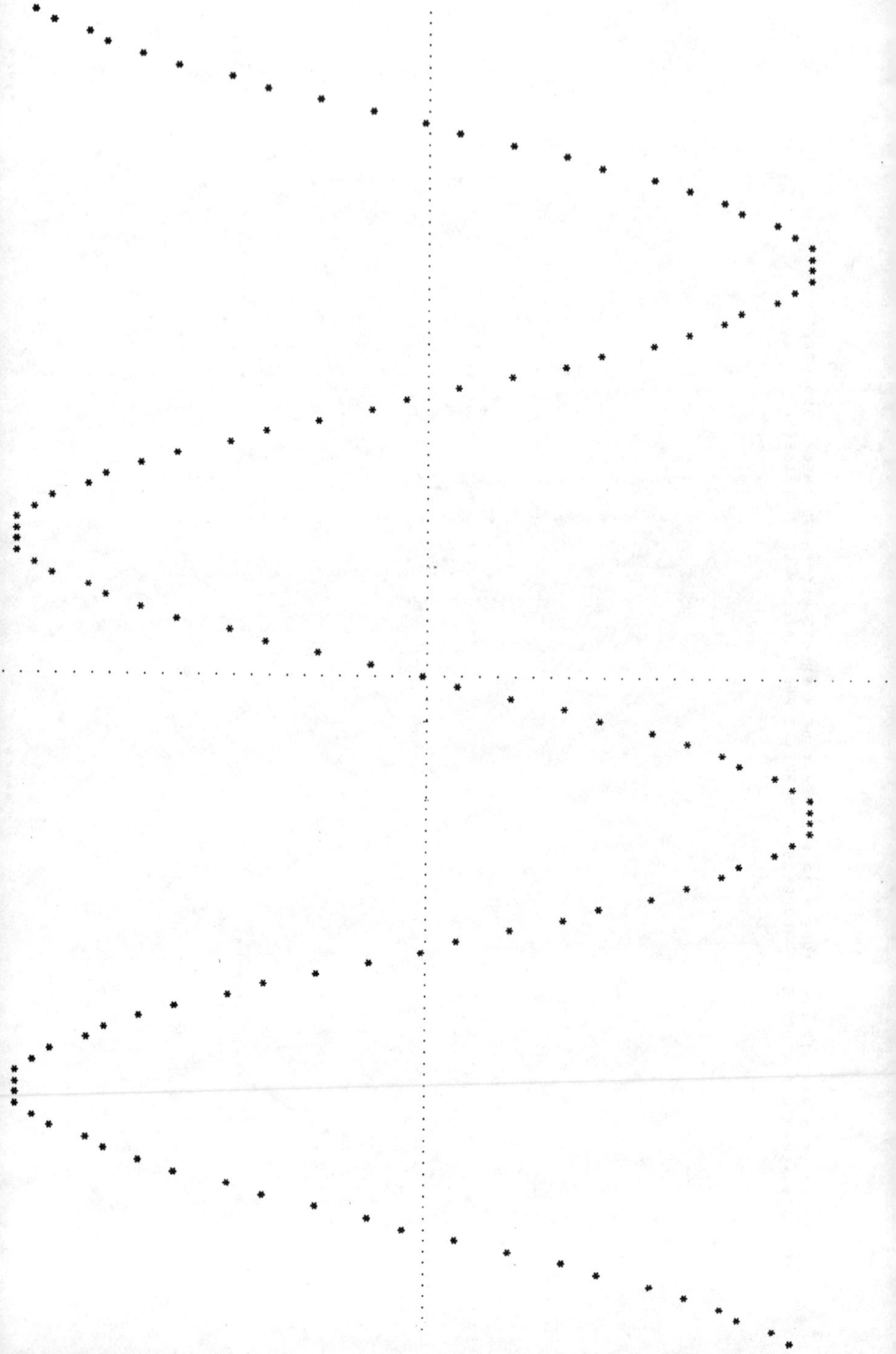

Main program: *The first line of this program states that the four variables named BLANK, DOT, EKS and Y1 are to be treated as integers and not as real variables as their names would ordinarily imply. The COMMON statement which follows is a declaration that the variables in the list which follows it are to share the same locations in memory as the variables of the same name in the subroutine (see the third line of the subroutine called CLEAR). The next three lines assign values to the integer variables called BLANK, DOT and EKS. As they are integers they occupy one word, 16 bits, of memory but they are also to store characters which normally only take up one byte, 8 bits. Hence the allocation of two characters per variable. Then the subroutine CLEAR is called. The next eight lines of program allow the values of the variables used in any particular run of the program to be input. In this case we use ACCEPT which is the instruction used to allow input from the computer console which is a keyboard device such as teletype or VDU as shown in Fig. 1.3. These lines will assign values to the variables called A, F, P. A1, F1 and P1. The WRITE statement then causes these values to be printed at the line printer, device number 12, according to the format specified by the statement labelled 300. This will print the value of the variables as well as the text which is specified on the three lines of the FORMAT statement. The / indicates that printing of the subsequent characters is to take place on the next line, but note that the very first character in quotes after the / is a space, the carriage control character which will ensure that the words "WITH A WAVE ..." will come at the start of the line. The &, by the way, is a continuation character which indicates that what follows is a continuation of what was on the previous line. The next eight lines of program are concerned with the arithmetic of the program—the non-mathematical need not really concern themselves with the details. What is in fact happening is that the page is divided up into an array containing 61 rows and 121 columns and the result of the arithmetic causes the variable EKS to be placed in the Y1th row and the Kth column of the array IG. The loop, DO 100 . . ., is performed 121 times so that the characters which form the graph are placed in the correct row of the array as we scan from left to right. The subroutine CLEAR has already filled up the entire array with blanks except for the two sets of dots which form the axes of the graph. When we come to the printing of the array IG at the WRITE statement, according to the format in line 200, we will get output as shown in the second half of the figure. The use of the A1 format causes only one of the two characters stored in each word in the array to be printed.*

Subroutine CLEAR: *This subroutine announces its name in the first line. There are no variable names in brackets after the name and so there are no variables transmitted between the main program and the subroutine. The next two lines fulfil the same function as the first two lines of the main program. However, the variable Y1 is not in the list of integers used in the subroutine as it does not occur in this part of the program. Then there is a loop within a loop which places blanks in every position of the array of 61 rows and 121 columns called IG. The loop DO 20 . . . places a DOT character in the 121 positions across the centre of the array thus forming the horizontal axis. The DO 30 . . . loop places 61 DOT characters vertically down the centre of the array to form the vertical axis. Then control is returned to the main program. This subroutine is necessary because there could well be all sorts of rubbish left in the addresses in memory allocated to the array IG by a previous program and these would be printed out and produce an incomprehensible graph if CLEAR were not used.*

SELECT INPUTA ASSIGN TO DISC

which informs the computer that the file called INPUTA will be stored on magnetic disc, as opposed to tape. This information is held in a *paragraph* headed FILE CONTROL.

(3) *The Data Division* consists of two sections: the FILE SECTION and the WORKING-STORAGE SECTION. The first of these defines the structure of the files used by specifying the names to be assigned to each field of each record and the number and type of characters in each field. (For more detailed information about this see G. G. L. Wright, *Mastering Computers*, Chapter 5.) The descriptions of the fields are achieved by using the PIC or PICTURE keyword. For example

PIC 9(5) means 5 decimal digits.
PIC 9(5) V99 means a number with 5 digits before the decimal point, V, and two digits after it.
PIC ZZZZ9.99 means a decimal number in the range 9.99 to 99999,99. The Zs imply that any zeros in these position are suppressed (floating zeros).
PIC X(4) means four alphanumeric characters, that is, any of the set A–Z, 0–9.
PIC A(6) means six alphabetic characters.

Remember that a file consists of a series of *records* each of which are made up of a series of *fields*. The WORKING-STORAGE SECTION defines the variables and constants to be used in the program; again they are defined by PIC statements.

(4) *The Procedure Division* specifies the actual processing to be carried out and uses words to instruct the computer to perform its various tasks. Because words are used instead of symbols the program reads

rather like a stilted piece of English prose. Separate parts of the program are referenced by *labels* so that a COBOL sentence can look like this

IF STOCK-IN-HAND IS LESS THAN 200 GOTO REORDER-STOCK

where REORDER-STOCK is a label attached to a particular routine in the program. Labels are easy to spot in a COBOL program as the section of program they are attached to is always indented from the label.

As with FORTRAN, COBOL is formatted according to the restraints of the 80-column punched card. A card used for COBOL programs is shown in Fig. 10.5. Again, one card is used for the punched code for one line of program. This does not mean that all COBOL and FORTRAN programs have to be prepared on punched cards, but the compiler programs, which interpret the source language, expect the format of the program to be in 80-character chunks where the position of characters within the 80-column format has a certain meaning. Fig. 10.6 shows a COBOL program, our electricity bill again, written in COBOL on a COBOL coding sheet. There are several things to be noticed in this example. One is that the Identification Division merely consists of the program name, and the Environment Division is empty. These divisions have to be there even though they have nothing in them. Note also that there are a lot of full stops in the program. They provide essential information to the compiler program and omission of any one of the full stops would cause the compiler to generate program error messages. As with FORTRAN the program is laid out in a rather formal way with the labels always starting in column 8 and the indented sections starting in column 12 (see the printing on the card in Fig. 10.5).

Fig 10.5

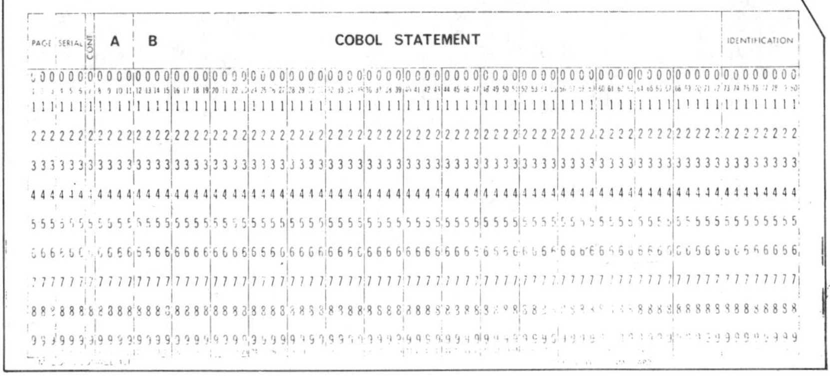

Fig 10.6

COBOL Coding Form

SYSTEM		
PROGRAM	CALCULATION OF ELECTRICITY COSTS	
PROGRAMMER		DATE

```
SEQUENCE    CONT  A   B
(PAGE)(SERIAL)
001010      IDENTIFICATION DIVISION.
001020      PROGRAM-ID. CALCOST.
001030      ENVIRONMENT DIVISION.
001040      DATA DIVISION.
001050      WORKING-STORAGE SECTION.
001060      01  UNITS              PIC 9(5).
001070      01  COST               PIC 9(5)V99.
001080      01  EDITED-COST        PIC ZZZZ9.99.
001090      PROCEDURE DIVISION.
001100      INPUT-UNITS.
001110          DISPLAY "TYPE IN UNITS OF ELECTRICITY" UPON CONSOLE.
001120          ACCEPT UNITS FROM CONSOLE.
001130          IF UNITS IS LESS THAN 150 OR EQUAL TO 150
001140              THEN GO TO CALCULATE-COST
001150              ELSE GO TO AMEND-UNITS.
001160      CALCULATE-COST.
001170          MULTIPLY UNITS BY 0.07 GIVING COST.
001180          IF COST IS LESS THAN 3.64
001190              THEN GO TO REVIEW-COST
001200              ELSE GO TO EXTEND-COST.
001210      REVIEW-COST.
001220          MOVE 3.64 TO COST.
001230      EXTEND-COST.
```

SYSTEM

COBOL Coding Form

PROGRAM CALCULATION OF ELECTRICITY COSTS CONTD.

PROGRAMMER   DATE

COBOL STATEMENT

SEQUENCE (PAGE) (SERIAL)	A	B
002010		MULTIPLY 1.15 BY COST.
002020		MOVE COST TO EDITED-COST.
002030		DISPLAY "£" EDITED-COST UPON CONSOLE.
002040		STOP RUN.
001050	AMEND-UNITS.	
002060		SUBTRACT 150 FROM UNITS.
002070		COMPUTE COST = (UNITS * 0.05) + 10.5.
002080		GO TO EXTEND-COST.
09		
10		
11		
12		
13		
14		
15		
16		
17		
18		
19		
20		

Fig. 10.7 shows another COBOL program, this time one which uses a file. Even with a very sketchy knowledge of the language it should be possible to read the program and discover what it does.

COBOL is a language which is very heavily committed to handling large quantities of data which will be stored on tape or disc files. The amount of computation in most COBOL programs is relatively small, but the manipulation of that data is considerable. In particular it should be noted that the program is split up into a series of clearly defined sections of *paragraphs* thus aiding the clarity of the program for the reader.

Fig 10.7

```
IDENTIFICATION DIVISION.
PROGRAM I.D. SORTER.
AUTHOR D.CHAPMAN.
ENVIRONMENT DIVISION.
INPUT-OUTPUT SECTION.
FILE CONTROL.
     SELECT FILE1 ASSIGN TO DISK.
DATA DIVISION.
FD FILE1.
01 INREC.
     03 INKEY PIC X(4).
     03 FILLER PIC X(52).
WORKING STORAGE SECTION.
01  SORT-CONTROL.
     03 I PIC 9(5).
     03 J PIC 9(5).
     03 K PIC 9(5).
     03 L PIC 9(5).
     03 M PIC 9(5).
     03 N PIC 9(5).
01 HOLD-TABLE.
     03 IN-FIELD OCCURS 250 TIMES
        06 KEY1 PIC X(4).
        06 FILLER PIC X(52).
01 ITEM-STORE PIC X(56).
PROCEDURE DIVISION.
BEGIN.
     OPEN INPUT FILE1.
     MOVE 1 TO N.
READIT.
     READ FILE1 AT END GOTO SORTIT.
     MOVE INREC TO IN-FIELD (N).
     ADD 1 TO N.
     GO TO READIT.
SORTIT.
     SUBTRACT 1 FROM N.
     CLOSE FILE1.
     MOVE N TO M.
SORT1.
     DIVIDE 2 INTO M.
     IF M EQUALS 0 GO TO SORT5.
     SUBTRACT M FROM N GIVING K.
     MOVE 1 TO J.
SORT2.
     MOVE J TO I.
SORT3.
     ADD I TO M GIVING L.
     IF KEY1 (I) IS SMALLER THAN KEY1 (L) GO TO SORT4.
     IF KEY1 (I) EQUALS KEY1 (L) GO TO SORT4.
     MOVE IN-FIELD (L) TO ITEM-STORE.
     MOVE IN-FIELD (I) TO IN-FIELD (L).
```

```
        MOVE ITEM-STORE TO INFIELD (I).
        SUBTRACT M FROM I.
        IF I IS GREATER THAN 0 GO TO SORT3.
    SORT4.
        ADD 1 TO J.
        IF K IS SMALLER THAN J GO TO SORT1.
        GO TO SORT2.
    SORT5.
        OPEN OUTPUT FILE1.
        MOVE 1 TO J.
    SORT6.
        MOVE IN-FIELD (J) TO INREC.
        WRITE INREC.
        ADD 1 TO J.
        IF J IS GREATER THAN N GO TO FINISH.
        GO TO SORT6.
    FINISH.
        CLOSE FILE1.
        STOP RUN.
```

*Program outline: The File Control section states that there is to be a file
called FILE1 and it is to be a disc file. The FD section states that the
records, each called INREC, are divided into two fields—INKEY and
FILLER. INKEY will contain four alphanumeric characters and FILLER,
which is the name given to any elementary item which cannot be referred
explicitly, but which contains 52 alphanumeric characters. The variables
used during the program are called I, J, K, L, M and N and they are each
numerics of up to nine digits. IN-FIELD is a subscripted variable, a list,
which can contain up to 250 items. This is the COBOL equivalent of the
DIM statement in BASIC and the DIMENSION statement in FORTRAN.
The elementary items of the list contain two fields each called KEY1 and
FILLER matching the fields within the records of the file. Finally there
is a variable called ITEM-STORE which can hold 56 alphanumeric characters. The procedure division starts with an instruction to open the file and
then assign the value 1 to the variable N. The READIT set of instructions
are to read the records from the file one at a time and allocate them to the
list IN-FIELD: one record to one item in the list. When the last record has
been read we go to the next set of three instructions, reduce the value of
N by one, close the file and set the variable M to take the value of N. The
rest of the program is, in fact, a shell sort (see Fig. 4.6) to sort the contents
of the list IN-FIELD. When the list has been sorted on the key to the
record called KEY1 then the sorted list is written back to the original file
from IN-FIELD. Notice how it is possible in COBOL to read in large pieces
of data, irrespective of what that data might be, and only examine part of
it. Hence the use of FILLER which is really saying that we are only
interested in the first four characters of the record as that is the part
of the record we are going to use as our sort key. We sort on that and then
transfer the whole lot back to original file. Another point to be noted is
the instruction*

> DIVIDE 2 INTO M

which is the COBOL way of saying 'divide M by 2, take the integer part and allocate that to M' which is the equivalent of line 140 in the program Fig. 4.6.

10.4 PASCAL

Here, for once, we have a computer language whose name is not an acronym. It is a recently (1970) designed language named after the seventeenth-century French mathematician Blaise Pascal, inventor of one of the earliest mechanical calculating machines. It is a development of an earlier language, ALGOL (ALGOrithmic Language) whose name implies that it is based on a more organised and mathematically orientated approach to programming than other languages. In fact, the mathematical aspect refers to the ideas relating to the proofs of theorems rather than the mathematics of computation. The whole concept of the language is the *structural* approach to the solution to a problem. Such an approach not only makes the writing of the program easier but also improves its clarity for an outsider who may have to take over the development of the program from the original author.

Programs written in Pascal, or any other structured language, are notable for their lack of GOTO statements which tend to obscure the understanding of programs written in more loosely organised languages. Writing a computer program should always be approached in a 'top-down' manner (meaning that the development of the program should go from the general — top — to the particular — down). This technique was shown in detail in the development of a program in Chapter 8. In this example the solution of the problem started with a generalised flowchart which was then refined further and further until a detailed flowchart and finally a complete program emerged. Structured languages take away the need for detailed flowcharts.

A structured language such as Pascal generally contains six types of instructions and these are

(1) FOR loops, as in BASIC and FORTRAN
(2) REPEAT/UNTIL loops
(3) WHILE loops
(4) decision instructions of the IF/THEN/ELSE type
(5) multiple decisions
(6) PROCEDURES, subprograms.

A set of instructions such as these should be quite adequate to cover a wide range of applications since they can be combined, essentially, in three possible ways

(1) Sequential instructions as in a series of arithmetical operations.
(2) Subordinate operations — selected loops of instructions embedded within other operations.
(3) Procedures that are freestanding in the sense that they can be written separately. Hence, this approach is ideal for creating programs in a modular manner. This is rather like the use of FORTRAN subroutines. The concept of a procedure is also found in COBOL.

A very easy-to-follow example of how this works and how widely applicable the concept of structuring is to a non-computing activity is shown in Fig. 10.8. It is easy to follow and makes sense. Just try and do the same thing in BASIC or COBOL and see how long it is before you get stuck! Notice that there is not a GOTO in sight.

Fig **10.8**

A football manager's approach to problem analysis and the stored program concept

A programmer's job is something like a football manager's. The manager must inculcate certain concepts into his players so that when a game starts they play good football without further interference from him.

His job is to analyse the problem (football) and formulate a set of rules for play, after which he must 'program' his players with these rules by training and coaching sessions.

The following 'program' is based on a somewhat simplified analysis of the game. It is in some ways more specific than a coach would be but its purpose is to illustrate good problem analysis using fundamental concepts.

```
REMARK Football manager's instructions to his players
FOR half = one TO two
    REPEAT
        WHILE the ball is in play
            IF opponents have ball THEN
                play in defensive positions
            ELSE
                REPEAT
                    pass safely to team-mate
                UNTIL good attacking opportunity occurs
                EXECUTE attack
            ENDIF
        ENDWHILE
    UNTIL half time or final whistle
    leave the field and go to dressing room
NEXT half
STOP
PROCEDURE attack
    REPEAT
        IF you have the ball THEN
            keep moving forward or pass
        ELSE
            run into space to receive a pass
        ENDIF
    UNTIL ball is in penalty area AND shot is possible
    shoot
ENDPROC
END
```

Note All structures must be opened and closed.

Opening keyword	Closing keyword
FOR	NEXT
REPEAT	UNTIL
WHILE	ENDWHILE
IF	ENDIF
PROCEDURE	ENDPROC

What happens between the opening and closing keywords is the content of that structure. Structures may be properly 'nested' or they may follow in sequence.

Now look at the BASIC program in Fig. 10.9. It is used to search for a specific element in a list using the *binary search* technique, which works as follows. The list must be in ascending order to start with and is initially divided into two equal parts, an upper and a lower half. The number being searched for is tested against the number in the middle of the list. The

Fig 10.9

```
10 DIM A(100)
20 GOSUB 190
30 INPUT U
40 L=1
50 U=I-1
60 F=U
70 IF L<=U AND A(F)<>U THEN 0090
80 GOTO 150
90 IF A(F)>>U THEN 120
100 L=F+1
110 GOTO 130
120 U=F-1
130 F=INT((U+L)/2)
140 GOTO 70
150 IF A(F)<>U THEN PRINT "NOT FOUND"
160 IF A(F)<>U THEN STOP
170 PRINT A(F),"FOUND"
180 STOP
190 FOR I=1 TO 100
200 READ A(I)
210 IF A(I)=999 THEN RETURN
220 NEXT I
230 DATA 3,8,12,13,40,56,67,87,88,89,90,92,94,100,101
240 DATA 123,134,145,167,176,188,199,200
250 DATA 999
```

result of the test will show if the number is in the upper or the lower half of the list. Once this has been established the relevant half is again sub-divided, tested and then halved again and so on until the position of the number in the list is finally discovered. The technique would be of use, for example, if a telephone number was being searched for in a list which held all the numbers and the subscribers with those numbers in ascending order of numbers. A linear search through a list of any size will always take an unreasonable time to complete since every search would have to start at the beginning of the list and continue entry by entry until the required number was found. A binary search reduces the search time by a very large amount. Such a description in words is fairly easy to follow and a language which allows us to put those words directly into the keywords of a computer language has many obvious advantages. The program in Fig. 10.10 is in Pascal and is far easier to follow than the meandering of the equivalent BASIC program. No wonder Pascal programmers talk of 'spaghetti' programming.

As with COBOL we make declarations about the type of data we are going to use in the Pascal program. We can state what names we are going to use for what variables and how the data is to be structured. The constants in a Pascal program can be declared at the start.

A programmer can make *type* declarations and write, for example

MONTH = (JAN, FEB, MAR, APRIL, MAY, JUNE, JULY, AUG, SEPT, OCT, NOV, DEC)

Fig 10.10

```
type LISTA = array(LBND..UBND) of integer;
procedure BSEARCH(LBND:integer;UBND:integer;VAL:integer;
                  var FOUND:integer);
var LOW:integer;
    HIGH:integer;
begin
  LOW:=LBND;
  HIGH:=UBND;
  FOUND:=UBND;
  while LOW <= HIGH and LISTA(FOUND)<> VAL do
  begin
    if LISTA(FOUND)>VAL then HIGH:=FOUND-1 else LOW:=FOUND + 1;
    FOUND:=(HIGH+LOW) div 2
  end;
  if LISTA(FOUND)<>VAL then FOUND:=LBND - 1
end;
```

meaning that the variable called MONTH can take any one of the values listed. In addition one can say

SUMMER-MONTH = (JUNE .. AUG)

meaning that SUMMER-MONTH is a subset of MONTH and can take the values JUNE, JULY or AUG.

A list of variables, *var*, and constants, *const* is made at the start of the program. Standard types are *integer, real* and *array* but new types of variables can be defined by the *type* statement.

By allowing the programmer to list variables and constants and specifying special data types the programmer is able to get the program organised, in a similar manner to COBOL, before the actual computing starts.

Fig. 10.11 shows our electricity bill again. Notice how the program proper is bracketed by the keywords *begin* and *end*. This section is a Pascal procedure and all procedures are delimited by these two important words.

Fig 10.11

```
program ELECTRICITYBILL (input,print);

const BASERATE = 7;
      LOWRATE = 5;
      BASEUNITS = 150;
      MINCHARGE = 364;
      STANDINGCHARGE = 325;
      VATRATE = 15;

var UNITS : integer;
    CHARGE : real;
begin
  read (UNITS);
  write (print, UNITS, ' UNITS £');
  if UNITS <= BASEUNITS then CHARGE := UNITS * BASERATE else
  CHARGE := BASEUNITS + BASERATE + (UNITS - BASEUNITS) * LOWRATE;
  if CHARGE < MINCHARGE then CHARGE := MINCHARGE;
  CHARGE := (CHARGE + STANDINGCHARGE) * (VATRATE + 100) / 100;
  writeln (print, CHARGE)
end.
```

Fig 10.12

```
Program MERGE (print, file(1..3));

(* Reads and lists files 1 and 2. Merges files 1 and 2 in
   numerical order.  If the same number appears in both files,
   then the data from file 2 is used. The merged file is
   written to file 3, which is then listed. *)

type STRING = packed array (1..24) of char;
var  NUMBER : array (1..2) of integer;
     NAME   : array (1..2) of STRING;


Procedure PRINTFILE (FILENUM : integer);

(* Lists File (FILENUM) *)

begin
  writeln (print, 'CONTENTS OF FILE NO', FILENUM);
  writeln;
  read (file(FILENUM), NUMBER (FILENUM), NAME (FILENUM));
  while not eof (file (FILENUM)) do
  begin
    writeln (print, NUMBER (FILENUM), NAME (FILENUM));
    read (file (FILENUM), NUMBER (FILENUM), NAME (FILENUM))
  end
end; (*PRINTFILE*)


Procedure OUTIN (FILENUM : integer; OUTENABLE : boolean);

(* If OUTENABLE = true, writes the record last read from
   File(FILENUM) to File (3) and reads the next record
   from File (FILENUM).
   If OUTENABLE = false, reads new data from File (FILENUM).
   If End of File encountered during read, assigns the
   maximum positive integer to NUMBER (FILENUM). *)

begin
  if OUTENABLE then
      writeln (file(3), NUMBER (FILENUM), NAME (FILENUM));
  read (file(FILENUM),  NUMBER (FILENUM), NAME (FILENUM));
  if eof (FILENUM) then NUMBER (FILENUM) := maxint
end; (* OUTIN *)

begin (* Main Program *)
  open (1, read, 'INPUT');
  PRINTFILE (1);
  reset (1);
  open (2, read, 'BROUGHTFWD');
  PRINTFILE (2);
  reset (2);
  open(3, write, 'CARRYFWD');
  OUTIN (1,false);
  OUTIN (2,false);
  while (NUMBER (1) < maxint) or (NUMBER (2) < maxint) do
  begin
    if NUMBER (1) < NUMBER (2) then OUTIN (1,true) else
    if NUMBER (1) > NUMBER (2) then OUTIN (2,true) else
    begin
      OUTIN (2, true);
      OUTIN (1, false);
    end
  end;
  reset (3);
  PRINTFILE (3)
end.
```

The final example, in Fig. 10.12, is a file merger program similar to that shown in Fig. 5.19. Notice that the version in Pascal contains two procedures which are placed outside the main procedure of the program for calling in whenever the need arises — a mixture of the best features of subroutines in BASIC and FORTRAN.

These programs are only intended to give the flavour of Pascal and the other languages mentioned in this chapter. Any detailed study should be made with the help of an appropriate programming manual or textbook devoted to an in-depth study of the language. There is, of course, no substitute for actually writing and running programs. No one can hope to learn programming simply from a book. Access to a suitable computer is essential for the programmer to gain skill and experience. In the early days of programming in a new language the only test one can apply to oneself is that of whether the program works or not. When the skill and experience have been gained then one's programming will become better and better. Practice, and plenty of it, is essential.

CHAPTER 11

COMPILERS

AND

INTERPRETERS

11.1 INTERPRETERS

We shall deal with interpreters first of all since they are the most likely to be used by a newcomer to programming. If one writes a program in BASIC the program is typed in line by line at a keyboard. Depending on the type of computer being used one of two things happen. One possibility is that your program is constantly being submitted to a program called BASIC which scans it line by line as each one is entered. If an error is discovered in a line then BASIC rejects it and attempts to tell you why—SYNTAX ERROR covers a multitude of sins! The program can be entered in any order, even backwards if one wants to, and BASIC sorts it out into an order dictated by the line numbers. On the command RUN, BASIC will convert all the acceptable lines into machine code. A typical example of this happening is shown in Fig. 11.1.

An alternative to this taking place is common to most microcomputer BASICs. In this instance we enter our program line by line as before but even if there are errors in any lines these are not picked up until the RUN command is issued. This means that the scanning of the program and its conversion into machine code does not take place until *run time*. The speed of execution of BASIC programs is therefore very slow because much of the computer's time is taken up with the *interpretation* of the program into the final runnable machine code. Fig. 11.2 shows the entering and running of a BASIC program in a microcomputer.

Interpreted languages have the advantage that errors can rapidly be detected, put right and the program tested and run repeatedly under the control of the programmer sitting at his keyboard.

Fig 11.1

```
   10 IMPUT X
ERROR 2 - Syntax
* 10 INPUT X
* 20 LET Y=X=4
ERROR 2 - Syntax
* 20 LET Y=4
* 30 LET Z=3(X*Y)-5
ERROR 2 - Syntax
* 30 LET Z=3*(X*Y-5
ERROR 11 - Parentheses
* 30 LET Z=3*(X*Y-5)
* 40 OUTPUT Z
ERROR 2 - Syntax
* 40 PRINT Z
* LIST
0010 INPUT X
0020 LET Y=4
0030 LET Z=3*(X*Y-5)
0040 PRINT Z
* RUN
 ? 6,7
ERROR 46 AT 0010 - Input
* RUN
 ? 6,7
 65.4

END AT 0040
*
```

Fig 11.2

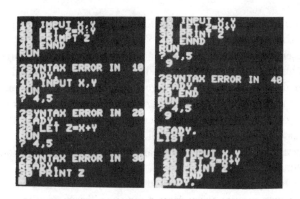

```
1Ø IMPUT X,Y
2Ø LET Z = X:Y
3Ø PRIMPT Z
4O END
```

11.2 COMPILERS

The use of a compiler to produce the final object code which is run is a rather more complex process than the use of an interpreter. For one thing, the production of the object code takes far longer than it does when an interpreter is used. The editing of a source program in FORTRAN or COBOL is more time consuming, but the final program in machine code runs several hundred times faster than the same program written in an interpretive language. When the speedy running of programs is of commercial importance (time is money) there is a very big advantage in having programs which don't spend their time being translated but spend all their time in useful computation. A programmer who has full control over his programs at all times can sometimes write sloppy programs because this tends to encourage bad, or little, planning of programs before they are actually written. When using a compiler the time which elapses between a program being entered and run can be quite considerable, several hours in some cases. It is therefore well worth planning one's work well in advance.

The reason for the time delay is that although the entering of the program is fully under the control of the programmer, its compilation and running are often under the control of the computer operator. It may well be that compilation of programs may only be undertaken at certain times of the day when a sufficiently large *batch* of programs is ready—hence a possible slow turnround of programs. The process usually falls into four main parts

(1) Entering the program in its source code, under the control of the programmer.

(2) Presentation of the source code to the compiler appropriate for the language of the source code. This detects any non-legal statements and detects other types of errors such as GOTO statements with no destinations and labels which are not referenced by other statements. The output from this is an assembler program, just as ACE produces an assembler program first of all.

(3) The assembler program is then assembled into a machine code, usually in binary.

(4) The binary code is then linked with any subroutines which the program may require either from a run-time library or other sources. The run-time library provides file input/output routines and standard facilities such as square roots and so on. Programmer-written subroutines are linked in at this stage and the final object code is stored on disc. It is this code which forms the runnable program. Because there is no interpretation taking place at run time the execution of the

program will be as fast as possible, possibly at the rate of 10 million machine instructions per second.

Stages 2, 3 and 4 are under the control of the operator, who on their completion will hand the results and any error messages back to the programmer for any modification he may need to make. How these modifications are done will be dealt with later on in this chapter.

Fig. 11.3 shows a FORTRAN program containing some errors and below it, the error messages generated by the compiler. Error 60 is an error claiming that there is a syntax error due to the line

K = SQRT(I)

being one space too far over to the left. Error 31 is an error because the compiler thinks that there are two statements labelled 10. Fig. 11.4 is an amended version of the program which still contains errors which were concealed by the previous errors. Error 72 says that there is a clash of data types—square root in integers. Error 35 detects an unclosed DO loop, there being no label 40. Error 61 tells us that there is an undefined label, label 40 again. Error 76 tells us that there is an unreferenced label, label 10. Finally Fig. 11.5 shows the same program with all the errors corrected.

Fig 11.3

```
C THIS IS A DEMONSTRATION PROGRAM CONTAINING ERRORS
  10  DO 40 I=1,25,1
      K=SQRT(I)
      WRITE(12,100),I,K
  100 FORMAT(1H ,I4,3X,F10.4)
      END


; C THIS IS A DEMONSTRATION PROGRAM CONTAINING ERRORS
;   10  DO 40 I=1,25,0.5
;       K=SQRT(I)
;       K=SQRT(I)
; *** 060 *** CHR 07
;       WRITE(12,100),I,K
;   100 FORMAT(1H ,I4,3X,F10.4)
)   100 FORMAT(1H ,I4,3X,F10.4)
; *** 031 *** CHR 06
;     END
```

To see how the progress from source code to object code and final run is made, look at Fig. 11.6. These would be the instructions issued by the operator at the keyboard of the console of the computer. Each set of instructions represents a different stage in the production of the final object code. The instruction FORT calls on the FORTRAN compiler

202

Fig 11.4

```
.C THIS IS A DEMONSTRATION PROGRAM CONTAINING ERRORS
 10 DO 40 I=1,25,1
    K=SQRT(I)
    WRITE(12,100),I,K
100 FORMAT(1H ,I4,3X,F10.4)
    END
```

```
;  C THIS IS A DEMONSTRATION PROGRAM CONTAINING ERRORS
;  10  DO 40 I=1,25,1
;      K=SQRT(I)
;      K=SQRT(I)
;  *** 072 *** CHR 15
;      WRITE(12,100),I,K
;  100 FORMAT(1H ,I4,3X,F10.4)
;      END
;      END
;  *** 035 *** CHR 11
;  40
;  *** 061 *** CHR 11
;  40
;  *** 076 *** CHR 11
;  10
```

Fig 11.5

```
;  C SAME PROGRAM WITH ERRORS REMOVED
-;     AI=1.
;      DO 40 I=1,50,1
;      AK=SQRT(AI)
;      WRITE(12,100),AI,AK
;  100 FORMAT(1H ,F10.5,4X,F10.5)
;      AI=AI+0.5
;   40 CONTINUE
;      END
```

Fig 11.6

```
FORT FIG95 $LPT/L
R
ASM FIG95
PROGRAM IS RELOCATABLE
                        .TITL  .MAIN
R
RLDR FIG95 FORT.LB LMAP/L
R
FIG95
STOP
R
```

to scan the source file and produce an assembler code if possible. The program called ASM takes the output from the previous operations and assembles it into binary code. The message

PROGRAM IS RELOCATABLE

is printed if this is successful. Finally the binary codes contained in the output from ASM and the run-time library are linked together by a program called RLDR. The program is finally executed by typing its name, which is incidentally the original name of the source file. The output from the program is shown in Fig. 11.7.

Fig 11.7

1.00000	1.00000
1.50000	1.22474
2.00000	1.41421
2.50000	1.58114
3.00000	1.73205
3.50000	1.87083
4.00000	2.00000
4.50000	2.12132
5.00000	2.23607
5.50000	2.34521
6.00000	2.44949
6.50000	2.54951
7.00000	2.64575
7.50000	2.73861
8.00000	2.82843
8.50000	2.91548
9.00000	3.00000
9.50000	3.08221
10.00000	3.16228
10.50000	3.24037
11.00000	3.31662
11.50000	3.39116
12.00000	3.46410
12.50000	3.53553
13.00000	3.60555
13.50000	3.67423
14.00000	3.74166
14.50000	3.80789
15.00000	3.87298
15.50000	3.93700
16.00000	4.00000
16.50000	4.06202
17.00000	4.12311
17.50000	4.18330
18.00000	4.24264
18.50000	4.30116
19.00000	4.35890
19.50000	4.41588
20.00000	4.47214
20.50000	4.52769
21.00000	4.58258
21.50000	4.63681
22.00000	4.69042
22.50000	4.74342
23.00000	4.79583
23.50000	4.84768
24.00000	4.89898
24.50000	4.94975
25.00000	5.00000
25.50000	5.04975

Fig. 11.8 shows the compilation and running of the program called GRAPHPLOT whose listing was originally shown in Fig. 10.4. Notice how the main program and the subroutine called CLEAR have to be compiled separately and then finally linked and loaded together with the FORTRAN run-time library.

Fig 11.8

```
FORT GRAPHPLOT $LPT/L
R
ASM GRAPHPLOT
R
PROGRAM IS RELOCATABLE
                                  .TITL  .MAIN

R
FORT CLEAR $LPT/L
R
ASM CLEAR
PROGRAM IS RELOCATABLE
                                  .TITL  .CLEAR

R
RLDR GRAPHPLOT CLEAR FORT.LB LMAP/L
R
GRAPHPLOT
AMPLITUDE - NOT GREATER THAN 1 .7
FREQUENCY - NOT GREATER THAN 10 4
PHASE ANGLE - DEGREES 35
AMPLITUDE - NOT GREATER THAN 1 .4
FREQUENCY - NOT GREATER THAN 10 8
PHASE ANGLE - DEGREES 60
STOP

R
GRAPHPLOT
AMPLITUDE - NOT GREATER THAN 1 1
FREQUENCY - NOT GREATER THAN 10 5
PHASE ANGLE - DEGREES 0
AMPLITUDE - NOT GREATER THAN 1 .5
FREQUENCY - NOT GREATER THAN 10 5
PHASE ANGLE - DEGREES 0
STOP

R
```

The progress of a COBOL program from compilation to execution is shown in Fig. 11.9. Although all these examples have been run using one particular minicomputer system, the phases through which the original program has to pass before execution are much the same for all systems.

The fundamental difference, therefore, between a compiler and an interpreter is that a compiler works in the same way that a translator works to convert a piece of text from one language to another. The translator has the whole of the text in front of him and can check backwards and forwards to ensure that the translation makes sense. An interpreter does exactly the same job as a language interpreter who translates one sentence at a time as he hears it from the speaker. The interpreter does not bother about the relevance of each translated phrase to what has gone before, and he certainly does not know what is coming next. This is just how the BASIC

Fig 11.9

```
COBOL DEMO1 $LPT/L
R
ASM DEMO1
R
PROGRAM IS RELOCATABLE
                        .TITL  .MAIN
R
RLDR DEMO1 COBLIB LMAP/L
R
```

interpreter works: it relies on the author of the program to have the overall picture clear before entering it at the keyboard. Preparation is therefore essential and it is generally considered to be bad practice to sit down and just write programs without any prior thought or planning.

11.3 EDITORS

We have seen how easy it is to amend BASIC programs: line numbers are the clue. To change a single line merely consists of retyping it with a different instruction in it. But what of compiled programs where there are no line numbers? How are FORTRAN or COBOL programs scoured of their errors? The answer is quite simple: we use an *editor*.

An editor is a program which allows us to change a file of text by the execution of a few simple commands. An editor allows us to search through a file of text for characters we wish to change and then inserts replacement characters as required. If we have a FORTRAN program stored on disc under the name of FIG910 our editor program can edit it in the following way. If, for example, we wish to change the number 0.1 to 0.01, the first thing to do is to find the characters 0.1. This is done by asking the editor to search for them by typing

SO.1

(S stands for Search.) When the required line is found we issue the instruction to change 0.1 to 0.01 by the code

C/0.1/0.01/

(C stands for Change.) The slashes, /, are called *delimiters* and show when the two sets of characters, the new and the old, start and finish. The @ symbol terminates the editor and the TYPE command causes the current version of the file to be typed out at the terminal. Fig. 11.10 shows the editing sequence taking place. The revised file must then be presented to the compiler, compiled, assembled and loaded ready to be run.

Most computer manufacturers provide text editors and although they may differ in detail they all follow the same pattern as in the previous example. In general, facilities offered by an editor will be

(1) Search for a specified set of characters.
(2) Change one set of characters for another.
(3) Delete a line or a specified number of characters.
(4) Insert a specified set of characters at a given point in a text file.
(5) Define and execute a *macro*. This is an instruction which says 'search through the file of text and every time you find character set A replace it by character set B'. For example you may need to change every occurrence of X1 into XONE.
(6) Display the contents of the file being edited.

Fig 11.10

```
Command ? TYPE FIG910

COMMENT DEMONSTRATION PROGRAM 1
        X=1.0
        DO 40 I=1,100,1
        X=X+0.1
        Y=X**2
  40    TYPE Y
        END

Command ? EDIT FIG910

COMMENT DEMONSTRATION PROGRAM 1
E: S0.1
        X=X+0.1
E: C/0.1/0.01/
        X=X+0.01
E: @

Edit ends

Command ? TYPE FIG910

COMMENT DEMONSTRATION PROGRAM 1
        X=1.0
        DO 40 I=1,100,1
        X=X+0.01
        Y=X**2
  40    TYPE Y
        END

Command ? END
```

Fig. 11.11 shows a typical editing session with a similar, but more comprehensive, editor than the one shown in the previous example. It contains a macro command, XMCX$A$$, which says that every time you meet the character X it is to be changed into the character A. The 4X$$ command tells the editor to execute the macro four times, since there are four changes to be made. A compilation and run of this program is shown in Fig. 11.12.

Very sophisticated editors form the basis of *word processors* which are either *packages* run on a computer, which also runs programs in any of the

Fig 1.11

Fig 11.12

```
EDIT FIG910

*T$$
COMMENT DEMONSTRATION PROGRAM 1
        X=1.0
        DO 40 I=1,100,1
        X=X+0.01
        Y=X**2
40      TYPE Y
        END

*B$$
*S.01$$
*LIT$$      X=X+0.01

*L$$
*C.01$.1$$
*LIT$$      X=X+0.1

*B$$
*XMCX$A$$
*4X$$
*B$$
*T$$
COMMENT DEMONSTRATION PROGRAM 1
        A=1.0
        DO 40 I=1,100,1
        A=A+0.1
        Y=A**2
40      TYPE Y
        END
*E$UE$H$$
R
```

```
FORT FIG910 $TTO/L
R
ASM FORT910

PROGRAM IS RELOCATABLE    .TITL   .MAIN

R
RLDR FIG910 FORT.LB LMAP/L
R

FIG910
        0.121000E  1
        0.144000E  1
        0.169000E  1
        0.196000E  1
        0.225000E  1
        0.256000E  1
        0.289000E  1

        0.102010E  3
        0.104040E  3
        0.106090E  3
        0.108160E  3
        0.110250E  3
        0.112360E  3
        0.114490E  3
        0.116640E  3
        0.118810E  3
        0.121000E  3
STOP

R
```

usual languages, or dedicated specialised computer systems, which exist solely for the production and editing of text. Such systems are gaining more and more use in, for example, solicitors' offices for the production of wills, leases and formal letters.

WHY NOT STRUCTURE YOUR PROGRAMS?

12.1 A NEW LOOK AT PROGRAM DESIGN

During one's early days of program writing there is often great difficulty experienced in seeing the dividing line between the 'program', which is the logical construction of the operations which lead to the solution of a problem, and the 'coding' of that program into a particular computing language. In the early part of this book we approached the devising of the logical approach by means of the traditional flowchart. Then this flowchart was converted into the coded program. However, it is not uncommon to find people who draw a flowchart with BASIC statements in the boxes—so we get boxes containing DIM and REM statements. Flowcharts are really about ideas and logic and should not be restricted by particular computing languages. In addition there is a further problem caused by the fact that a flowchart is two-dimensional, and a program, because it is a *list* of instructions, is only one-dimensional. Hence the conversion operation is made quite complex and leads very often to too many GOTO instructions. Ideally, only about 5 per cent of the total effort should have to be put into the coding; the vast majority of the thought should be devoted to the logical steps which allow the problem in hand to be solved.

There is an alternative to the flowchart approach and it consists of laying out one's 'program' in the way that Figure 10.8 is laid out, even if one is not very familiar with English soccer. The sequence of events described in that figure is very easy to follow. Just consider how easy it would be to give the instructions in that form over a telephone, compared with the difficulty of doing the same thing with a flowchart. Think about that, and you will begin to appreciate some of the problems we can get with flowcharts. A program outlined in the manner of Figure 10.8 is often described as being written in 'pseudo-code'. One particular advantage of constructing a program in this way is that the use of the GOTO instruction, that generator of spaghetti code, is eliminated. The use of

REPEAT, WHILE and more sophisticated IF statements enable the coding of a program from such a design to be much quicker and less error-prone than was previously possible. This form of programming is known as 'structured' programming, and since this book was first published a number of improved versions of BASIC have appeared which take advantage of this new approach. The Pascal language provides highly structured code and is becoming more readily available for the evergrowing microcomputer population.

12.2 THE ELECTRICITY BILL AGAIN

An example of the structured approach to a problem is shown next; it is our electricity bill once more, but stated in much clearer and more readable terms. One of the satisfying things about writing a program in this structured way using pseudo-code is that so long as we use standardised looping and decision statements we can invent our own version of the common statements such as the assignment, input and output statements. Notice that, for example, in the following programs we use the word 'Set' followed by the := symbol. This is intended to convey the assignment operation in an unambiguous manner. Then we can have no confusion about the two uses of the = symbol used in many computer languages; i.e. for assignment and for equality.

```
1. Read units
2. If units<150
3.    Then
4.       Set Cost:=units*.07
5.    Else
6.       Set Cost:=10.5+(units-150)*.05
7. Ifend
8. If Cost<3.64
9.    Then
10.      Set Cost:=3.64
11.   Else
12.      Skip
13. Ifend
14. Set Cost:=(Cost+3.25)*1.15
15. Print Cost
16. End
```

```
          In BASIC we can write
```

```
10 INPUT UNITS
20 IF UNITS<150 THEN COST=UNITS*.07 ELSE COST=10.5+(UNITS-150)*.05
30 IF COST<3.64 THEN COST=3.64
40 COST=(COST+3.25)*1.15
50 PRINT COST
```

12.3 IMPROVING BASIC

Now, one version of BASIC has been devised to take a real step forward in the use of the IF . . . THEN . . . ELSE construction and it enables us to write the program coded as shown in Figure 12.1. Notice how easy it

Fig 12.1

```
0010 DIM C$(20),S$(20)
0020 INPUT "CURRENCY:";C$
0030 PRINT"HOW MANY ";C$;" ";
0040 INPUT"TO THE POUND";P
0050 INPUT"CONVERT 'TO' OR 'FROM' STERLING ";S$
0060 IF S$="TO" THEN
0070     PRINT "HOW MANY ";C$;" ";
0080     INPUT N
0090     S=N/P
0100     PRINT N;C$;"=";S;"POUNDS"
0110 ELSE
0120     INPUT "HOW MANY POUNDS";N
0130     S=N*P
0140     PRINT N;"POUNDS = ";S;C$
0150 EIF
0160 END
```

becomes to read the program and discover how it works. This construction
is also available in the latest version of FORTRAN known as FORTRAN
77. The program performs currency conversion and is, in fact, an improved
version of the program which is listed in Figure 3.4.

The structured approach to programming helps to rid us of the 'spaghetti' type of programming which has already been illustrated and it was
shown that a language such as Pascal helps us to write programs which are
easier to understand, and hence to amend should the necessity arise. Now
there are various additions to the BASIC language which give us some
Pascal-type features. These are the enhancement of various versions of
the language by the addition of REPEAT ... UNTIL or WHILE ...
statements, or both. Here are some examples of programs written in the
newer forms of BASIC using these features. To start with here is an
amended version of the program shown in Figure 3.3. It is first shown in
Figure 12.2 with a WHILE loop, a feature offered with Microsoft (R)
BASIC. (Microsoft is the registered trademark of Digital Research.) The
same program written using REPEAT is shown in Figure 12.3. This feature

Fig 12.2

```
10 REM*** BETTER VERSION OF FIG. 3.3 USING WHILE***
20 S=0
30 C=0
40 X=1
50 WHILE X <> 0
60    INPUT X
70    S=S+X
80    C=C+1
90 WEND
100 C=C-1
110 A=S/C
120 PRINT A
```

Fig 12.3

```
20 S=0
30 C=0
40 INPUT X
50 REPEAT
60    S=S+X
70    C=C+1
80    INPUT X
90    UNTIL X=0
100 A=S/C
110 PRINT A
```

is offered on the popular BBC microcomputer. You should be aware by now that the *program* is the same in every one of the examples, Figure 3.3, Figure 12.2 and Figure 12.3, but the *coding* of the program is different in every case.

Notice that in Figure 12.2 the loop starts at line 50 and if X has a value not equal to zero the loop will be entered and executed. If X at that point had a value of zero then the loop would not even be entered. That is why we give X a value of 1 at line 40 and then immediately into the loop input another value. The object of this is to force the program into the loop in the first place. The WEND in line 90 signifies the end of the loop which will only be repeated if the value of X in line 60 is not zero. If a value of X of zero had been input at line 60 then the loop will not be executed again and the instructions on lines 100 to 120 will be the next ones carried out. This is why we have to reduce C by one after the last execution of the loop—the addition of zero to S in line 70 has no effect. In the second version—Figure 12.3—of the program we do not have to 'seed' the loop with a spurious value of X since all REPEAT loops are executed at least once—WHILE loops do not have to be traversed at all if the test value of the control variable is the one which stops the loop. In the second example the loop is repeated 'until' the value of X input at line 80 is zero, at which point the program goes on to line 100 where the average is calculated.

The next example is another coding of the program listed in Figure 3.6. First of all using a WHILE is shown in Figure 12.4. and in REPEAT . . . UNTIL . . . format in Figure 12.5.

Fig 12.4

```
10 REM***VERSION OF FIG. 3.6 USING WHILE***
20 INPUT A
30 X=1
40 D=1
50 WHILE D>.0005
60    X1=(X+A/X)/2
70    D=ABS(X-X1)
80    X=X1
90 WEND
100 PRINT X
```

Fig 12.5

```
10 INPUT A
20 X=1
30 REPEAT
40    X1=(X+X/A)/2
50    D=ABS(X-X1)
60    X=X1
70 UNTIL D<.0005
80 PRINT X
```

The third example of these very useful loops is of programs written to do the same as the program listed in Figure 4.2 where we find the smallest number in a list. The first is listed in Figure 12.6 and the second is shown in Figure 12.7.

Fig 12.6

```
10 REM***IMPROVED VERSION OF FIG. 4.2 USING WHILE***
20 DIM L(50)
30 I=0
40 WHILE L(I)>=0
50    I=I+1
60    INPUT L(I)
70 WEND
80 N=I-1
90 I=1
100 S=L(1)
110 WHILE I<=N
120    IF S>L(I) THEN S=L(I)
130    I=I+1
140 WEND
150 PRINT "THE SMALLEST NUMBER IN THE LIST IS ";S
```

Fig 12.7

```
20 DIM L(50)
30 I=0
40 REPEAT
50    I=I+1
60    INPUT L(I)
70    UNTIL L(I)<0
80 N=I-1
90 I=1
100 S=L(1)
110 REPEAT
120    IF S>L(I) THEN S=L(I)
130    I=I+1
140    UNTIL I>N
150 PRINT S
```

These additional looping instructions are really condensed and easier-to-understand versions of existing constructions which have to be made using IF . . . THENs and GOTOs. Their use makes the programming easier for other people to understand since the coding of a program is not always the final word on any problem. Very often our programs are taken over and modified by other people long after we have forgotten them, and been forgotten ourselves, and so it is a much easier task if those coming after us are left with a cleanly written and logically simple program to amend.

12.4 MERGING TWO LISTS AGAIN

Our problem which involved the reading in of two sorted lists and then merging them into one single list can be dealt with by using the 'top down' approach which leads to a structured program. This approach consists of first of all writing down our general thoughts on the matter by saying that the program is going to consist of several parts. The first of these is to read the two lists into memory. Then we have to merge the two lists in such a way that we compare pairs of numbers from each list and allocate the appropriate one to the new list. Finally we print out the two original lists and the new merged list. At this point we at least know what our objectives are and so we could write them down in the following way

(1) Read the two lists into memory.
(2) Loop while there are numbers left in each list.
(3) Allocate the next number in turn from each list according to their size into the new list.
(4) Print out original lists and the new merged list.

These steps have now to be expanded to give us more detail, since we should now have realised that we have continually to compare pairs of numbers, one from each list, and place the smaller of the two in the new list. Then we have to pick up the next number from the list which provided the smaller number and perform another comparison. This we continue until we have used up all the numbers from one list. Then we write the remaining numbers from the other list onto the new, merged, list. To start the program off we have to compare the pair of numbers taken from the head of each list. Then we have to pick up the next number from the list which provided the one just written out to the new list. Here is an IF . . . THEN . . . ELSE type of situation. There is also a hint of two subroutines; one to collect the next item from one of the two lists and the other to write a number into the new list, which is what we did with the versions of the problem in Figure 6.9, Figure 10.3 and Figure 10.12.

If we call the two original lists "A" and "B" and the new merged list "C" then we can write our program in more detail

```
1. Read the lists "A" and "B" into memory.
2. Set the first number in list "A" to the variable P.
3. Set the first number in list "B" to the variable Q.
4. Loop
5.    If P<Q
6.       Then
7.          Place P into list "C"
8.          Get next number from list "A"
9.          Set this number to the variable P
10.      Else
11.         Place Q into list "C"
12.         Get next number from list "B"
13.         Set this number to variable Q
14.   Ifend
15.Repeat until one of the lists is exhausted
16.Place rest of remaining list onto list "C"
17.Print list "A"
18.Print list "B"
19.Print list "C"
```

Notice that we have written our program with no GOTO statements. The loop has been defined by the statements in lines 4 and 15 and all the instructions contained within these are executed as required by the decision in line 5. You will notice that this is becoming more like the Pascal version of the program as shown in Figure 10.12.

The program outline lends itself very well to the insertion of subroutines and we can now identify four of these. They are a subroutine to read a list into memory, another to print it out, one to get the next number from one of the lists and to allocate this to P or Q as appropriate, and finally a subroutine to add either P or Q to the list "C".

Let us look at these subroutines separately. First of all the LISTREAD routine

```
SUBROUTINE LISTREAD(NO,L)
1.Read NO
2.For counter=1 to NO
3.   Read item
4.   Set L(counter):=item
5.Repeat
RETURN TO MAIN PROGRAM
```

In the main program we will write

```
CALL LISTREAD(N1,A)
```

if we want to read a set of numbers into the list A. N1 will hold the number of numbers in the list.

Similarly a subroutine called LISTPRINT will print out the contents of a specified list

```
SUBROUTINE LISTPRINT(N,L)
1.For counter = 1 to N
2.   Print L(counter)
3.Repeat
RETURN TO MAIN PROGRAM
```

We have already seen the subroutines GETNEXT and ADD forming part of the previous versions of this program, so let us write them down in this structured way

```
SUBROUTINE GETNEXT(H,X,M,E,N)
1.Set E:=0
2.If M>N
3.   Then
4.      Set E:=1
5.   Else
6.      Set H:=X(M)
7.      Set M:=M+1
8.Ifend
RETURN TO MAIN PROGRAM
```

E is the variable which tells us whether we have reached the end of the list named X.

ADD looks like this

```
SUBROUTINE ADD(H,C,K)
1.Set C(K):=H
2.Set K:=K+1
RETURN TO MAIN PROGRAM
```

So now we can construct our complete program in the following way

```
1.CALL LISTREAD(N1,A)
2.CALL LISTREAD(N2,B)
3.Set P:=A(1)        **P set to 1st number in A**
4.Set Q:=B(1)        **Q set to 1st number in B**
5.Set L:=2           **L points to next number in A**
6.Set K:=1           **K points to next number in C**
7.Set J:=2           **J points to next number in B**
8.Loop
9.   If P<Q
10.     Then
```

```
11.        CALL ADD(P,C,K)
12.        CALL GETNEXT(P,A,L,E,N1)
13.    Else
14.        CALL ADD(Q,C,K)
15.        CALL GETNEXT(Q,B,J,E,N2)
16. Ifend
17.Repeat until E=1
18.Loop
19.    If P<Q              **This decides which list has
20.    Then                     been exhausted**
21.        CALL ADD(Q,C,K)
22.        CALL GETNEXT(Q,B,J,E,N2)
23.    Else
24.        CALL ADD(P,C,K)
25.        CALL GETNEXT(P,A,L,E,N1)
26.    Ifend
27.Repeat until E=1
28.CALL LISTPRINT(N1,A)
29.CALL LISTPRINT(N2,B)
30.Set N:=N1+N2
31.CALL LISTPRINT(N,C)
```

To illustrate this program in action we are going to code it in the version of BASIC available on the Open University Academic Computing Service. This is a structured version of the language which allows us to use called subroutines, REPEAT ... UNTIL and WHILE as well as the IF ... THEN ... ELSE construction mentioned earlier. The subroutines are defined at the end of the program and will be called READ, ADD, GET and PRINT. Notice how the lists are referred to in the subroutine calls and in the parameter lists for the subroutines themselves by having the name followed by an empty pair of brackets. The program is listed in Figure 12.8 and the listing is followed with a demonstration run of the program.

Fig 12.8

```
10 DIM A(100),B(100),C(100),X(100)
20 PRINT "FIRST LIST :-";
30 CALL READ(N1,A())
40 PRINT "SECOND LIST :-";
50 CALL READ(N2,B())
60 PRINT
70 P=A(1)
80 Q=B(1)
90 L=2
100 K=1
110 J=2
120 REPEAT
130    IF P<Q THEN
140        CALL ADD(P,C(),K)
150        CALL GET(P,A(),L,E,N1)
```

```
160    ELSE
170       CALL ADD(Q,C(),K)
180       CALL GET(Q,B(),J,E,N2)
190    EIF
200 UNTIL E=1
210 REPEAT
220    IF P<Q THEN
230       CALL ADD(Q,C(),K)
240       CALL GET(Q,B(),J,E,N2)
250    ELSE
260       CALL ADD(P,C(),K)
270       CALL GET(P,A(),L,E,N1)
280    EIF
290 UNTIL E=1
300 PRINT
310 PRINT "FIRST LIST"
320 PRINT "=========="
330 CALL PRINT(N1,A())
340 PRINT
350 PRINT
360 PRINT "SECOND LIST"
370 PRINT "==========="
380 CALL PRINT(N2,B())
390 PRINT
400 PRINT
410 N=N1+N2
420 PRINT "MERGED LIST"
430 PRINT "==========="
440 CALL PRINT(N,C())
450 END


460 SUB READ(NO,L())
470 PRINT "HOW MANY NUMBERS ";
480 INPUT NO
490 FOR C=1 TO NO
500    INPUT L(C)
510 NEXT C
520 END


530 SUB ADD(H,C(),K)
540 C(K)=H
550 K=K+1
560 END


570 SUB GET(H,X(),M,E,N)
580 E=0
590 IF M>N THEN
600    E=1
610    ELSE
620    H=X(M)
630    M=M+1
```

```
640 EIF
650 END

660 SUB PRINT(N,L())
670 FOR C=1 TO N
680    PRINT L(C);
690 NEXT C
700 END

RUN

FIRST LIST :- HOW MANY NUMBERS?12
?3
?5
?6
?8
?9
?14
?16
?18
?19
?20
?26
?28
SECOND LIST :- HOW MANY NUMBERS?10
?1
?2
?7
?11
?17
?30
?32
?45
?50
?55
```

```
FIRST LIST
==========
 3     5     6     8     9     14    16    18    19    20
26    28

SECOND LIST
===========
 1     2     7     11    17    30    32    45    50    55

MERGED LIST
===========
 1     2     3     5     6     7     8     9     11    14    16
17    18    19    20    26    28    30    32    45    50    55

DONE
```

12.5 SUMMARY

The new approaches to programming introduced in this chapter can be summarised fairly simply and can be used even if you do not happen to be able to use a version of a language, particularly BASIC, which has not had the new features incorporated. If you approach the programming of a problem, as opposed to the coding of the solution, and write it in this structured form you can write the code using a standard version of BASIC. If you do so you will have to use a few GOTOs, but in general they will be less in number than if you drew a conventional flowchart. First of all the IF . . . THEN . . . ELSE . . . construction. In outline it will look like this

```
IF (assertion) THEN
    statements to be executed if
    (assertion) is true.
ELSE
    statements to be executed if
    (assertion) is false.
IFEND
```

The WHILE . . . construction will appear as follows where WHILE and ENDWHILE, or WEND, bracket the loop

WHILE (assertion)

```
┌─────────────────────┐
│ Body of the         │
│ loop.               │
└─────────────────────┘
```

Note that the loop need never be executed.

ENDWHILE

In 'ordinary' BASIC a typical coding for a program to input a set of numbers, terminated by zero, then calculate and print their total and average, would be written as shown in Figure 12.9 with the same program written using WHILE is shown in Figure 12.10.

Fig 12.9

```
10 T=0
20 C=0
30 INPUT N
40 IF N=0 THEN GOTO 80
50 T=T+N
60 C=C+1
70 GOTO 30
80 A=T/C
90 PRINT T,A
100 END
```

Fig 12.10

```
10 T=0
20 C=0
30 INPUT N
40 WHILE N<>0
50    T=T+N
60    C=C+1
70    INPUT N
80 WEND
90 A=T/C
100 PRINT T,A
110 END
```

Exactly the same program but using coding which allows REPEAT and UNTIL is shown in Figure 12.11 and the layout of this type of construction is shown below

REPEAT

```
┌─────────────────────┐
│ Body of the         │
│ loop.               │
└─────────────────────┘
```

Note that the loop must always be executed at least once.

UNTIL (assertion)

Fig 12.11

```
10 T=0
20 C=0
30 INPUT N
40 REPEAT
50    T=T+N
60    C=C+1
70    INPUT N
80    UNTIL N=0
90 A=T/C
100 PRINT T,A
110 END
```

You should be now be in a position to attempt to rewrite some of your existing programs in this structured way and it is very likely that you will end up with programs which are less tortuous, shorter and more efficient than the earlier versions. What is more, you stand a better chance of writing programs which work first time and are easier to debug.

FURTHER READING

VIDEO INSTRUCTION COURSES

These are available from
  Guild Sound and Vision Ltd
  Woodston House
  Oundle Road
  Peterborough PE2 9PZ

BASIC: *An Introduction to Computer Programming*, devised by Miles Ellis, University of Sheffield—video tape and course manual with exercise sheets.

FORTRAN: *Structured FORTRAN Course using FORTRAN 77*, devised by Miles Ellis, University of Sheffield—video tape and set of handbooks.

COBOL: *The COBOL Language, ANSI Standard*, devised by the University of Manchester and the National Computing Centre—video tape and workbooks with student notes and a course project.

Pascal: Devised by Lawrence Atkinson, University of Sheffield—video tape and book, *A Guide to Programming in Pascal* (Wiley, Chichester, 1980).

BOOKS

Calderbank, V. J., *A Course in Programming in FORTRAN IV* (Chapman & Hall, New York, 1969)

Davis, W. S., and Fisher, R. H., *COBOL, an Introduction to Structured Logic and Modular Program Design* (Addison-Wesley, Reading, Mass., 1979)

Gosling, P. E., *Beginning BASIC* (Macmillan, London and Basingstoke, 1977)

Gosling, P. E., *Continuing BASIC* (Macmillan, London and Basingstoke, 1980)

Gosling, P. E., *Program Your Microcomputer in BASIC* (Macmillan, London and Basingstoke, 1981)

Gosling, P. E. *Structured Programming – a first course for students and hobbyists* (McGraw-Hill, 1983)

Hartley, P. J., *Introduction to BASIC: a case study approach* (Macmillan, London and Basingstoke, 1976)

Hutty, R., *FORTRAN for Students* (Macmillan, London and Basingstoke, 1980)

Interactive COBOL, Programmer's Reference (Data General Corporation Publication No. 045-011-03—this is one of the few manufacturers' manuals that is easy to follow)

Jackson, B., *Approaches to Programming* (Blackie, Glasgow, 1981).

Kernighan, B. W., and Plauger, P. J., *Elements of Programming Style* (McGraw-Hill, New York, 1974)

Sanderson, P. C., *An Introduction to Microcomputer Programming* (Butterworth, London, 1980)

Wilson, I. R., and Addyman, A. M., *A Practical Introduction to Pascal* (Macmillan, London and Basingstoke, 1978)

Wright, G. G. L., and Evans, D., *Commercial Computer Programming* (National Computing Centre, London, 1974)

INDEX

225